Home Design in an Aging World

HOME DESIGN
IN AN
AGING WORLD

JEFFREY P. ROSENFELD
Hofstra University and Nassau Community College

WID CHAPMAN
Parsons The New School for Design

FAIRCHILD BOOKS, INC.
NEW YORK

Director of Sales and Acquisitions: Dana Meltzer-Berkowitz
Executive Editor: Olga T. Kontzias
Senior Development Editor: Jennifer Crane
Development Editor: Joseph Miranda
Senior Production Editor: Elizabeth Marotta
Photo Researcher: Erin Fitzsimmons
Art Director: Adam B. Bohannon
Production Manager: Ginger Hillman
Assistant Development Editor: Blake Royer
Interior Design: Tom Helleberg
Cover Design: Adam B. Bohannon

Library of Congress Catalog Card Number: 2007930695

ISBN: 978-1-56367-472-3

GST R 133004424

Printed in the United States of America

CH08, TP13

TO THE WOMEN IN MY LIFE
Sue, Julia, and Claire Elizabeth

CONTENTS

Acknowledgments

Four years ago a student of mine at Parsons The New School for Design waited after class to show me an article from a Japanese newspaper. I had been teaching the class about nursing-home design in the United States and had explained that the number of older people entering U.S. nursing homes was steadily increasing. This student explained that the same thing was happening in her hometown in Japan. It turns out that her mother had clipped this article from a local Japanese newspaper and had mailed it to her daughter, who was studying interior design at Parsons in Manhattan. Handwritten across the newspaper article was this message from her mom: "Come back and help us make beautiful nursing homes here."

Home Design in an Aging World has been shaped by my experiences at Parsons The New School for Design, including those from a senior seminar I teach there. From time to time, over the past three years, I have asked my students to create environmental genealogies that trace all of the homes where their families have lived. I have been especially interested in where their grandparents had been housed. It became clear from these environmental genealogies that intergenerational housing patterns were changing and that this was true both in developing and developed nations. The environmental genealogies led to conversations with my students, and I became aware that older people in a variety of nations were being housed in new ways. With the help of my colleagues, family, and friends, I decided to examine this in a more systematic way, and so *Home Design in an Aging World* was born.

Home Design in an Aging World explores home design and community creation in seven of the world's most rapidly aging nations. This includes local, vernacular approaches to senior housing and also the impact of globalization. Together, the local *and* the global are shaping the form and function of senior housing around the world.

Most important, I want to thank Wid Chapman for working with me on this project. His skill, sensibilities, and dry humor have helped me focus on the architecture and design of senior housing. I could not ask for a better friend, colleague, and collaborator. From the beginning, Wid has had faith in this project.

The creation of this book, like its contents, has been international. With generous support from Fairchild Books, Wid and I have been privileged to work with researchers and architects in each of the nations that are covered in this book.

The Swedish research team included Boel Kierulf, Fred Andersson, Martin Presson, and Anna Hanson. Mikael Sodersten provided many wonderful photos of senior housing in Sweden.

Our Japanese research team was headed by Nobuko Iijima and included Tsubasa Kamei and Yuka Uehara. Sakiko Yoshinami was once a student of mine and now lives in Japan. She generously agreed to visit some of the nursing homes mentioned in this book, and in one case, contacted a Japanese designer to get permissions for one of the images in the Japan chapter. Thanks also to So Sugita.

The chapter on India benefited from the input and photography of Professor Phoebe Liebig, who is a gerontologist at University of Southern California. Vibhuti Patel has also been enormously helpful. An excerpt from her diaries appears in this chapter. Thanks also to Shelly Vasudeva for her insights on housing arrangements in India and to Jagat Sharma for his suggestions and reactions. Meeta Bhatti of *Harmony Magazine*, India's equivalent to *Modern Maturity*, supplied helpful information on local product designs to help people age in place.

Professor Jih-Jin, Young, of Nassau Community College, spent hours locating assisted-living facilities and nursing homes in China and Taiwan. Yilin Chen provided additional material and encouragement.

Research on Brazil was spearheaded by Saul Cunow and would have been impossible without his help. Special thanks to Brazilian architect Sandra Perito for sharing her work in the appendix of this book. Jessica Frank, of AARP, shared statistical data on Brazil that allowed us to make internal and international comparisons.

Israel is a small but complex nation. The research on senior housing in Israel was done with help from Gale Ginzburg, Sharon Furman, and Monte Pakuda. Thanks also to Lawrence Normie at Eshel for referring us to directors of Israeli nursing homes. Bruria Gefner and Esty Stern offered personal insights on Israeli senior housing. Dr. Paul Biersuck generously shared the story of Feyga and her move from the Ukraine to Israel. Miriam Herzog relayed the story of her grandmother's housing arrangements in Haifa, which was also much appreciated. And Hava Shilon made visits to nursing homes and assisted-living facilities in Israel during one of her visits to that country. She was our eyes and ears in Israel.

The chapters on the United States were shaped by ongoing dialogue and input from Coralina Mayer and Evan McCullough. They have been friends and supporters of this project from the beginning.

Thanks also to the architects and interior designers who have helped along the way. Doug Gallow, Ellen Gallow, and Marianne Cusato generously supplied architectural material for the appendix of this book. Two interior designers have also been very helpful: Barbara Paige, in Irvine, California, and Rosemary Bakker, in New York City, New York. Paige and Bakker often work with elderly clients, and these designers provided technical and anecdotal information that deepened my understanding of the interplay between gerontology and interior design.

Dr. Dale Lund, a gerontologist at University of Utah, has commented on the interplay between aging and family structure. Dr. Barbara DuBois, a gerontologist at San Diego State University, has been an unending source of information on home safety.

My editors at Fairchild Books have kept me focused and on schedule. I want to thank Olga Kontzias for believing in this project, and especially, Joe Miranda for his support and encouragement. Jason Moring, Jennifer Crane, and Erin Fitzsimmons have dealt with the challenges of working with content, jargon, and images from seven different nations.

My friends and family have been there to encourage me to keep thinking and writing about home design in an aging world. They give me something to look forward to in my old age. I have dedicated this book to my wife, my daughter-in-law, and my granddaughter because they help me appreciate my life, my good luck, and my future. I could not ask for more—except perhaps a place to retire in each of the nations I write about in this book.

—Jeffrey P. Rosenfeld
New York

Introduction

THE LESSON OF RAJAJI ELDERS' HOME

The Rajaji Elders' Home, near the Indian city of Chennai, now markets itself as a haven for old people with children "who live away in a foreign land" (Figure I.1) (Rajaji Elders' Home, 2006). The time-honored residential pattern in India was that a widow or an aging couple would move in with the oldest son and his wife or with another family member. Until recently, it was unthinkable for old people in India to live apart from their children. We can learn a great deal about home design in rapidly aging nations by understanding what is happening in India.

There are new homes and housing options for older people in India because the fabric of Indian society is changing. Just as these changes are impacting architecture and interior design in India, so too are they affecting other rapidly aging nations. The lesson of Rajaji Elders' Home is that the age wave is creating new architecture and even newer forms of community, not just in India but also worldwide.

People in India are living longer than ever before. In 2005, for example, the average life expectancy in India was 71 years (HSBC, 2004: 6). But Indian family life is being transformed at the very moment when people are living longer and becoming more frail. In India today, women are entering the workforce in record numbers, and more people are pursuing careers that take them far away from their aging parents.

Something similar is happening in Japan. Green Tokyo, a nursing home in Japan's largest city, now has a waiting list. Yet nursing homes were almost unheard of in Japan only 20 years ago. The story is the same in China and Brazil, where new residential options are now available for older people. It is no longer rare to be very old, and it is not a disgrace to live in senior housing.

Figure I.1. Rajaji Elders' Home, which welcomes people whose
children have migrated abroad to find work.

SENIOR HOUSING IS NO LONGER A DISGRACE IN INDIA OR OTHER DEVELOPING NATIONS

At one time it was a disgrace for an older person to end up in one of India's "Old Age Homes" (Ramanathan, 2003: 1). But Rajaji Elders' Home and others like it are responding to the social and demographic changes. It is now becoming more "respectable" for middle- and upper-class people in India to live in senior housing. In some sectors it has actually become a status symbol to live in one of the new retirement communities that are going up around Mumbai and New Delhi. These are luxurious gated communities that are "benchmarked to meet the needs of the elderly for comfort, care, security, and even entertainment" (Nayar, 2004: 1).

Something similar is happening in Hong Kong, where the first middle-class retirement home was built in 2004 (Lee, 2003: 1). In Hong Kong, as in Mumbai and Tokyo, senior housing is becoming more socially acceptable. It used to be that senior housing was a "last resort" for people whose families had abandoned them. However, it is now becoming a "lifestyle" and maybe even a status symbol for upwardly mobile families to have an aging relative in senior housing.

Figure I.2. Architects and interior designers are responding to India's Age Wave with innovative housing solutions, such as the Clasic Kudumbam in Chennai. It is now a status symbol for some older people to live in communities such as these.

Indeed, in most of the world's rapidly aging nations, architects and designers are responding to the demand for a variety of housing types: private homes for older people who want to age in place, communities for like-minded people who are getting on in years, and long-term-care facilities for those who can no longer take care of themselves (Figure I.2).

Of course, the architectural response not only is shaped by codes and regulations that are becoming standards around the world but also by social norms and family structures.

HOME DESIGN AND THE AGE WAVE

Home Design in an Aging World describes the interplay between the age wave and home design in seven of the world's most rapidly aging nations. In nations such as China and India, the majority of older people live in the homes of their children or on their own. In Sweden most older people live independently until they need to move into a *servicehus*, which is the Swedish equivalent of a nursing home. Older people in Israel, Brazil, and the United States are housed in a variety of ways: at home with their children or independently, in retirement communities, in assisted-living facilities (ALFs), or in nursing homes.

But in all of these nations, the aging of the population has prompted architects and designers to create new and more geriatric-appropriate housing. *Home Design in an Aging World* explores the form and function of senior housing and explains how it is being shaped by local norms and global trends.

LOCAL NORMS AND GLOBAL TRENDS

We now live in an aging world. According to data from the United Nations, older people (65 or older) made up 8 percent of the world's population in 1950 and are 10 percent of the world's population today. The projection for year 2050 is that 21 percent of the people on this planet—an estimated two billion people—will be aged 60 or older (HSBC, 2005:3). Developing nations are actually aging more rapidly than developed nations, and it is estimated that by 2050 more than two-thirds of all older people will be living in the developing nations of the world (AARP, *Aging Everywhere*, 1998: 6).

This book discusses senior home design in seven rapidly aging nations. Ironically, each one claims to be the *most* rapidly aging nation in the world. This is not the place to dispute or reconcile this demographic claim. It is more important to appreciate the fact that all seven of these nations are now faced with the challenge of housing populations that are living longer than ever before. The sheer number of old (60 or older) and very old (80 or older) people is enough to challenge existing residential patterns. But also there are social transformations that impact architecture and interior design. The most important of these is the transformation of family structures worldwide.

Developed nations, such as Israel, Sweden, Japan, and the United States, are experiencing an unprecedented increase of women in the workforce. And in developing nations, such as India, China, and Brazil, people are migrating from rural or urban areas or are moving abroad in search of work. The result is that older people cannot necessarily turn to their children for care and shelter.

Architects and interior designers worldwide are responding to this need, though the response takes different forms depending on local norms and the social class of potential residents.

Home Design in an Aging World explores how worldwide trends and local norms are impacting home design and housing options for older people. Globalization is shorthand for the worldwide spread of ideas, technologies, and information that are shaping home design. The Internet and the blogosphere are making home design more collaborative than ever before. Tapscott and Williams, writing on the social impact of the blogosphere, conclude that "Mass collaboration changes everything" (Tapscott and Williams, 2006). This is most certainly true in the area of senior housing.

COLLABORATIVE DESIGN IN AN AGING WORLD

Products, ideas, and information are now being created and shared worldwide. With the help of the Internet and the blogosphere (Tapscott and Williams, 2006: 25), architects and designers are keeping abreast of recent trends in geriatics and gerontology and are incorporating them into the design of homes and long-term-care facilities. The online revolution is even bringing new and modern forms of senior housing to developing nations like China (French, 2005: 1).

SENIOR HOUSING GOES GLOBAL

Paradigms and principles of universal design are now accessible to architects and designers all over the world. And in addition, design professionals are collaborating, sometimes internationally. The design of homes and long-term-care facilities can easily involve partnerships, franchises, and consultancies that cross borders and continents. Developers of nursing homes in China, for example, are hiring consultants from the United States and Europe who have more experience with nursing-home design (Liaoning, 2004: 1). News of these projects then travels via blog and e-mail from large cities like Shanghai and Beijing to more remote regions of China (Yan, 2003: 122). As another example, Japanese corporations are developing, and then sharing, information about networked appliances and robotics, which then make their way online to architects and designers around the world.

For example, Lifetime Homes, based in London, builds homes that are accessible and adaptable so that residents can live there for a lifetime (www.lifetimehomes.org.uk, 2007) instead of moving to a nursing home (Figure I.3). Lifetime Homes incorporates 16 principles of universal design that are beginning to impact home design in nations as diverse as England, Brazil, the United States, and China.

Just as the "Hypernet" (Tapscott and Williams, 2006: 20) is creating a more collaborative environment for designers, the quest for community is doing the same for older people around the world. There is a small but growing number of senior-to-senior groups that share ideas about the design of homes and communities for older people.

Figure I.3. Lifetime Homes is a London-based firm offering homes that are intended to last a lifetime because they meet the needs of people at all stages of life.

PRODUCT DESIGN GOES GLOBAL

Home Design in an Aging World explores home design for older people in rapidly aging nations. The picture that emerges is fascinating: Local products and vernacular architectural forms are now combined with international products and postmodern architectural style (Figure I.4). This calls attention to the new and sometimes hybrid (i.e., local and global) solutions to the challenge of housing the growing number of older people around the world.

THE QUEST FOR COMMUNITY

The collaborative environment extends beyond architects and designers. Older people are beginning to collaborate on the purpose and design of places where they live. In a growing number of cases, they are "peer-producing" (Tapscott and Williams, 2006: 13) the blueprints for retirement communities and senior

Figure I.4. This assistive device, Up n' Go Dynamic Body Weight Support System, was developed by Easy-Walking Inc. and is being marketed worldwide.

housing. In Sweden, Israel, and the United States, there is now a quest for community that began as grassroots activity but is now enhanced by access to e-mail, websites, and blogs. The result is that more older people than ever before can create the homes and communities of their own choosing. At this point in time, many of the most exciting experiments in cohousing are happening in the United States.

SENIOR COHOUSING AND RETIREMENT COMMUNITIES

The Elder Co-housing Network, for example, is helping older people to create "new housing choices" (ElderCo-housingNetwork.com). In a growing number of cases, this includes the actual design and development of the communities where they will live. At Glacier Circle, a recent example of senior cohousing, the residents (most of whom are 75 or older) designed a community where they would each have separate houses, but would own a share in a specially designed commons hall where they could socialize and dine together (Brown, 2006: 1).

The website for the Elder Co-housing Network indicates that in 2006 there were 195 such communities across the United States, communities that had been created and designed by the older people who lived there (directory .cohousing.org). Also, older people are peer-producing communities for themselves in Sweden, Holland, Canada, and Israel.

SUSTAINABLE AND ALTERNATIVE COMMUNITIES FOR OLDER PEOPLE

In some cases, community design reflects the desire for sustainable and green communities; in others the focus is on religious or political beliefs or goals (Williams, J. 2005: 196–205). Community building can result in age-mixed housing, as in Hope Meadows in Rantoul, Illinois (Generations of Hope.com), or social networks of older people in urban areas, such as the Beacon Hill community in Boston. The quest for community is resulting in some communities for older gay and lesbian people (Levine, 2006: 76) and even communities for college alumni who relocate to residential communities near their alma mater (Kerkstra, 2006: 18).

The popularity of senior cohousing is also evident in Sweden's "adult communities" and in the naturally occurring retirement communities that now dot the Israeli landscape. Recently, the *residencial* has come to Brazil. The *residencial* is a cross between a luxury hotel and a retirement community and is the first example of senior cohousing in cities like Rio de Janeiro and Curitiba.

CHANGING NORMS IN AN AGING WORLD

Web 2.0—the world of the blogosphere, chat rooms, and electronic bulletin boards—makes new forms of communication and peer production possible. But it is the changing norms and values in rapidly aging societies that make them *necessary*.

MORE WOMEN ARE ENTERING THE WORKFORCE

One of the most dramatic changes is the weakening of what gerontologists call *the norm of filial piety*, or caregiving. In many cultures, especially the traditional cultures of Asia, sons and daughters were supposed to take care of aging, widowed parents. In daily practice, this obligation rested on a daughter or daughter-in-law.

But women all over the world are now entering the workforce in record numbers. The result is that fewer daughters or daughters-in-law are able or willing to be caregivers. The British banking giant HSBC did a cross-cultural survey in 2005 called *The Future of Retirement*. The survey found that the norm of filial piety is losing its prescriptive power. Especially in Asian cultures, the traditional extended family "where the old move in with their children, and expect to be cared for, is on the way out" (HSBC, 2005: 7). This has increased the demand for congregate housing, such as ALF and nursing homes. And this is true in nations as diverse as China, India, and Brazil, all of which are discussed in Part II of this book.

But it is not just the attitudes of younger people that are changing. Older people are also thinking about themselves and their families in new ways. Slowly but surely, older people in Japan, the United States, and Sweden are enjoying their independence and are more reluctant than ever before to move in with their children. And there is a similar trend in China, where surveys in China's largest cities find that more older people want to live independently (HSBC, 2005: 6; Hui, 2004: 2). It is no surprise, then, that the *South China Morning Post* recently proclaimed that "older people want to be more independent" (Hui, 2004: 1).

MORE OLDER PEOPLE ARE LIVING ALONE

It is also true that more older people now insist on *remaining* independent. Nations like Sweden have a long tradition of independence, and an estimated 74 percent of elderly people now live independently, and do so mostly by choice. In China, this is a new development that is spurring the construction of nursing homes (*Shanghai Daily*, 2004: 1) and universally designed apartments (Lai, 2004: 1).

The majority of older people around the world say that they want to live independently for as long as possible. The change is especially striking in Japan, where only 57 percent of older people now assume they will eventually move in with a son or daughter, and only 29 percent assume their children will support them financially. Forty years ago, a sample of older Japanese people would have overwhelmingly expected to move in with one of their children (HSBC, 2004:7).

Instead of assuming they will move in with one of their children—or that a child will move in with them and become a caregiver—more older people worry about being a burden to their family. This is true for older people in Brazil, China, and the United States (HSBC, 2004: 8). This has huge implications for the future of senior housing. There is growing interest worldwide in remaining independent or finding alternative housing arrangements.

LIVING ALONE? OR LIVING INDEPENDENTLY?

Global data collected by the AARP (AARP, *Aging Everywhere*, 1998: 13) indicates that the percentage of people aged 65 or older who are living alone has increased steadily since 1960. This is true for the United States, the United Kingdom, Sweden, Japan, and Denmark.

LIVING ALONE IN DEVELOPING NATIONS

In developing nations, this has been accompanied by an increase in institutionalization. Developing nations "rely extensively on nursing homes and other residential arrangements to solve the problem of older people who can no longer manage on their own" (AARP, *Aging Everywhere*, 1998: 13–14). This has been the case in China, where, as Eric Eckholm has observed, "Homes for the elderly are replacing family care as China grays" (Eckholm, 1998: A1).

LIVING ALONE IN DEVELOPED NATIONS

In developed nations, such as the United States, the United Kingdom, Sweden, and Australia, older people are more likely to live in their own apartments or houses. Japan is an excellent case in point. Gone are the days when housing for older people was an afterthought. A growing number of architects and interior designers are now creating "stylish homes" for older and disabled people (Hoevel, 2007: 1).

LIVING MORE INDEPENDENTLY THAN EVER BEFORE

Architecturally, there have been important breakthroughs in home design for seniors.

ADULT COMMUNITIES

In Sweden, home design for seniors is taking the form of adult communities that are designed to house adults aged 45 and older. There are now waiting lists of people eager to live in such adult communities. Very often, they contain private residential space and common areas where members of these age-integrated communities enjoy meals and activities together. Another notable example is "the Eden Alternative," designed by Bill Thomas, who calls himself a "nursing home abolitionist" (Gawnde, 2007:27). Thomas has built green houses in Tupelo, Mississippi. These are houses for no more than 10 residents, and each house contains a kitchen, living room, and private bedrooms. The goal, says Thomas, is to keep residents engaged in daily life despite the fact that many of them have Alzheimer's disease (Gawnde, 2007: 27).

Sometimes members of an entire community grow older and more frail together. The resulting community needs services and repairs to make homes safe. This is what is happening on many of Israel's kibbutzim, or collective settlements, where almost a third of them are being retrofitted and made more accessible to retain residents because the original settlers have aged in place. The way to retain residents is not only to retrofit existing homes but also to build long-term-care facilities on-site. These kibbutzim originally specialized in farming or manufacturing. But over the years they have become naturally occurring retirement communities (NORCs). Architecturally, this has required kibbutzim to rethink the community and redesign many of the buildings. In this way, architecture has been responding to the age wave in Israel's collective settlements.

SMART HOUSES AND ROBOTICS

In addition to such planned communities, the desire for independence has spurred the development of adaptable and accessible housing. As previously mentioned, this is especially striking in Japan, where it was once almost unthinkable for older people to live on their own. Yet in recent years, older people in Japan have expressed interest in living near but not with their children; this has prompted Japan's home builders to begin marketing homes specifically to older people (Brown, 2003: 62). In addition to designing barrier-free housing for older people, Japan's home builders are now creating "smart houses"—prototypes that feature robotics and networked appliances. These experiments are also fueled—perhaps for the first time—by the knowledge that older people in Japan can and will live apart from their children. The *Japan Times* recently predicted that it will not be long before older people have robots to carry heavy packages, do light housework, and even serve tea (Nakamura, 2006: 1). Robots cannot take the place of human caregivers, but they can most certainly help older people maintain their independence.

DO-IT-YOURSELF REPAIRS

Home repair and do-it-yourself projects are the most popular strategies for people who want to remain in their homes. The United States has witnessed a significant increase in do-it-yourself projects, which are promoted by major retailers like Home Depot and Lowe's and also by the AARP. The AARP's handbook on home repair, entitled *Fixin' to Stay* (AARP, 2000: 25) is one of its

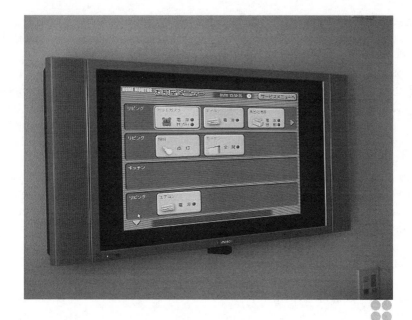

Figure I.5. Appliances in this Japanese home can be operated via the monitor on the wall in the living room.

most popular and influential publications. India is also a growing market for do-it-yourself projects. *Harmony Magazine*, which is India's equivalent to *Modern Maturity*, runs monthly stories on home repair and renovation—the better to help readers age in place. There is also great interest in home repair and renovation in Sweden and Japan. One Japanese website, for example, runs an ongoing series of "Before" and "After" images so that older readers can learn how to make their homes safer and more user-friendly (www.careful.Japan.com, 2006).

INFORMATION TECHNOLOGY AND PRODUCT DESIGN

Networked home appliances, though still in the experimental stage, show the potential for allowing appliances to regulate one another, as when a broken washing machine automatically e-mails the repair service and requests a service call (*Networked Home Appliances*, 2006). The goal of producing these appliances is to create safer, more manageable environments for the elderly (Figure I.5). Japan, long a leader in technological innovation, now "leads the world in developing new products for the elderly" (*The Economist*, 2005: 59).

All of these examples—robotics, networked appliances, do-it-yourself repairs, and community retrofitting—have something in common. All of them reflect a gerontological fact: *Older people now want control over the homes and communities where they live.* The design of home and community is now, in large part, a response to the quest for independence and control.

Even when older people can no longer live on their own and must move into long-term-care facilities, they still desire to maintain as much control and independence as possible. The architecture and design of long-term-care facilities are beginning to reflect these gerontological needs.

THE NEW NURSING HOMES ARE MORE "HOMELIKE"

The old, institutional approach to nursing-home design is being replaced by facilities where residents live in smaller, homelike clusters, as is occurring in the United States and Holland. At some of these homelike facilities, residents even get involved in selecting the color that their room will be painted and are consulted about the choice and placement of the furniture in their rooms. The idea is to create smaller, more cohesive settings where residents will feel "at home" (Hamilton, 2005: A1; Baldwin, 2006: F1). Architecturally, this is expressed in details, floor plans, and way-finding systems that reinforce the homelike quality of small residential clusters.

Architects and designers are also helping to reshape the interaction between nursing homes or ALFs and the surrounding community. For decades, long-term-care facilities stood apart from the communities where they were located. Architecturally, they were shut off and self-contained, but designers in Holland have pioneered in the design of long-term-care facilities. Many of the urban assisted-living facilities in Holland now have health clubs and Internet cafes on the ground floor. These are meant to be places where residents of the ALF and members of the community can mingle and interact (Bakker, 2005:2).

Architects and interior designers can expect more opportunities to create long-term-care environments that look more homelike and integrate the facility with its surroundings. Some of the more innovative approaches in nursing-home design are explored in Chapter 3 of this book.

BOOMERS WILL NEED MORE, AND DIFFERENT, HOUSING

Many of the world's developing nations will soon face the next age wave as Boomers begin to retire. There are already indications that Boomers will want different housing as they get older. More Boomers are divorced or living alternative lifestyles. They are more involved with sports and hobbies that they will want to pursue during retirement; they are less willing to leave the culture and fine dining that are available to them in big cities. Most important, Boomers will not necessarily want to retire. There are already indications that they will continue working, perhaps from home, either by choice or by necessity.

Home Design in an Aging World examines the beginnings of community design, home design, and product design for aging Boomers. There are already indications that Boomers will consider living in communities that are closer to large metropolitan areas and that they will want to live in age-mixed settings.

The developer Del Webb almost single-handedly launched the concept of the retirement community with the first Sun City near Phoenix, AZ, in the 1950s. Sun City became synonymous with relocating, often thousands of miles away from children and grandchildren. But Del Webb has recently launched an age-mixed community where people can retire but be able to live next door to their younger relatives, even their grandchildren (DelWebb.com/lifestyle/Adult_Lifestyles). The newest wrinkle in the design and construction of adult communities is to locate them in or near cultural centers. This is a change from the more familiar pattern of relocating to Sunbelt communities in retirement. Boomers may want to retire, but they do not want to move too far from museums, theaters, professional sports, and good restaurants.

Boomers are very mindful of their eventual aging and decline. And so, their home-design preferences reflect the need for gracious living in the present and the possibility of a frail or infirm old age down the road. This translates into retirement communities that adapt to both possibilities. They will have hiking trails, gym and spa facilities, tennis courts, and more. This is a nod to the Boomers' interest in health and fitness. And within these health-oriented retirement communities, Boomers live in homes that are smaller than their previous homes but still luxurious. Retired Boomers do not necessarily want to mow their own lawns, but they do want homes that feature loft space or spare rooms that can be converted into a home office, home gym, or guest room.

These same homes are being designed for the contingencies of old age. Typically, the master-bedroom suite will be located on the ground floor, and some Boomers are installing residential elevators in their homes (http://otis.com/products/detail/residential elevator). Residential elevators are added insurance for the day when it will be difficult for them to walk up or down stairs.

THE UNITED STATES TAKES CENTER STAGE

The United States has been perhaps the most important source of home-related ideas, experiments, and product design. The first chapter in this book examines competing strategies for housing older people. The first of these is reactive and is based on the medical model of aging. Reactive home design is typically in response to declining physical health or cognitive impairment.

It is significant that many older people and their families only begin to grapple with issues of housing when physical or cognitive problems arise. Reactive home design often involves do-it-yourself repair, though in recent years, a growing number of older people are working with Certified Aging-in-Place Specialists (CAPS).

The second strategy is universal design, which is derived from an active aging paradigm (and *not* the medical model). Through universal design, homes are created to be safe and accessible for people of all ages. With the help of universal design, it is possible for people to age in place without making urgent or hasty changes to their homes later in life.

The United States is also the world leader in *community planning and design* for older people. What first comes to mind are the retirement communities that dot the Sunbelt, but the United States is home to a much more dynamic and sociologically significant movement: senior cohousing. A small but growing number of older people are taking the initiative and opting to live with people of similar beliefs and orientations. Senior cohousing often includes community planning and home design. Chapter 2 focuses on the quest for community and summarizes many of the important trends and prototypes emerging from the senior cohousing movement in the United States.

Finally, there are important developments in the field of long-term care: the design and construction of ALFs, skilled nursing facilities, and Alzheimer's units. Chapter 3 examines contributions to the design and construction of long-term-care facilities.

Together, these three chapters comprise Part I of *Home Design in an Aging World*. Part I acknowledges the pivotal contribution of the United States to the housing and long-term care of older people. But the United States is not the only nation dealing with issues of housing and long-term care for the elderly. And, more to the point, the solutions emerging in other nations, especially developing nations, are different from those that are coming out of the United States. In the spirit of globalization, this book presents norms, designs, and architectural strategies for housing and long-term care throughout the world.

GLOBAL HOUSING OPTIONS FOR OLDER PEOPLE

This book closes with a look at the future and what it could bode for the design of housing and long-term care of older people. Web 2.0 is a more collaborative world. Architecturally, the result is that ideas for the housing and care of older people are beginning to spread from one nation to another. Some of these are fanciful, but all of them point to the possibilities for synergy and collaboration as ideas and designs are shared internationally.

FLOATING HOTELS

At this time, Japan is the source of at least two innovative housing ideas that are receiving international attention. The first of these is floating hotels for older people (*Trends in Japan*, 2004: 1; Parker, 2004: 1; Weil, 2006: 81). The floating hotel is an ocean liner that specializes in long-term care, or becomes a floating adult community. Floating hotels extend the pleasures of a cruise to retirees and those in need of long-term care. Japan is already experimenting with floating hotels, and they are attracting attention in the United States, Australia, and Israel.

CORPORATE RETIREMENT VILLAGES

Another prospect for senior housing and long-term care is called "corporate retirement villages," which have also originated in Japan, a country that practices life employment. In a very real sense, these corporate retirement villages are an extension of Japan's corporate culture. They are communities where retired workers from Japan's close-knit corporations can relocate to "happy corporate villages" (Wiejers-Hasegawa, 2003: 1). It is not clear whether there could be a market for corporate retirement villages in the United States. There is a functional equivalent in the retirement communities being built near some colleges and universities, where alumni can now live (Kerkstra, 2006: 18).

POST-RETIREMENT COMMUNITIES

As of 2007, the first retirement community for affluent Boomers was being built in China (www.orangecounty.com.cn), where there is a small but growing market for them (Figure I.6). And their counterparts in India are now moving to post-retirement communities where they live in studio apartments that have air-conditioning, closed-circuit TV, refrigerators, and microwave ovens. Internet access helps them stay in touch with sons and daughters living outside of India (Ramanathan, 2003: 1).

Figure I.6. China is beginning to build Western-style retirement housing for affluent Chinese retirees. These private homes in Orange County, China, are very similar to ones being built and designed for affluent Boomers in the United States.

COMMUNITY-FACILITY INTERFACE

The Dutch are rethinking the relationship between nursing homes and the surrounding towns and cities across Holland. Traditionally, the nursing home stands apart from the rest of the community. Most nursing homes might as well have walls around them, so isolated they appear. But the Dutch are creating long-term-care facilities that are integrated into the surrounding community. These spaces include cyber cafes, health clubs, and retail space at the street level (Bakker, 2005: 2). Instead of just walking by, people on the street are now tempted to stop and visit—if only to check e-mail or have a cup of coffee.

Building on the Dutch model, Age Song, an ALF in San Francisco, features retail space at the street level, and elderly residents of Age Song are encouraged to staff these stores and interact with shoppers from the community (Gwynn, 2006: 9). The traditional barriers between nursing home and community are being replaced by a more interactive paradigm.

VIRTUAL RETIREMENT HOMES

The future may see even more barriers giving way to interactive models. Belkin, for example, speaks of virtual retirement homes (2006: 9) where people essentially live on their own but are connected to friends, caregivers, and neighbors with the help of Net 2.

The design of homes and long-term-care facilities for older people was once done locally or regionally. Today, however, home design is becoming global in scope. *Home Design in an Aging World* salutes global change and also applauds the ways that ideas and designs are adapted to reflect local norms.

Home Design in an Aging World

PART I
AMERICAN SUCCESS STORIES

"*The Goal: Smart People, Not Smart Homes*"
—Stephen S. Intille, PhD, 2006

"*Change is accelerating, but the places we create are largely static and unresponsive.*"
—Statement from House_n, Department of Architecture research group, Massachusetts Institute of Technology

1

Home as Proactive and Home as Reactive
Designs for Aging in Place

OVERVIEW

According to the AARP, 83 percent of older people say that they want to age in place, which means they want to remain in their own homes. There are currently three options for people who want to age in place.

The first is the Home Depot approach, which entails making home repairs or remodeling on one's own. Many homeowners do their own home modification, although the do-it-yourself approach sometimes creates more problems than it solves.

The second approach is to work with a local contractor or Certified Aging-in-Place Specialist (CAPS). This approach to home modification is called "gerontologic design," and it is derived from a medical, or geriatric, perspective. Gerontologic design usually takes the form of remodeling or modifying an existing space—often in response to the deteriorating health of a homeowner. Gerontologic design is therefore *reactive*. It prescribes modifications or home remodeling, just as health-care providers prescribe medication, physical therapy, or psychological counseling. Home design becomes a way of treating problems and preventing them from getting worse.

The third approach to home design is proactive and inclusive. It involves the creation of environments that work for people of all ages. Known as "universal design," this approach focuses on change that lasts a lifetime. It requires planning and a vision of a future that involves aging in place.

Older people are interested in making the modifications that will allow them to age in place, though there are differences within this age group. People aged 75 and older are interested in making existing space safer and barrier-free. People aged 60 to 74 are more open to the idea of universal design, which will enhance a greater number of relationships and arrangements in late life.

There are assistive digital technologies on the horizon that will dramatically reshape opportunities to age in place. They will make information, medication, and caregivers more accessible than ever before. The home of the future will have proactive computing applications that monitor health and safety in the home and send alerts to health-care providers and family members when problems are detected.

The digital home could also contain therapeutic lighting systems that adjust or respond to the inhabitants' moods, and sensors to detect the progress of physical therapy, to name but a couple of digital possibilities. Major corporations, such as Intel, are developing digital technologies for aging in place (Intel, 2004), and the result will be a longer, healthier old age for consumers.

In the future, the focus of aging in place will shift from the digital home to clusters or communities of digital homes that pool information and caregiving. Some gerontologists speculate that digital communities will cluster into digital cities dedicated to aging in place. This chapter opens with home modifications and ends with a glimpse of the gerontopolis. All of this is possible because of the overwhelming desire by older Americans to age in place.

UNIVERSAL DESIGN AND GERONTOLOGIC DESIGN: HELPING PEOPLE AGE IN PLACE

Michael Thomas, a founder of the Design Collective Group, has stopped telling older clients that they need to modify their homes. Many people are still in denial about aging, whether it is their homes or their bodies. Thomas knows that most clients will react by saying, "I don't want any of that old-people stuff; I don't want my house to look like a nursing home." He now "just designs houses this way" and doesn't mention that he has in fact added "the old-people stuff" (Holstein, 2006: 173).

Michael Thomas is one of the growing number of designers trained in universal design. One goal of universal design is to make homes safe and comfortable for older occupants without making them look *geriatric*. He is successful because he offers state-of-the-art universal design (*Interiors*, March 2007: 1). His interiors are inclusive and are designed to work for people of all ages and abilities.

However, not all clients are in denial about aging. Older people often realize that they need to modify their homes because the older people have become ill or disabled or are caring for an aging spouse. Very often they will turn to a geriatric-care manager to help them with home modifications, or they can work with interior designers like Barbara Paige or Rosemary Bakker, who know how to do home modification but bring to it the flair and good taste of interior design. In other words, they *excel* at designing "the old-people stuff."

Clients often come to designers like Barbara Paige or Rosemary Bakker because they help elderly people improve their homes. For example, Ada and Jesse were an elderly couple in Orange County, California, who commissioned Paige to remodel the home where they planned to spend their final years. They had married late in life, after each had lost a spouse. They were still in good health when they came to Paige in 2001, but they were adamant about the fact that they needed her to design an interior in which they would be comfortable and could live out the rest of their lives. "They were already slowing down," says Paige, whose practice is based in Irvine, California. "My job was to design and remodel a home they bought together so they could age in place. . . . I created a guest room [that] could easily become the bedroom where a caregiver would sleep. I encouraged Ada and Jesse to select tile floors for easy maintenance, but Ada still regrets not putting down stone floor. So don't think that the desire to "decorate" ends with aging. New sofas were built to their specifications. They had to be able to sit and lie down comfortably. They already knew that they would be lying down on that sofa more than they might be sitting on it. Special neck pillows were added to the design, and why not? I wanted their home to make them happy because they were already beginning to slow down. When I work with seniors, I think about that aspect of my design product" (Barbara Paige, personal correspondence, 2005).

Barbara Paige works mostly with private clients, while Rosemary Bakker has begun working with elderly outpatients at Manhattan's Wright Center for Aging. The Wright Center is an outpatient clinic at the Weill Cornell Medical College, and Bakker's input on the modification of their apartments and homes enhances the patients' overall rehab. Bakker helps the patients make their homes safer and barrier-free (Wilkinson, 2006: 18). Gone are the days when doctors made home visits and could see barriers to mobility when they visited their patients' homes. Bakker and Paige see themselves as providing safer—and more beautiful—environments to older people whose needs *are* geriatric. They operate in much the same way as geriatric-care managers who will offer advice on home modification as part of the plan that they develop for a client.

Rosemary Bakker remembers when her elderly mother had been discharged from the hospital. "Suddenly, the house that had suited her well for 42 years became a time bomb just waiting to go off " (as quoted in Wilkinson, 2006: 1). Designers like Bakker and Paige work in the tradition of geriatric-care managers, but with a difference. Geriatric-care managers are concerned primarily with home safety and help their clients avoid the kind of "explosions" that could have happened in the home of Rosemary Bakker's mother. The difference is that interior designers who work within this framework bring style and good taste to home modification. Their work is called "gerontologic design."

Universal design and gerontologic design are very different paradigms for working with older people and their homes. Universal design is proactive. The focus is on inclusive design for people of all ages and abilities. Gerontologic design is reactive. Some actually see it as a subspecialty of geriatrics. Gerontologic designers expect that their clients will be elderly and possibly in crisis. The gerontologic perspective is that home and design are an extension of rehabilitation or accident prevention for an older person. These perspectives are polar opposites. But they both succeed brilliantly at helping clients age in place. If there is one thing that older people want, it is the peace of mind that comes with not having to relocate to a nursing home.

THE DESIRE TO AGE IN PLACE

A recent AARP survey finds that 83 percent of people over 60 want to stay in their homes [Wilkinson, 2006: 1; NAHB, Older Adult Housing Survey, 2005: 49]. And 63 percent of older people surveyed in 2000 by the AARP say that their current residence "is where they will always live" (NAHB, 2005: 5). Older people are more likely to remain in their homes when they feel they can control and enjoy their living space (Hansen and Gottschalk, 2006: 41). Data on home modification indicates that 14 percent of older people surveyed by the AARP have already made modifications that will let them live on the first floor of their homes; 17 percent have added handrails on both sides of the stairs in their homes; and 18 percent have added handrails or grab bars (Figure 1.1) in their bathrooms (NAHB, 2005: 5). The desire to age in place is evident. The challenge is to give older people the information and resources they need to do so. For example, 79 percent of the older people surveyed by the AARP agreed that bathroom grab bars are important, but only 32 percent of those respondents actually had them (National Association of Home Builders [NAHB], 2005: 7).

DO-IT-YOURSELF: THE HOME DEPOT APPROACH

Despite the availability of architects and interior designers, most older people get their home-renovation information either from the Internet or magazine articles. In fact, the AARP's *The Do-able, Renewable Home* (AARP, 1991, revised in 2000) is one of its most successful publications ever. The book empowers older people by giving them enough advice and information so that they can

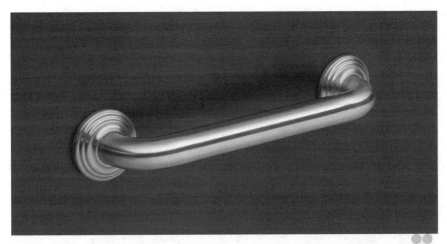

Figure 1.1. Grab bars provide safety and accessibility for older people.

make their own modifications. This is referred to here as the Home Depot approach, which involves homeowners going to local stores, buying parts or materials, and making changes themselves.

The AARP's *The Do-able, Renewable Home* builds on the popularity of aging in place. The book's goal is to demystify home modification by not only giving many older people the information they need to modify their own homes but also encouraging them to think of modification as a series of do-it-yourself projects. In fact, the book begins by explaining that "most of the devices mentioned in this book—kick plates, hand levers, etc.—are available at local hardware stores. You can obtain other items from the sources listed in the resource chapter" (AARP, 1991: 12). *The Do-able, Renewable Home* has spawned many how-to books, websites, advice columns, and home-modification checklists. For example, Rebuilding Together, in partnership with the U.S. Administration on Aging, developed a checklist for assessing many areas of the home. The section called "Telephone and Door," for example, asks homeowners the following yes/no questions about their homes' doorbells, mailboxes, and telephones:

Yes/No	Phone jack location near bed, sofa, chair?
Yes/No	Able to get phone, dial, hear caller?
Yes/No	Able to hear doorbell?
Yes/No	Able to reach/empty mailbox?

Figure 1.2. Installing a rocker light switch that is reachable from the bedside will help reduce the risk of slips and falls.

Some of the best how-to books list room-by-room physical considerations, and some show before and after images of older people's homes. Figure 1.2, for example, shows readers how they can install a rocker light switch, reachable from the bedside. A rocker light switch is easier for an older person to turn on and off than a standard light switch and can help older people avoid slips and falls that can occur in the dark.

If there is now a growing need for architects and interior designers, it is in part because so many people have been able to stay in their homes as a result of the advice they have obtained from the AARP book and others like it.

Checklists and how-to books are as far as some homeowners ever go, or ever need to go. Some do go further but without consulting an architect or designer. Instead, they turn to smart-house prototypes, either in real-time or virtually, and get ideas from those visits.

SMART HOUSES: NEW IDEAS FOR AGING IN PLACE

Smart homes are intelligent and futuristic models of what homes could be. They are designed to be sustainable and barrier-free, which makes them attractive for at least two reasons: Smart homes help people age in place and are environmentally appropriate. They are often experimental labs where computer technologies and robotics are being tested in the hopes of creating more livable homes in the future. Smart homes are not places where people actually live. But older people visit them online or in real time to look for ideas that will help them make their own homes more livable. These smart homes offer the promise of a safer, more computerized future. Here, for example, is a description from Reuters' newswire:

> In the future, people could live in "Smart Homes" that will tell them when to wake up or remind them to lock the back door. . . . The "Caring Home" [a British "Smart House"] would be equipped with electronic sensors connected to a computer that will remind people to take their medicine or turn off the oven. . . . The aim of the "Smart Home" would be to allow elderly people to live independently in their own homes for as long as possible ("Homes of the Future," 2002: 1).

The home-building industry is beginning to showcase smart-house technology. The goal is to encourage people to adapt smart-house technologies to their own homes. In fact, the NAHB has designed a prototype or model house filled with cutting-edge technologies. This prototype, called LifeWise Home, is open to the public and often visited online (www.NAHBrc.org).

According to the NAHB, LifeWise Home, whose opening in Bowie, MD, in 2004 was timed to coincide with National Aging in Place Week, was designed with technologies and features that can make aging in place a reality. It is energy-efficient and wheelchair-accessible and contains an upstairs suite for "a live-in caretaker or boomerang child" (Figure 1.3).

A number of research institutes have also developed smart-house prototypes. Table 1.1 contains a recent listing of smart homes across the United States.

TABLE 1.1 SELECTED WEB ADDRESSES FOR SMART HOUSES IN THE UNITED STATES

The Duke University Smart Home program. www.smarthome.duke.edu

Smart Medical Home Research Laboratory: www.futurehealth.rochester.edu

What Is a Smart Home?: www.smarthome.com

Adaptive House, University of Colorado: www.cs.colorado.edu

NC State Solar Center: www.ncsc.ncsu.edu

Center for Universal Design: www.design.ncsu.edu

E-House: www.michaelmcdonough.com/e-house

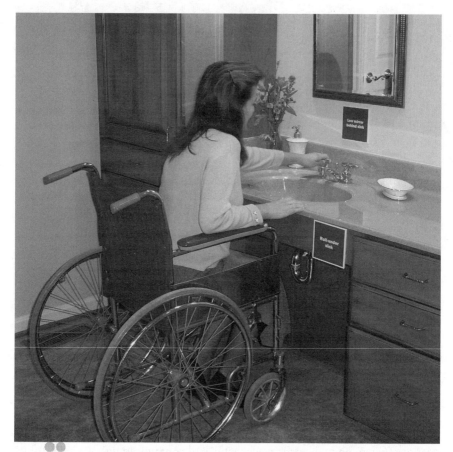

Figure 1.3. LifeWise Home is an example of how the home-building industry has supported seniors' wish to age in place. The roll-under sink in this figure is designed to accommodate people with different needs.

It is possible to get ideas and encouragement to age in place by visiting these places in person or online. Checklists and smart homes are great sources of ideas. But there usually comes a time when it is necessary to locate a trained professional.

There are basically two possibilities for locating a trained professional. It is possible to locate somebody who will intervene because there is already a problem, or somebody who will work with the homeowner long before there are any problems. Geriatric-care managers, local contractors, and CAPS do interventions, and their work can best be called *gerontologic design*. Architects and interior designers try to focus more on universal design that will last a lifetime and projects that will work for people regardless of their age or ability.

GERONTOLOGIC DESIGN: GERIATRICS AND AGING IN PLACE

Gerontologic design builds on geriatrics, which is the medical treatment of the elderly. Because it is grounded in a medical model of aging, gerontologic design is an *environmental intervention* that usually occurs in response to a medical problem or to prevent a specific problem. For example, the AARP *Home Modification Book* (2006) is filled with room-by-room suggestions for home modification. Figure 1.4 is the suggested modification for the shower in a typical bathroom. The modification is not meant to be beautiful, but practical. It will help prevent accidents from happening in the shower.

Gerontologic design appeals to Boomers who have decided to make room in their home for an aging parent or in-law. An estimated 13 percent of seniors live in shared housing, often with one of their grown children. Boomers often hire designers or consultants to make the modifications or additions that will be necessary. This is a prime example of gerontologic design in response to a family transition or crisis.

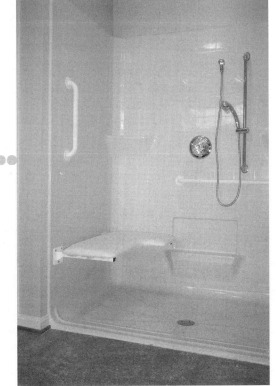

Figure 1.4. Gerontologic design helps people make their homes safer and more comfortable, but not necessarily more beautiful.

The first impulse for many homeowners is to contact local contractors or electricians to only make repairs. Most communities now have consultants who specialize in gerontologic design. There are two groups of professionals who do this: CAPS and geriatric-care managers.

The AARP has mobilized the talents of local architects, contractors, electricians, and some health-care professionals, and it now offers them the opportunity to study to become CAPS. Together with the Remodelers Council of the NAHB, AARP has developed the CAPS program. CAPS understand and explain why specific modifications will help homeowners age in place. The CAPS program teaches future consultants:

- The unique needs of the older adult population
- Aging-in-place home modifications
- Common remodeling projects
- Solutions to common barrier

As of 2006, more than one thousand remodelers had been trained to be CAPS consultants (NAHB, 2006:1). In fact, AARP publishes an annual CAPS locator that allows homeowners to locate CAPS consultants in their own communities (AARP.org/families/home_design). The CAPS credential improves consultants' chances of working with homeowners to help homeowners age in place (Higdon, 2006:2).

For example, CAPS consultants often visit the infinitec.org website to learn the geriatric or medical benefits of particular modifications. Figure 1.5 is the Kohler image of a sink with a single-lever faucet. This image helps consultants visualize how much easier it is for older, arthritic, or disabled people to use a single-lever faucet.

Infinitec.org includes geriatric and medical reasons for recommending such a sink to an aging homeowner. For example, ". . . [the single-lever faucet] is easiest to use for weak hands or hands with decreased sensitivity." Gerontologic designers can go to such websites, locate the appropriate bathroom sink(s), and learn the geriatric or medical reasons for installing them.

While CAPS training is limited to home modification, geriatric-care management is a more comprehensive approach to elder care that not only includes home modification but also focuses on crisis intervention and a variety of ongoing supports and supervision. Geriatric-care managers routinely make home-modification suggestions when they visit clients' homes. For some geriatric-care managers, the home-assessment process begins when they ring their clients' doorbells. Here is how one geriatric-care manager describes that moment: "I can't help myself," she says. "I walk up to the door,

Figure 1.5. Gerontologic designers suggest home modification ideas for seniors, such as this single-level faucet.

and I've already started thinking about how to make the home safer and more accessible. How many stairs are there? How accessible is the home? How far away is the mailbox? Can they hear the doorbell inside? By the time they answer the door, I have already started thinking about modifications" (Batsheva Schreiber, CareManagers Inc., personal correspondence, 2007). A good geriatric-care manager thinks about accessibility and home safety, even before ringing the doorbell.

UNIVERSAL DESIGN: INCLUSIVE MODIFICATIONS

Universal design is a different paradigm about home and the people who live there. Universal design incorporates people of all ages and all abilities (Pirkl, as cited in Luscombe, 2003: 26), and its goal is to prevent or avoid the need for home modification. A recent interview with James Joseph Pirkl, known as the father of universal design, confirms that good design should not be just a stopgap. The architect or designer should be doing more than environmental interventions after an illness or crisis, says Pirkl. Home design in an aging world has a different mission. It can resolve "pressing social concerns" for people of all ages (Kelly, 2004: 2). It should give people what they "want and need their whole lives" (Pirkl, as cited in Luscombe, 2003: 35). Architect Douglas Gallow adds that universal design is even bigger than giving people what they want or what they think they want. It's the fact that a well-designed home will work for people of *different ages* who are living in the same space. Gallow, who designed his own home, recalls that "I interviewed my own children. I made the *family* the client because people of different ages would be living there" (Douglas Gallow, personal correspondence, 2006). The house was designed to work for a lifetime, and for the entire family.

This calls attention to how universal design can best be defined: as an inclusive design paradigm and as design for all. The universal design paradigm is human-centered design that is created with everyone in mind (adaptiveenvironments.org, "Universal Design"). The universal design paradigm emphasizes equitable use, flexibility in use, and design that is both simple and intuitive (www.design.ncsu.edu/cud). In other words, universally designed spaces offer benefits that can work for everybody and be appreciated—though perhaps for different reasons—by everybody living in the space (Figure 1.6). Richard Duncan, senior project manager for the Center for Universal Design, calls this "the social equity component" because universal design works for everyone living in the home (as cited in Chamberlain, 2007: 10).

The Center for Universal Design in North Carolina offers the lever-style door handle as an example of human-centered design. The lever-style door handle requires little physical effort. It allows doors to be opened with minimal repetitive action (www.ncsu.edu). This paradigm is making inroads among educators, architects, and home builders. All three of these groups are developing projects to educate the public about the importance of universal design in an aging society.

In this context, it is worth mentioning that Prince William County, Virginia, opened the Universal Design Demonstration House in 2006. The county encourages group tours and group meetings at the house, which combines "upscale design with functional ease" (pwc.gov.org/ud).

The following features will help homeowners to adapt as their needs change (pwc.gov.org/ud):

- Wider doorways
- Lever-style door handles

- No-step entryways with attractive railings and nonslip flooring
- Thermostats installed lower on the wall and rocker light switches
- Kitchen and laundry appliances at convenient heights
- Attractive but safe features: nonslip floor tiles, single-lever faucets

Universal design is also featured in some model homes, which makes them very different from Smart Homes. Smart Homes are showcases for future technologies and for the systems that link them to home and community. Heartland House, which is shown in Figure 1.7, is a model for universal design today.

Homebuilders are beginning to include technologies and detailing in the homes they create that work for people of all ages. In fact, a recent national survey of home builders (NAHB, 2005: 12) finds that 71 percent of home builders now routinely include the following universal design features:

- Doors with a minimum clearance of 32 inches
- Easy-to-use climate controls
- Windows that open easily
- Wider hallways
- Bigger bathrooms with separate showers and tubs

Figure 1.6. Retractable bread boards and mounted mixers are some of the features in this universally designed home by Tapestry Custom Homes, McKinney, TX.

Figure 1.7. Heartland House was developed by the IDEA Center at the
University of Buffalo. This is not a "house of the future." It is
ready to be built and sold today.

COMBINING TWO PARADIGMS: GERONTOLOGIC *AND* UNIVERSAL DESIGN

Architects and designers often work within both of the gerontologic *and* universal design paradigms. One client may come to the architect or designer with a specific problem, while another client seeks the help of an architect or designer to plan for a lifetime. Recent media coverage (Knox, 2006: 5B) presents a combination of reactive and proactive designs. Noelle Knox, writing in *USA Today*, explains that some changes, such as under-cabinet lighting or toggle light switches, can be installed by the homeowner, while others—stair treads that are 11 to 12 inches deep or railings 34 inches from the floor—are best installed when the house is being built (Knox, 2006: 5B). Design professionals are learning to incorporate both of these paradigms. For example, Ellen Gallow is a gerontologist and also an interior designer. She not only appreciates the importance of universal design but is also CAPS-certified. This gives her the flexibility to work with people who have immediate needs and to do what she and architect-husband Douglas Gallow call life-span design. She mentions that most of her clients "don't want to even hear about aging" (Ellen Gallow, personal correspondence, 2007). They are planning for the future and want peace of mind rather than a quick fix. They want to age in place, though aging in place means something different to each segment of the senior population.

Home design for seniors is being driven by what gerontologist Ken Dychtwald calls "the age wave," the rapidly increasing percentage of older people in the U.S. population. But within that age wave, there are market segments with distinct housing needs. For example, there are people aged 75 or older who often own their own homes. Seniors have the highest homeownership rate of any age group. Studies by the Joint Center for Housing Studies (Schafer, 2000: Executive Summary) and the NAHB (NAHB, National Older Adult Housing Survey 2000) find that more than 25 percent of all U.S. homeowners are seniors. But the first Boomers turned 60 in 2006 and officially joined the Age Wave, and with them, they bring their own distinctive housing needs and wants. Statistically speaking, Boomers will not need "the old-people stuff " for at least 15 more years, at least not for themselves. And yet many Boomers are adding or renovating rooms to house an aging family member. Senior home design now addresses not only the needs of traditional seniors but also those of Boomers.

BOOMERS: PLANNING FOR THE NEXT STAGE

There are more than 75 million Americans over the age of 50, and 20 million of them are Boomers. In addition, there are 55 million Boomers between the ages of 41 and 50 (Taylor, 2004:37). The original Age Wave of people who are now in their late 70s will soon be dwarfed by a "silver tsunami" when these 75 million Boomers reach retirement age.

Boomers have already begun to impact senior home design (Esterbrooks, 2006:1). Most important, most Boomers expect to be working past retirement age, and most of them come to retirement—or semiretirement—with different attitudes than earlier generations. Forty-six percent of Boomers aged 50 to 59 and 62 percent of Boomers aged 60 to 69 say they want to stay in their current homes (NAHB National Older Adult Housing Survey, 2005: 140). They may not be thinking about aging in place, but that is what they say they will do.

"Today's 55 [or older] segment wants to downshift but not necessarily to be shipped out to . . . a seniors-only community" (Peter Dennehy, as cited in Esterbrooks, 2006:2). Many Boomers are children of people who packed up and moved, sometimes thousands of miles away, to active retirement communities in the Sunbelt. Boomers are more likely to live close to their children and large cities that offer cultural sites, sporting events, and fine dining. Boomers are more apt to avoid seniors-only communities. They explore new housing options in their own communities, as when Boomers sell a larger home and downsize but live in the same community (Gordon, 2005; *Behind the Aging Curve*, August 3, 2004).

NEXT-STAGE HOUSING AND NEXT-STAGE COMMUNITIES

Boomers are also entering the senior-housing market with different attitudes about aging from their predecessors—attitudes that will have enormous impact on home design. For example, boomers are often in denial about aging. "They think they will never get old." Retirement housing is not even on the radar screen for most Boomers. What they *are* ready for is next-stage housing (Nyren, 2006: 1), which might only be located a few miles away from where they currently live. Chuck Nyren has written perceptively on the architectural meaning of next-stage housing and how different it will be from the retirement housing that came before it. "Communities like Sun City or Century Village, which opened in the 1960s, based their appeal on instant relaxation: the more features, the better. The more 'planned' the better," writes Nyren. "It was time to start a new life. Time . . . to relax" (Nyren, 2006:2).

The Boomers typically do not need or want *new* lives. And the last thing they want is instant relaxation. They want to continue, or perhaps modify, the lives they have. They are looking for next-stage housing and next-stage communities.

Boomers typically want to live close to their families (Wylde, 2001: 42), and they want access to the amenities of urban areas. They are open to building or buying homes in communities that offer "entertaining education, excellent college sports, gated communities, conservative government, and great cops" (Taylor, 2004: 38). In other words, the next-stage communities for which Boomers are looking allow for change while still keeping life recognizable—the *sine qua non* of baby-boom aging.

Next-stage housing is a flexible, open-ended approach to home design. Boomers want to create homes and communities that reflect their own needs and interests. They are open to the simplicity and style of universal design for that reason. The fact that it will help them age in place is important, but it is less important than the aesthetics of a universally designed home. The NAHB did a survey of Boomers' housing preferences and published those findings as a book in 2001. *Boomers on the Horizon: Housing Preferences of the 55 + Market* (Wylde, 2001) describes what Boomers are looking for when they buy or retrofit their homes. Many are living in an empty nest and do not need as much room as they once did. Although they may want to scale back on size, they are often reluctant to give up luxury.

UNIVERSAL DESIGN

Boomers respond to the simplicity and bold, modern look of universal design (Fiure 1.8). Kohler Co., one of the nation's most influential home suppliers, has incorporated this understanding into its marketing efforts. Kohler products appeal to upscale Boomers because the products are well-designed, and not because they require low physical effort (Kamerick, 2005: 2). Architects, home builders, and designers are learning to emphasize the utility *and* beauty of universal design when they market homes and home products to Boomers.

SMALLER CASTLES WITH GROUND-FLOOR MASTER BEDROOM SUITES

Boomers want to buy or build smaller market-rate homes that require less upkeep than their current homes but still allow for gracious living. In other words, ". . . they want to cut down on the time and energy they have to expend on the upkeep of their castles" (Gopal Ahluwalia, of NAHB, as quoted in Esterbrooks, 2006: 2). They want to downsize but want a house with lots of amenities (Sluis, 2006: 19). Boomers are perhaps the first generation of home buyers who will perceive the purchase of a home after the age of 60 as an upgrade. And although these new castles are smaller than the homes the Boomers vacate, these homes are larger than the homes seniors lived in 20 years ago (NAHB, 2005: 15). These next-stage homes allow boomers to enjoy the present while preparing for the future. There might very well be a dining

Figure 1.8. A simple and modern universally designed house that
"works" for people of all ages.

room, even though it only gets used four or five times per year. There will probably be two bedrooms and two baths (NAHB, 2005: 15). But there will also be a ground-floor master bedroom suite—a nod to the fact that climbing stairs to a second-floor bedroom may someday be out of the question (Trager, 2006: 2).

APPLIANCES AND GRANITE-COVERED COUNTERS

Next-stage housing includes appliances, but not necessarily for the purpose of timesaving. There is a steady demand for gourmet kitchens with granite countertops and high-end appliances (Trager, 2006: 2) (Figure 1.9). The universal kitchen appeals to Boomers because it can have continuous wet surfaces, pop-up dishwashers, retractable burners, and more (Rhode Island School of Design, 1999: 2). Boomers may not want to cook every day, but they do want opportunities to make gourmet meals, or even linger over a cup of espresso. One aging boomer explains that he put a leather club chair in the dining room of his new home because "I like to sit here every morning [in this new leather chair], read the newspaper, and drink my morning coffee" (Richard Bradspries, personal correspondence, 2007). Next-stage housing allows for high-tech relaxation without the feel of retirement.

BOOMERS WHO DESIGN SPACE
FOR THEIR AGING PARENTS OR IN-LAWS

There has been a role reversal in growing numbers of American families, as Boomers invite aging parents or family members to live with them. In fact, a recent cover of *U.S. News & World Report* shows an aging mother and her baby-boom daughter. The cover reads "Taking Care of Mom & Dad: A Boomers' Guide" (Larson, 2006).

An estimated 13 percent of Americans aged 65 or older are living with their adult children or other family members (Larson, 2006: 64), up from 12 percent in 1999 (Greenwald, 1999: 45; but only 6 percent of seniors sampled for an NOAHS survey in 2000 were living with a child).

This role reversal—the child taking care of the parent—usually involves home design or modification. Boomerang parents—Boomers who are making

Figure 1.9. Universal design makes this kitchen attractive, safe, and appropriate for people of all ages.

space in their home for an aging parent, in-laws, or often turn to gerontologic design for the modifications they need.

The arrival of an aging parent or in-law involves retrofitting a bedroom, or perhaps the entire home. (The NAIPC has a website, www.NAIPC.org, that offers gerontologic design options.) There are some modifications that involve the entire home: Doorways may need to be widened everywhere in the house, for example. There are also room-specific modifications that may be necessary. The bathroom, for example, may need a higher toilet, slip-resistant tile on the floors, grab bars, anti-scald shower valves, and a safer, larger area for showering (Figure 1.10).

Figure 1.10. This room has been modified for an aging family member who is living with her children. Notice the grab bars along the walls.

Remodeling involves more than just home design. It also impacts relationships within the home. The following case study—taken from the NAIPC website—is a reminder that gerontologic design also involves social dynamics. The case study is called "Making Room for Mom," and it involves a married couple, Claire and Steve, who will soon become boomerang parents. They have invited Steve's mother, Ursula, to move into an unused space in their home. We learn that gerontologic design has made a world of difference for Claire, Steve, and Ursula. "The home apartment now includes a new accessible and attractive bathroom, bedroom, kitchen, and living room. Ursula is happy to have an accessible home . . . and she gets to see her grandchildren every day." The NAIPC website provides a number of such case studies in gerontologic design involving home modifications and additions, including accessible bathrooms and kitchens, walk-in showers, new rollout shelving in closets, wider doors, and slip-resistant floors, to name a few. The more important point is that gerontologic design can have long-lasting social consequences, including quality time with grandchildren, companionship, and peace of mind.

CAPS consultants are often called on to do the remodeling. And even though CAPS consultants help the families that retain them, there are "hundreds of thousands of seniors [living] without handrails, grab bars, ramps, and other structural modifications" (Schafer, 2000: 2). As a result, organizations like the NAIPC, AARP, and Institute on Elder Environments are reaching out to Boomers to provide safer environments for their aging parents or in-laws. It is not enough to invite an aging parent or in-law to live in the same home. It is just as important to create living space that is barrier-free and accessible (Cotsalas, 2005: 12).

PEOPLE 65 AND OLDER: HOPING TO AGE IN PLACE

People aged 65 and older do not move from home to home as often as younger people do. Eighty-five percent of today's seniors own their own homes and have been living there for 21 years or longer (NAHB, 2005: 4). Most seniors surveyed assume that they will always live where they are currently living. Many seniors have already made at least three home modifications, and they worry that they will need even more if they become frail or incapacitated. Seniors aged 65 to 74 who have renovated their homes have made the following modifications:

- Raised the toilet (96 percent)
- Installed a wheelchair-accessible shower (70 percent)
- Added a shower seat
- Created a shower separate from the tub (67 percent)

(NAHB, 2005: 42)

COMFORTABLE, SAFE, AND INDEPENDENT AT HOME

There are gaps between what seniors say they need and what they have. There is a gap between seniors who want and who actually *have* nonslip floor surfaces (26 percent), an entrance without steps (40 percent), and a personal alert system (66 percent) (NAHB, 2005: 8).

Nine out of every 10 people aged 60 or older still live independently (Schafer, 2000: 1). National surveys find that those living in smaller, easier-to-manage homes are the most optimistic about continuing to live independently (NAHB, 2006:1).

HOMES THAT ARE SMALLER AND EASIER TO MANAGE

People aged 65 and older want homes that are smaller and easier to manage. This includes less outdoor maintenance and fewer stairs to climb (Hansen and Gottschalk, 2006: 41). People aged 65 and older also want homes that are barrier-free, have accessible storage areas, and areas to entertain visitors and family members. Square-shaped kitchens work better than linear kitchens for people aged 70 or older (Percival, 2002: 735), and this can be an important selling point for senior home buyers. Less obvious, but equally important, is the view from windows in the home. Windows with outdoor views help older people remain connected to the world around them, even as they become too frail or disabled to venture out of their homes (Ellen Gallow, LifeSpan Designs, personal correspondence, 2007).

Older people in search of new homes often find that modern homes meet most of these needs. As Dutch architect Paul de Ruiter observes, "Elderly people and modern architecture fit together very well" (Paul de Ruiter, as quoted in Holstein, 2006: 175). Universal design of modern homes can make spaces appealing and can stretch the notion of what is suitable for older people. Amara Holstein, for example, describes an aging couple in Minneapolis who created loft space for themselves. Loft space is usually the habitat for young urban hipsters, but architects Meyer, Scherer & Rockcastle created an urban loft for an older couple. The loft space even includes a guest room that could one day become sleeping quarters for a home-health aide (Holstein, 2006: 175).

HOMES THAT DO NOT FEEL INSTITUTIONAL OR GERIATRIC

Older people also want homes that meet their functional needs without feeling institutional or geriatric. The National Health Care Corporation (nhccare.com) offers a list of considerations for people aged 70 or older who are looking for someplace new to live. Selected items on that list include:

- No steps from garage to house
- Door handles with levers instead of knobs
- Floors that are not highly shined
- Higher toilets and countertops
- Buzzers instead of doorbells (because buzzers have a lower frequency)
- At the bathtub, grab bars, grip mats, bath benches, and handheld showerheads
- Storage at waist-level and rollout shelves
- Shallow shelves rather than deep ones
- Large dials on stove
- Pullout racks in ovens
- Master bedroom on main level
- Senior-friendly bed heights

(Knox, 2006: 5B)

The IDEA Center has designed model homes that include most or all of these features. These are not fantasy homes. They are model homes that are ready "to be built and sold today" (ap.buffalo.edu/idea/projects).

THE FUTURE: DOMOTICS AND DIGITAL HOME TECHNOLOGIES

Senior home design is already being shaped by new technologies and the linkages that they create. Just as people are becoming "Older, Wiser, and Wired" (Title of AARP conference on aging and technology, 2005), so will their homes. The future of aging in place will involve the interconnection of people, homes, and communities. Domotics refers to these interconnections, which will have a large impact on aging.

DOMOTICS: INTEGRATING SERVICE WITH TECHNOLOGIES

Domotics is the science of integrating service with technologies. The goal of domotics is to improve safety, security, comfort, communication, and technical management in the home. For example, new digital technologies in domotic homes make it possible to create a lighted pathway as somebody walks from one part of the house to another, such as from the bedroom to the bathroom and then to the kitchen. This has enormous gerontological potential. Digitally controlled lighting can help older people to avoid slipping and falling inside the home. It can also offset the effects that occur with people who suffer from Sundowning Syndrome. Sundowning is agitated behavior that is often triggered by the change of light at sundown. Digitally controlled lighting can regulate levels of light and prevent the darkening shadows.

Digital home technology is the third, and perhaps the most radically different, wave of technology, and it has important implications for aging in place. The first wave of technological change brought timesaving appliances to the American home. At the end of the nineteenth century, household appliances began making homes safer and more comfortable. By now it is common that appliances reduce the time and labor necessary to operate a home (Rybczynski, 1997: 7, 163). The second wave brought the mediated environments of the 1990s (Gumpert and Drucker, 1998: 423) when the Internet made it possible to link appliances and technologies. Mediated environments empower people by widening the scope of what they are able to control in their homes—a room, a system, an entire home. The next wave will be the digital home technologies of the twenty-first century (Intel: Digital Home Technologies, 2004:1). Digital home technologies are creating new patterns of home control, and in this way, they will impact on aging in place.

DIGITAL HOME TECHNOLOGIES

Until now, control has been entirely in the hands of the people who live in the home. Digital home technologies are now creating proactive home computing that creates new partnerships for aging in place. Digital home technologies are based on domotics, or the application of digital technologies to domestic appliances throughout the home (Wikipedia, 2006: 1). Digital technologies in the home will enhance day-to-day living and link older people to health-care providers and family members who live elsewhere. Intel Corporation sees digital home technologies as electronic partnerships in which people and even the home itself will be able to monitor health and behavior. The digital home will contain a wireless network that includes sensors, computers, and a variety of consumer electronic (CE) devices. With the help of such wireless networks, it will be possible to monitor the health of people as they age in place. Health-care providers and family members can access this data and then "take action to meet [medical] needs on their behalf" (Intel: Digital Home Technologies for Aging in Place, 2004:1). Health monitoring will be only one of the smart residential technologies that will help people age in place.

SMART RESIDENTIAL TECHNOLOGIES:
THE FUTURE OF AGING IN PLACE

Smart and caring homes (Kovach, 2005: 1) will help create living spaces that address the health problems of older, homebound people. Architect Michael Rojkind envisions a bathroom with preventive medical features, including a shower that performs body scans (McKeough, August 2006: 69).

SMART AND CARING HOMES

A house wired for health monitoring will include telemedicine technologies that feature biosensors, activity sensors, and bodily diagnostics capabilities. They will monitor traditional vital signs, such as blood pressure and respiration. There will also soon be new technologies to monitor the progress of physical therapy (Center for Future Health: 2005: 1). Telemedical technologies will facilitate "remote diagnostics and virtual physician visits" (Mathew, 2006:1). There will be computerized reminders for older people to take their medication. New technologies enable family members or health-care providers to be alerted if a homebound person falls or does not get out of bed in the morning. Despite fears that this will result in "spying on Mom" (Armour, 2006:29) or that the technologies will take over the home, the more optimistic view is that digital technologies will "watch out for you" (http://infinitec.org, 2005:1) as you age in place.

There will soon be therapeutic lighting that responds to the resident's mood (McKeough, 2006: 69) and home technologies that will help older adults with medication compliance, fitness, and safety (NAHB, 2005: 2). The goal of these technologies is to promote physical and mental health. Other technologies will monitor and encourage social contacts outside the home. Intel Corporation has developed a telephone with a rich visual display, a PC, and a sensor network that looks for sudden declines in social contact. Declines in social contact— which are a symptom of clinical depression—are noted and relayed to caregivers ("Digital Technologies for Aging in Place," www.intel.com/research).

SMART PANTRIES, MEDICINE CABINETS, AND MAILBOXES

Digital technologies will also create smart pantries and medicine cabinets that monitor availability and expiration dates on food items or medicines. Those same technologies can automatically generate shopping lists and digital reminders to take medication. There are even plans for a smart mailbox, which will tell residents if they have mail (Kovach, 2005: 1). Aging in place in the digital home will not only be easier but it may also be more fun.

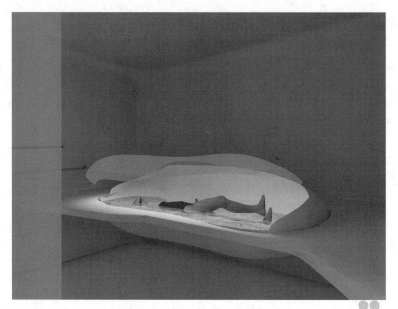

Figure 1.11. This futuristic bathroom contains preventive medical features, including a shower that does body scans, systems that analyze bodily fluids, and a floatarium that relaxes users.

Most important, the very meaning of "home" is changing, and this has already begun to affect the design of housing for older people. Home is no longer just a retreat, or what Christopher Lasch (1995) has called "a haven in a heartless world." Instead, home has become a communications hub where messages and input are "mediated." In other words, it is a place to receive, process, and then respond to information from the larger society. Gumpert and Drucker (1998: 442) insist that mediation is one of the newest functions of home.

The University of Rochester, for example, is developing a smart medical home that will help older people to communicate more effectively with healthcare providers. Sensors and digital scanners in the medical home will compile health profiles so that a change in blood pressure, body temperature, or other vital signs will be electronically noted by the nearby hospital or clinic. The smart medical home will also be wired with telemedical technologies that allow for virtual doctor visits and robotic physical therapy (www.futurehealth.Rochester.edu). Home fitness centers, for example, can create interactive environments where older people can work with cyber-trainers to increase strength and stamina. Other aspects of life, including education, financial planning, and even spirituality, will be mediated in the home ("Smart Homes and Beyond," International Conference on Smart Homes and Health Tememarics, 2006, www.healinghomes.com).

Wired homes can be linked into clusters, which are then managed by a single provider or caregiver. This is already happening in Sweden (see Chapter 6). Home-health workers are now assigned to clusters of elderly residents in some Swedish apartment buildings. They are responsible for monitoring the health and well-being of the people in these clusters, who are neighbors and often friends of one another.

In some rapidly aging nations, such as Germany, there are already plans to link homes, neighborhoods, and communities to maximize delivery of services to older people ("Gerontopolis 2030," www.Bauhaus-dessau.de. "Gerontopolis 2030"). The future for growing numbers of older people could be safer homes that are connected to more livable communities.

NOW THAT YOU'VE READ CHAPTER 1

KEY TERMS AND CONCEPTS

boomerang parents
digital home technologies
domotics
environmental interventions
ergonomics
gerontologic design
integrated personal health system
medical model of home design
next-stage communities
next-stage housing
proactive computer-assisted health
sensor networks: smart house
universal design

QUESTIONS FOR STUDY AND DISCUSSION

1. Eighty-three percent of older people surveyed by the AARP say that they want to age in place. Why is this such a popular option?
2. The do-it-yourself approach appeals to people aged 65 and older. Do you think that Boomers will be as interested in making home modifications on their own?
3. In what ways are CAPS different from architects or interior designers?
4. What is universal design, and how does it compare with gerontologic design?

5. How will the housing choices of Boomers be different from the housing choices of people who are now aged 65 or older?
6. What are Boomers looking for in retirement housing?
7. Which rooms in the house require the greatest number of modifications for people aged 65 or older?
8. What are the three waves of technological change, and why does technological change impact aging in place?
9. Digital technology will soon be able to control the level of lighting in digital homes. How will this benefit people with mood disorders or Alzheimer's disease?

HELPFUL WEBSITES

aahsa.org/advocacy/housing [American Association of Homes & Services for the Aging (AAHSA)/housing site]

aarp.org/families/home_design/rate_home (AARP. Rate Your Home Special Needs Checklist for Home Design)

aarp.org/families/home_design (AARP Home Design)

activeandable.com (Active & Able: Products with Age-Friendly Features)

adaptiveenvironments.org (Adaptive Environments)

AgingBeautifully.org (Design secrets for aging beautifully)

aging.state.ny.us/explore/housing (Housing alternatives for seniors in New York State)

agingtech.org [Center for Aging Services Technologies (CAST)]

aia.org (AIA, Design for Aging Review)

ap.buffalo.edu/idea/projectsindex.asp (Center for Inclusive Design and Environmental Access. The IDEA Center: Diversity in design; home modifications; model homes)

architectureweek.com (*Architecture Week*, "House Wired for Health")

bauhas-dessau.de "perantolopolis2030"/en/projects.asp?p=alter

CAPS.org (Certified Aging in Place Specialists)

claudiaault.com (Single-Family Homes Rule!)

communitiesforalifetime.org (Physical spaces)

design.ncsu.edu/cud (Center for Universal Design)

futurehealth.rochester.edu (Smart Medical Home)

Gero-tech.net (Smart-homes: A bibliography of smart houses)

Healinghomes.com

Infinitec.org (Information on bathroom modifications and "Homes of the Future: Smart Home Watches Out for You")

intel.com/research exploratory/digital_home.htm ("Digital Technologies for Aging in Place")

kitchenbathdesign.com (Kitchen and Bath Design Review)
NAIPC.org (NAIPC Case Studies: "Home Modification" and "Making
  Your Home Senior Friendly")
RebuildingTogether.org (Home modification checklist developed in
  partnership with the U.S. Administration on Aging)
smarthome.com (Smart Home website)
unca.edu/NCCCR/CIC_conference (Creating International Communities
  for the Second Half of Life)
wikipedia.org/wiki/domotics (Domotics)
wikipedia.org/wiki/Universal_design (Universal design)

"*Think about Keith Richards falling out of a palm tree. That's the generation we built this for. The building says, 'Let's pretend that everyone is happy and healthy, but if you need anything, you can get it. It's a back door to being old.*"

Dutch architect Arnoud Gelauff, speaking about his design for a high-rise for seniors 55 and older.

2

Quest for Community

OVERVIEW

Older people now live longer, healthier lives than previous generations. They do not necessarily need or want long-term nursing care. Instead, many older people are moving to, or actually creating, communities. This chapter looks at unassisted communities in which older people have friends or like-minded neighbors close by. They are on a quest for community in old age, and home or community design is very much a part of it. This chapter examines home designs that grow from the quest for community in old age and looks at the following types of senior housing:

- Senior Housing by Design: Active Retirement Communities
- Senior Housing by Intent: Cohousing
- Senior Housing by Coincidence: NORCs

SENIOR HOUSING BY DESIGN

The earliest senior communities in the United States were known as *active retirement communities*. People who moved there in the 1960s were buying into planned or designed communities. The good life meant relocating—very often to the Sunbelt—and leaving family or friends behind. Today's active retirement communities are adapting to demands for new types of housing and urban development. There is now an effort to design communities—in the Snowbelt as well as in the Sunbelt—that appeal to Boomers.

SENIOR HOUSING BY INTENT

There are more than 100 cohousing communities in the United States today. Such communities are often designed and operated by the people who live there. Cohousing typically involves between 4 and 30 households, which can be private homes, town houses, or apartments. These communities are typically intergenerational. There are also nearly 20 elder-cohousing communities, which were designed and then populated by elderly people.

SENIOR HOUSING BY COINCIDENCE (NORCS)

Lastly, there are communities in which the entire apartment buildings or neighborhoods have grown old together. The result is a NORC. NORCs often require increased medical and social services, and pressure is placed on the NORCs' municipal government to meet those needs.

In years to come, senior housing in unassisted communities will be shaped by changes in community goals and the aging of the baby-boom generation, which will have a very different set of housing needs and preferences.

THE QUEST FOR COMMUNITY

Metropolis Magazine refers to this Dutch building as a "rock 'n' roll retirement community" because it targets the Netherlands' aging Boomers. Holland's boomers, like our own, are now eligible to live in active adult communities. But they are far from being elderly or frail.

This rock 'n' roll retirement community called Plussenburgh is nothing like the senior housing in American towns and cities (Figure 2.1). Instead, it consists of futuristic apartments and an adjacent nursing tower painted in psychedelic colors. The designers, two Dutch architects named Arnoud Gelauff and Floor Arons, say that it speaks to the new meanings of home—and home design—in an aging world.

Plussenburgh consists of 104 living units. Half of them are located in a rectangular bloc that seems to float on huge diagonal stilts. There is a facade of wavy balconies that gives the rectangle a psychedelic look. The remaining units are located in the adjacent vertical tower—an equally psychedelic nursing home—that is painted in shades of vermillion and shocking pink.

Architecturally, the building makes a statement about what senior housing can mean now that Boomers are growing old. Plussenburgh appeals to what gerontologist Ken Dychtwald has called "Middlescence"—the Boomers' sense of adventure and entitlement (www.dychtwald.com/Highlights). The rectangle, with its undulating balconies, harks back to the Boomers' experiences in the late 1960s, which were all about playfulness and experimentation. But Plussenburgh also provides the necessary backup that older people need. Residents

Figure 2.1. "Rock 'n' roll apartments" at Plussenburgh for Boomers offer independent living in the elevated slab and a supportive nursing home in the attached, vertical tower.

know that their free-form apartments are just a short distance from the vertical nursing tower.

BUILDING ON THE DREAMS AND REALITIES OF OLD AGE

Like Plussenburgh in the Netherlands, senior housing across the United States is now building on the dreams—and realities—of old age. Many older people are now living in homes that reflect their dreams and desires. The rock 'n' roll retirement community in Plussenburgh may pay homage to shared memories

Figure 2.2. Glacier Circle is one of the growing number of self-planned housing communities for older people.

of the past (i.e., the psychedelic 1960s). American home design is giving seniors a way to realize their dreams and goals for the future.

Sometimes these dreams are social or political, and have led older people to create cohousing experiments for themselves. In 2006, for example, twelve like-minded friends created a cohousing community called Glacier Circle Senior Community. Glacier Circle, near Davis, California, has been described as the first "self-planned housing development for the elderly" in the United States (Brown, 2006: 1) (Figure 2.2).

In Abingdon, Virginia, 37 people who belonged to the same Christian con-gregation created ElderSpirit, which is their own "spiritual community" (Brown, 2006: 26). Glacier Circle and ElderSpirit are examples of communities by intent, cohousing that was designed by or with the guidance of the older people who live there.

NORCS: UNINTENTIONAL COMMUNITIES

It is also true that some of today's senior communities happen unintentionally—by coincidence—but become just as close-knit as Glacier Circle or ElderSpirit. A good example is Co-op City, in the Bronx, New York. Co-op City is a huge

Figure 2.3. Thousands of people living in Co-op City in the Bronx, New York, since the 1960s have grown old together.

development of more than 15,000 apartment units. There are 36 high-rise apartment buildings in Co-op City, ranging in height from 24 to 36 stories (Figure 2.3). Many of today's residents had moved to Co-op City back in the late 1960s when it was still new—and they were still young. Forty years later, many of the residents are still there, but they are now elderly. As they grew older, the residents of Co-op City became more politically active and friendlier with one another. What began as a collection of people living in the same apartment buildings has morphed into a close-knit community with a social and political agenda.

And because they are now friends and allies, these residents have been able to bring social services and other amenities to Co-op City.

DESIGNING FOR ACTIVE ADULTS

Finally, there are communities like Del Webb's new Festival, an active retirement community west of Phoenix, Arizona. Festival can be appreciated as the prototype for active retirement living in the twenty-first century (Figure 2.4). The community has been designed to appeal to aging Boomers. Unlike Century Village or Sun City—the prototype for retirement in the twentieth century—Festival will be intergenerational and will attract people who plan to remain employed and want to have access to everything, from museums to department stores. Instead of having to relocate thousands of miles away, aging boomers are now able to relocate to Festival and other active retirement communities that have opened.

In all three cases, home design and community development have been shaped by the hopes and dreams of older people. These communities do not "admit" older people, the way that nursing homes or ALFs do. Instead, these homes and communities have taken shape because older people created them. In this sense, the design and construction of many senior communities is a reflection of quests for community in old age and is gerontologically significant for that reason.

AGING AND THE QUEST FOR COMMUNITY

In 1972, sociologist Gerald Suttles wrote *The Social Construction of Communities*, which explains how people create a sense of community for themselves. Communities, says Suttles, require physical space, boundaries, and consensus as to who belongs there (1972: 93). American communities involve a combination of administrative details (e.g., the official boundaries of a neighborhood or community) and the cognitive maps (i.e., ways that people identify their turf). Architecture becomes significant, says Suttles, when it helps people identify their communities in the administrative sense (as in a gated community with clear-cut boundaries) and gives them cognitive maps that help them know where their turf begins and other turfs end. This interplay of architecture, official boundaries, and cognitive maps is what Suttles calls "the social construction of community" (1972:42).

Figure 2.4. In the twenty-first century, active-adult communities, such as Festival in Arizona, are appealing to Boomers who do not want to leave friends or family behind when they retire.

The lesson behind Glacier Circle and Plussenburgh is that senior housing can be actively shaped by the needs and wants of older people. Nursing homes and assisted living may be important options for America's older people, but they are not the only options. Older people are living healthier, more active lives, and often they want more of a say in how and where they live. As Ken Dychtwald (1999: 21–25) observes, America's elderly people have already begun flexing their financial and political power. Home design is another way of expressing age power (Dychtwald, 1999: 1).

More seniors than ever before are actively involved in the design, planning and, occasionally, the construction of their homes and communities. A recent study of living arrangements for America's seniors shows that 7 percent of older people in the United States now live in unassisted communities (Schafer, 2000: 10). This includes people who chose active retirement and cohousing. The AARP's president, William D. Novelli (2005: 2), mentions that "people overwhelmingly want to live in their own homes and communities as they age. . . . The challenge, then, is to create livable communities with appropriate and affordable housing. . . . [that will] facilitate personal independence and continued engagement in civic and social life." Seniors are creating livable communities by intent, design, and sometimes coincidence.

CREATING COMMUNITIES: RESPONSIVE AND FLEXIBLE SPACES

From a design perspective, the goal is, wherever possible, to create communities that are responsive and flexible. This is how one architect explains the success of Hope Meadows, a three-generational community in Rantoul, Illinois: "Hope Meadows is . . . a *living* architecture [italics in the original] that emerges and adapts, and which allows for environment shaping by residents that would normally be excluded from such processes" (Hopping, 2006: 13). Whatever form the community takes—designed, intentional, or coincidental—residents should be able to make the spaces their own—and remake them as social and spatial dynamics continue to change. Aging is an active and ongoing process. Community buildings can and should be as well. The remainder of this chapter shows that this is very much the case.

SENIOR HOUSING BY DESIGN: THE QUEST FOR ACTIVE-RETIREMENT COMMUNITIES

Active-retirement communities in the United States came to be on January 1, 1960. On that day, Sun City began selling homes to older people (SunCityAZ. org). Located west of Phoenix, Arizona, Sun City now has more than 38,000

Figure 2.5. Retirement no longer means relocating thousands of miles from home. Retirees at this active-adult community Swan's Market cohousing, will have easy access to business opportunities, culture, and sports in their hometown.

residents. Back in 1960, Sun City proclaimed itself to be a "self-sustaining community" that offered older people a new vision of the good life. Most of the original residents gladly relocated—sometimes from thousands of miles away—to a Sunbelt community that gave them easy access to shopping, recreation, and health care.

Active-retirement communities in the twenty-first century still promise the good life, although they are being designed differently because the good life now means something very different. "It's not like it was back in the 1960s," says Mark Merymee, a spokesperson for Pulte Homes, the company that now owns and operates Sun City. "[In the 1960s] people waved good-bye to their family and friends and moved away to start new friendships, find new churches, and all that" (NewRetirementCommunities.com, 2006: 1). Today's active-retirement communities appeal to Boomers who tend to be middle-aged and tied more closely to the communities where they have lived most of their lives (Figure 2.5). See page 43 for further discussion on cohousing. "Retirement today no longer means that you stop working," says Merymee (NewRetirementCommunities.com, 2006: 2). They may be buying retirement homes, but Boomers will usually continue working either full- or part-time. They may work out of a home office or commute to work.

Active-retirement communities are now places where people can continue doing what they have always enjoyed (NewRetirementCommunities.com).

Many Boomers—now on the verge of retirement—are buying property as an investment "and often as their 'aging-in-place' home" (Esterbrooks, 2006: 1).

ACTIVE RETIREMENT COMMUNITIES: PREPARING FOR BOOMERS

As a result, Pulte Homes and other large developers have begun designing active-retirement communities that can be the bridge between "single family and senior housing" (Esterbrooks, 2006: 2). Active-adult communities are now being built closer to metropolitan areas, even in the Snowbelt. Many Boomers want to downsize their homes but not leave the metropolitan area where they reside. They want to live in communities where they can be retired but still take advantage of cultural and business opportunities in nearby metropolitan areas.

Active retirement communities are being redesigned to meet the needs of Boomers. And Boomers, like their counterparts at Plussenburgh, intend to enjoy themselves for as long as possible. "Empty nesters want all the amenities of suburbia without the usual maintenance and upkeep of a home. . . . They don't want to move to Florida or Phoenix" (Esterbrooks, 2006: 1). This translates into retirement homes that have a master bedroom, a bathroom suite, a laundry room, and a spare bedroom or two. Surveys show that Boomers want to retire to homes with larger bathrooms, often with a double-sink vanity, heated tile floors, heated towel bars, and even skylights (www.NewRetirementCommunities.com). Loft space is an acceptable substitute for spare bedrooms, especially in townhouse communities. But the intent is the same: Boomers want extra space that can sometimes be converted into guest rooms but will often be used as home offices, exercise areas, or libraries.

And yet Boomers contemplate their eventual aging. The average buyer of housing in an active retirement community is 61 years old—six years younger than a decade ago (Trager, 2006: B-4). And buyers intend to live longer in the homes they purchase. This has resulted in design that appeals to the Boomers' zest for life and the all-too-familiar fact that they will eventually be more frail and possibly incapacitated. For this reason, they look for retirement homes with the master bedroom and bath at ground level (NewRetirementCommunities.com).

HOME DESIGN FOR BOOMERS

Boomers are beginning to design homes that are enjoyable *now* and will be safe and secure as they get older. For example, Boomers seem to prefer homes that have wider hallways, nonslip floors, and showers with grab bars and adjustable shower seats. They are sometimes even willing to pay thousands of dollars for residential elevators. This is what one homeowner—retired and in his early sixties—says about his new residential elevator: "Today our LEV [residential elevator] is mostly a convenience . . . but we also know that with our increasing age, it's going to become a real necessity down the line" (thelev.com). In other words, Boomers are moving to active retirement communities so that they can enjoy not only the here and now but also prepare for possible disabilities in the future.

On Long Island, New York, some of the newest upscale senior communities have two-story homes with built-in elevators or at least offer elevators as an option (otis.com). Elevators cost much more than chairlifts—$35,000 as compared to $7,000—but they have a contemporary look that appeals to Boomers, and they do not look or feel geriatric the way that chairlifts always do.

There is a broader range of active-retirement communities than there was even 15 years ago. It is now possible to live in resort-style environments, or more intimate communities, and communities that offer a combination of these two gerontological extremes. The housing stock in active-retirement communities is larger than it was 20 years ago. As Cara Trager points out, "In the 1980s, age-restricted homes averaged 1,100 square feet, as compared to more than 1,700 square feet today. In 2004, 39 percent of new senior homes were 2,400 square feet or more" (2006, B-4). Very often, new senior housing will take the form of town houses. This was unheard of in Sun City and twentieth-century retirement housing.

THE NEW GENERATION OF ACTIVE-ADULT COMMUNITIES

Sun City Festival is a new generation of active-adult community that is being built for today's Boomers. It is a far cry from the age-restricted senior housing of the original Sun City. Sun City Festival, which opened in 2006, advertises itself as intergenerational. Younger people are permitted to buy homes in this community, a nod to the fact that many retirees want to remain connected to their married sons and daughters. Sun City Festival even contains tot lots and children's playgrounds, along with more traditional golf courses and clubhouses. Other amenities, designed to appeal to active Boomers, include biking trails, walking trails, a fitness center, a wellness center, a business center, playing fields for baseball and basketball, and tennis courts (Delwebb.com/Homefinder/Festival).

The kitchen and dining area in Sun City housing of the 1960s was scaled down, as though cooking and entertaining would be less important in retirement. The new senior housing does not scale back these spaces in Festival and elsewhere (Trager, 2006: B-3). There will typically be granite-covered counters in the kitchen and bathrooms, cutting-edge appliances, and—as often as not—a separate dining room. Boomers know they will eventually be frail, but they intend to enjoy their senior housing while they can.

Sometimes it is not enough to buy a home. The goal for a growing number of older people is to create a community for themselves, their neighbors, and their friends. Cohousing appeals to people who are looking for this.

SENIOR HOUSING BY INTENT: THE QUEST FOR COHOUSING

There are older people who plan their own communities and who own and operate them as well (see www.ic.org, the Intentional Communities website). Most of these intentional communities are self-contained and focused on their own growth and development (Figure 2.6). They do not plan to franchise or replicate themselves.

INTENTIONAL COMMUNITIES

There are almost 200 self-contained cohousing communities in the United States today (Martin, B., 2006: 1; Wikipedia, "Cohousing," 2006: 1), and a third of the people living there are retirees. According to the *Cohousing Communities Directory*, there are now self-contained cohousing communities in 38 states and the District of Columbia (directory.cohousing.org, 2006). Older people are drawn to the social space and the living space of these intentional communities for at least two reasons.

First, these are socially inclusive places. *Cohousing*, as it is called, gives people a chance to create a sense of community for themselves. For example, when architects Katie McCamant and Chuck Durrett launched Nevada City (California) Cohousing, they recruited people who not only wanted to live there but also wanted to help plan the community; where possible, McCamant and Durrett involved residents in the construction process. Nevada City Cohousing was a multigenerational, child-friendly, and environmentally sustainable neighborhood from its inception. Part of that identity was derived from the input of older people who got involved at the planning stage.

Older people are also often attracted to cohousing because it gives them equity ownership and a sense that they are working toward shared goals and objectives. It is as though the commune—an experimental living arrangement of the 1960s—has been rediscovered and updated so that it showcases the talents of older people (Yeoman, 2006: 3).

COHOUSING: ARCHITECTURE WITH A GERONTOLOGICAL MESSAGE

The architecture of cohousing creates welcoming environments for all residents, but especially for seniors. Cohousing takes many forms, but consistently appeals to older people because residents of all ages live in private homes that cluster close to one another, and there are almost always common areas within walking distance. This could be a kitchen and dining area for communal meals or a meeting room where people from the community can socialize. Other examples of common areas include child-care facilities, laundry rooms, pool areas, TV

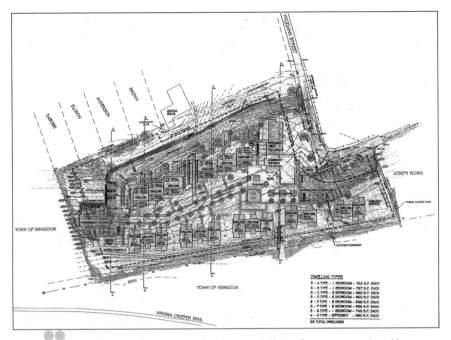

Figure 2.6. The Elder Spirit Campus bills itself as a community with intentional neighborhood design.

rooms, gyms, and computer rooms. Some cohousing communities also boast guest rooms in the common area (see, for example, Swan's Market at swans-info@swansway.com and Muir Commons Cohousing at muircommons.org).

At Nevada City (California) Cohousing, there are 4,000 square feet of common facilities on an 11-acre site, and Champlain Valley (Vermont) Cohousing offers a 4,500-square-foot common house around a central green. Older residents enjoy the easy access to common areas that allow them to remain involved in activities that interest them.

Some cohousing communities are going even further and building common areas adjacent to the homes or bedrooms of frail, older residents. By doing so, they literally bring the community to the residents when the residents can no longer go out into the community. Hope Meadows, in Rantoul, Illinois, is a good example of cohousing that remains inclusive even though its older residents are becoming frail (Belluck, 2007: F1). Hope Meadows has designed Hope House, which is now under construction. "[Hope House] will be a building with six apartments for elders and a large community kitchen/dining room. It is for seniors [from Hope Meadows] who either do not want to live alone in their current apartments, such as men who have lost their wives and now want communal dinners, as well as for seniors who can no longer be maintained in our current housing due to medical conditions. . . . I would like to see a removable wall [in Hope House] between the bedroom and the living room so that when a senior is bed-bound, family and friends do not have to gather in a small bedroom, but the bedroom can become part of the living room" (Brenda Eheart, Director of Hope Meadows, personal correspondence, 2006).

CREATING INTENTIONAL COMMUNITIES FOR OLDER PEOPLE

Cohousing is an attempt to create an intentional community, both in the social and architectural senses of the word. Cohousing takes many forms. For example, Songaia Cohousing Community in Washington State offers studio apartments, while Burlington Cohousing in Burlington, Vermont, is comprised of 21 houses that are clustered on 15 acres. Gaia Grove Ecovillage, near Gainesville, Florida, contains a mix of private housing and rental units (directory .cohousing.org, 2006). Yet, even though cohousing takes many forms, most of the people who live in cohousing strive to create a sense of community for themselves.

One architectural way of doing so is by clustering houses closer together and creating open areas where children can play and people can walk or socialize. A cohousing community could start from scratch or can recycle existing structures into something that is socially and architecturally new. There are cases where people create intentional neighborhoods by purchasing adjacent properties and removing the fences between them (Wikipedia, "Cohousing," 1–4). But in almost every case, there is an effort to create open, walkable space and green areas for gardening and recreation.

Parking is usually on the periphery, and residents must typically walk from one part of the community to another. This appeals to older people. Once they move into cohousing, they are absolved from the need to drive from one part of the community to another.

COHOUSING FOR OLDER PEOPLE

Older people have been welcomed into the intergenerational communities ever since Muir Commons opened in 1990. But in addition, there are now cohousing communities specifically for older people (Durrett, 2005). According to the Elder Cohousing Network, there are currently 13 such communities across the United States. Table 2.1 lists them by name and location.

They are in different stages of development. Some are complete and fully occupied, such as Glacier Circle Senior Community and ElderSpirit Commu-

TABLE 2.1 COHOUSING COMMUNITIES IN THE UNITED STATES

Arvada Generations	Arvada, CO
Avalon	Sherburne, NY
Community in the Cities	St. Paul, MN
Cohousing Lofts	Grass Valley, CA
Catholic Elder Community	St. Petersburg, FL
Elder Cohousing at Prospect	Longmont, CO
Elder Family in the Smokey Mountains	Whittier, NC
ElderGrace	Sante Fe, NM
ElderSpirit Community	Abingdon, VA
Galisteo Basin Preserve	Galisteo, NM
Glacier Circle Senior Community	Davis, CA
Oshara Village Commons	Santa Fe, NM
Silver Sage Village	Boulder, CO

nity. Some are only in the planning stage. The home page for Arvada Generations says, "This community will be located in Arvada, Colorado, next to an intergenerational community and within a New Urbanist neighborhood"; and the website for Oshara Village Commons in Santa Fe, New Mexico, reports plans for a 20-household Elder cohousing community adjacent to a 30-home multigenerational cohousing community. Both of these communities are being planned by older people who intend to create and enjoy their homes for years to come. And, in fact, there are seniors who go beyond this model and are now actively helping other seniors to create communities of their own. Avalon, in Sherburne, New York, is an excellent example of this process.

OTHER PEOPLE TRAINING OTHER OLDER PEOPLE TO CREATE COMMUNITIES

Avalon is senior cohousing with a different mission. The goal is to make Avalon the prototype for other senior cohousing communities that would replicate the design and gerontological goals of the original community. In this respect, Avalon represents the next wave of senior cohousing. In addition to creating a supportive and nurturing community for elderly residents, Avalon's founders— Bill and Jude Thomas and Arthur Rashap—aspire to make the community and its pioneering residents into "change masters" who will bring the Avalon concept to elderly people in other parts of the country. Bill and Jude Thomas developed the Eden Alternative (1999), which has become an important alternative to nursing homes. The Eldershire could do for independent living what the Eden Alternative did for long-term nursing care.

Avalon is an Eldershire Demonstration Project in Sherburne, New York. It consists of 30 homes surrounding a common house. Avalon has been designed to incorporate elements of cohousing and ecohousing. The community is located in a rural setting and offers residents opportunities for gardening, outdoor activities, an 11-circuit walking labyrinth, hiking trails, and a common dining area. In addition to enjoying an active, healthy lifestyle, residents have the opportunity to become mentors to older people who are interested in developing Eldershires of their own. The Avalon website explains that in the future, there will be an Eldershire Community Network throughout the country that will allow for local development while reflecting "core Eldershire Community concepts."

Elderspirit is another senior cohousing community that has already duplicated itself. Residents of Elderspirit refer to themselves as a mutual support and late-life spiritual community. They focus on doing good works for one another and for the Abingdon, Virginia, community in which they are located (elderspirit.net, 2006). The community is a mixed-income cohousing project that consists of 29 homes. Thirteen of the homes are purchased at market rate and 16 are low-income rental units. There is also a meditation hall and a common house with a large kitchen, a library, and space for dining, crafts, and social events. Residents pledge to respect the earth, care for one another, and serve the larger community. They do so by supporting the arts, doing volunteer work, recycling, and encouraging spirituality. Residents also pledge to give and receive support to one another as they age. Elder Spirit Development Corporation is building an ElderSpirit II nearby to accommodate older people on the waiting list for the original community (elderspirit.net, 2006), which is a sure sign of ElderSpirit's popularity.

OLDER FRIENDS SHARING A HOME

In addition to cohousing communities, there are many instances of older people designing shared housing for themselves. The arrangement has been called "the senior frat house" (Fornoff, 2005: 2), though that name does not do justice to the significance of the housing. The senior frat house represents an effort by older people to design their own shared housing—a house in which residents share common areas such as the kitchen and living room but have bedrooms of their own. In some cases, these aging housemates could not afford this lifestyle if they had not decided to share or pool their resources.

The arrangement is attracting widowed and divorced women, especially Boomers. Aging with friends (Gross, 2004: A1) is attractive to a small but growing number of women who have remained friends and now want to become roommates. Many women realistically expect to outlive their husbands, and "trust their [female] friends will be good caregivers" (Gross, 2004: 22).

Whether they come together as neighbors or as roommates, more older people than ever before are moving into intentional housing. Muir Commons, the first official cohousing development, was intergenerational from the beginning in 1990. Housing by intent has become even more specialized, so that there is now senior cohousing and also senior shared housing.

But not all community building is intentional. Some neighborhoods that weren't originally planned as retirement communities end up that way. They are home to people who had moved there years ago, when they were much younger, but who gradually aged in place. It is common for people to age in place, but it is becoming a gerontological fact that neighborhoods can do the very same thing. They become communities by coincidence.

SENIOR HOUSING BY COINCIDENCE: NORCS

NORCs are neighborhoods or buildings where a substantial portion of the residents are older adults. In general, NORCs are not designed to be senior housing or retirement communities. They became NORCs because residents have either aged in place over several decades or have moved to such buildings or communities in old age. But although they are strangers when they move to the building or community, they become political allies and advocates of change.

In New York's Pelham Parkway Houses, for example, residents mobilized to persuade the city council to reinstate $1,000,000 for NORC programs throughout New York City (Bleyer, 2006: 3). There are also cases where residents of NORCs petition landlords to upgrade the apartment buildings where they live (Rosenfeld, Chapman, and McCullough, 2006: 1). In other words, older people become actively involved in their communities, even when those communities are coincidental.

NORCS: NEW ARCHITECTURAL CHALLENGES

NORCs can be either suburban or urban. In either case they impose architectural challenges. For example, the Plainview and Old Bethpage area, in New York, has a population of over 30,000 with more than a third over the age of 60. It has been designated as New York State's first suburban NORC. It is difficult for older people to live in suburbia when they cannot move easily around their split-level homes and cannot drive (Manheim and Friedman, 2005: 1). With funds from local and state agencies, the Plainview–Old Bethpage NORC has been able to retrofit homes on an ad hoc basis, making them safer for older people by adding grab bars, ramps, and nonskid surfaces on bathroom floors (personal correspondence with the Adult Services division of the Mid-Island YM and YWCA, Plainview, NY, 2006). Efforts are being made in the Plainview–Old Bethpage area to encourage residents to walk in their neighborhoods and remain physically active. The community has added benches in U-shaped groupings, which encourages older people to congregate and socialize. There are also pedestrian paths that are landscaped with seating at strategic intervals so that older people can walk the neighborhood but sit down to rest when necessary.

Living in NORCs is perhaps even more difficult for older people in urban areas, where laundry rooms are often located in the basement of an apartment building and bathrooms or kitchens are not senior-friendly. This means that older people often find themselves aging in homes and communities that were never intended for older people, and these elderly people risk falls and poor nutrition because they are so isolated. The urban response has been to promote independence by making buildings safer and more navigable through supportive service programs (norcs.ujcfedweb.org, 2005).

NORCS: RETROFITTING FOR URBAN LIVING

Such programs can provide funds for retrofitting the premises. For example, lobby areas in some NORC apartment buildings have been redesigned by making them better lit and more accessible by adding ramps and handrails as well as eliminating stairs at the entryway. The mailroom is often reworked so that residents' mailboxes are larger and easier to reach. There are now benches in the mailrooms so that the elderly residents can sit while looking through their mail. Other improvements include the placement of decals on doors or windows to identify units with infirm or frail residents and the installation of improved hallway lighting (Poliakoff, 2004: 3).

There is currently no distinctive architecture associated with NORCs, but it is important to note their existence because they call attention to one of the challenges of home design in an aging nation and, indeed, an aging world. The design and planning of homes and communities must encourage residents to stay healthy and age in place (Ahrentzen, 2004: 1). NORCs require ongoing repair and renovation if they are to achieve these gerontological goals.

THE FUTURE

The lifestyles and aspirations of older people will continue to be reflected in home design and urban planning. And just as the roles and lifestyles of older people are changing, so are the homes and communities in which they live. Older people are living healthier and more dynamic lives than ever before. Their homes and communities are being shaped—often unexpectedly—mainly because of the three following three reasons:

1. A home or community can be built for one purpose, but may have to change as time goes on. Almost a third of Israel's kibbutzim, or collective settlements, have been redesigned to meet the needs of their aging populations (see Chapter 8). Most were originally designed as farming or light-manufacturing communities, but many of them are now retirement communities. Therefore, they have had to respond architecturally to meet these new needs.
2. The original goal can be intentionally changed, requiring new architectural forms. Such changes often happen "from the top down." For example, a company acquires a retirement property and converts it to an assisted-living facility or nursing home. Changes also happen "from the bottom up," such as when residents create new goals or options for themselves. This often happens when people decide to care for an aging family member and retrofit their homes accordingly.
3. The design may change when a home or community is marketed more widely or aggressively. New owners or tenants may have different needs than former occupants, which will lead to design adjustments.

THE PURPOSE OF A SENIOR COMMUNITY CAN UNEXPECTEDLY CHANGE

Hope Meadows, for example, is a cohousing community (i.e., a community by intent) that is unexpectedly aging in place and becoming a NORC. The implications for home design and community planning are already impacting Hope Meadows. The community was founded in 1993 with 64 housing units. Fifteen of those units were allocated to foster and adopted families, 44 to senior citizens, and five were reserved for administrative and community activities (Eheart, Happing, et al, 2005: 3; Belluck, 2007: F1).

Hope Meadows was originally driven by the need to create a safe and supportive community—a surrogate family of sorts—for the foster children who lived there. Over the years the children have grown into adolescents (with issues that come with being teenagers), and the elderly residents have grown more frail and incapacitated. The community has had to rethink home design because the original housing for elderly people is no longer suitable for some of them. The community is now planning a new building that has elements of a hospice and a nursing home. That building, which will be known as Hope House, was not part of the original plan, but reflects the fact that this intergenerational community has become very much a NORC. The future will see more communities in which senior housing by intent, design, and coincidence begin to merge.

THE INTENTIONAL GOAL OF A COMMUNITY CAN CHANGE

Beacon Hill Village is a community of 320 members who live independently for as long as they can, but whose lives gradually become intertwined as they grow older (Figure 2.7). A NORC consists of people, usually in apartment buildings, who are members of a community by coincidence. The 320 members of Beacon Hill Village are residents of the larger Beacon Hill community, which has intentionally joined together and whose goals change as they get older (Gross, 2006: F1; Gross, 2007: 1; Bosler, 2005:14). Beacon Hill Community offers the concept of active retirement to younger members and also provides support systems for members who are more frail or impaired. And

Figure 2.7. Residents of Beacon Hill, 52 to 58, grow old at home with support from a community group.

members of the community receive all of these benefits while remaining in the homes where they have always lived (Basler, 2005).

Residents live independently, but turn to their "concierge service" (Gross, 2007:1; Basler, 2005:14) for help with everything from home repair to sick pets. Neighborhood residents can—and do—join the Beacon Hill Village Association, which now includes people in their fifties and sixties, as well as people in their nineties.

Beacon Hill represents the transition from independent living to NORC, but with a gerontological difference. A NORC, like Co-op City in the Bronx, New York, is usually limited to a finite number of apartment buildings or town-houses. Beacon Hill Village is more dynamic and intergenerational. Residents remain in their own homes, but gradually become integrated into the Village Association as their needs change and they require more services.

Cohousing experiments can be just as dynamic as NORCs. Wild Sage Cohousing, in Boulder, Colorado, and Muir Commons illustrate how a cohous-ing experiment can have more than one goal and can successfully achieve them both. The two goals are to create an intergenerational community and build solar-powered, zero-energy housing. Figure 2.8 shows how these two goals have shaped home design at Muir Commons.

Figure 2.8. Muir Commons strives to be an intergenerational community that features solar-powered, zero-energy housing.

WHEN A DESIGN IS MARKETED MORE WIDELY OR AGGRESSIVELY

Until now, communities by intent—cohousing and intergenerational communities—have been small and intimate experiments. The architecture and design of cohousing communities is often managed by the small group of original residents, known sometimes as "settlers" (Martin, 2006: 2). In fact, a recent issue of *AARP: The Magazine* recently ran an article on the "bold pioneers" who are creating the new cohousing (Yeoman, 2006: 1). But designs that work well for a group of longtime friends may not satisfy more randomly selected homeowners. The resulting architecture is more about compromise than the quest for community, as the following two examples show.

Cohousing for the Gay, Lesbian, and Transgender Community

Communities such as Rainbow Vision (Levine, 2006: 1; Wilson, 2005: 16) are bringing senior housing to the gay, lesbian, and transgender community. Rainbow Vision consists of 146 condos and rental units on 13 acres of land (Ritter, 2006: 1). The few examples of senior housing for the gay, lesbian, and transgender community have been more like cohousing than active adult communities (Figure 2.9). They have been created by groups of friends or neighbors with a common vision of a retirement lifestyle. Also, Stonewall Audubon Circle in Boston has been designed to strengthen the ties to the surrounding gay community. Stonewall includes a neighborhood center that extends services to nonresidents who live nearby (Ritter, 2006: 2). Cohousing with space for outreach is new to the United States but is already a standard feature in Israeli cohousing.

Birds of a Feather Housing

There will be more intergenerational housing experiments, especially in or near college campuses. Some universities, including the University of North Carolina and Penn State, are developing active adult communities for alumni. More than 50 such communities, which can be called "alma mater housing" are operating nationwide (Kerkstra, 2006: 1). The original alma mater housing was more like cohousing: It was the brainchild of alumni and sorority sisters who wanted to live near one another in old age. As the concept takes hold, alma mater housing—like senior housing for the gay and lesbian community—will become more standardized across the nation. But the larger gerontological point is that there will be more senior housing for birds of a feather (Neville, 2007: F1). Rocinante, in Summerville, Tennessee, has been designed for aging hippies (Neville, 2007: F1). It calls attention to the fact that more older people will want to live with other people who share the same values, religion, or sexual orientation. The big selling point in the earliest retirement communities was sunshine;

Figure 2.9. In the past few years elderly cohousing has gained ground as aging boomers head into retirement. Some women have taken it a step further with plans for a collective living model that caters to retired lesbians.

it is no coincidence that Sun City was—and still is—larger than many American cities. But the selling point for the future will be norms, values, and sexual orientation. People are not only getting older. They are getting wiser, too.

NOW THAT YOU'VE READ CHAPTER 2

KEY TERMS AND CONCEPTS

accessory apartment
active-adult living
adult homes
aging in place
alternative housing
cohousing
commune
continuing-care retirement communities
Elder Cottage (or ECHO Housing)
Eldershire
enriched housing
family-type homes

humanistic design
intentional communities
naturally occurring retirement community (NORC)
senior frat house
social construction of communities
spiritual community
universal design

QUESTIONS FOR STUDY AND DISCUSSION

1. In what way(s) is humanistic design of senior housing different from the way(s) that senior housing has traditionally been designed?
2. What is a NORC, and how must a NORC be upgraded or retrofitted to meet the needs of aging residents?
3. Why has cohousing become so popular among older people in the United States, and what type(s) of older people are typically attracted to cohousing communities?
4. How is a cohousing community different from a NORC? Is it possible to plan or design a NORC in the way(s) that it is possible to plan or design a cohousing community?
5. How is the baby-boom generation impacting the design of senior housing?
6. As best you can, define an active-adult community. Now, explain how a community can be designed to support an active-adult lifestyle.
7. Is the design of assisted-living communities keeping pace with the needs of older people in the United States?
8. Which makes it easiest for people to age in place: cohousing, NORCs, or assisted living? How does the design of a building and community affect the process of aging in place?
9. How does home design in active-adult communities reflect the baby-boom focus on the here and now, and how does it also reflect the concern for aging and disability? Explain how the residential elevator reflects both of those concerns.
10. In what ways are senior communities changing, and how is this impacting home design in such places?

HELPFUL WEBSITES

1. General Websites
   aarp.org/families/housing_choices
   aahsa.org/advocacy/five_big_ideas.asp (AAHSA's Five Big Ideas)

aahsa.org/advocacy/housing (Housing: A Glossary)
aging.state.ny.us/explore/housing/housalt2.htm (Housing Alternatives
for Seniors in New York State)
dychtwald.com/highlights ("A New Stage of Life: Middlesence" and
"Re-visioning Retirement)
eldersource.org/living (Living Arrangements)
kodiakdailymirror.com (Author discusses alternative housing for seniors)
NPR.org/templates/story/story.php?StoryID=5149646 Ken Dychtwald
NewRetirementCommunities.com
senioroutlook.com/glossary.asp (Glossary of senior housing terms)

2. Active-Adult Lifestyles
delwebb.com/lifestyle/default.aspx (Del Webb Active Adult Lifestyle)
2young2retire.com
suncityaz.org (Sun City and Sun City West)
wikipedia.org/wiki/Retirement_Village

3. Cohousing and Alternative Housing for Seniors
cohousingco.com (Cohousing for seniors)
cohousingco.com (Real Estate Development Firm for Cohousing)
cohousing.org
elderspirit.net (Late-life spiritual community)
eldercohousing.org
eldershire.net
edenalt.com (The Eden Alternative)
ic.org (Intentional communities)
igstrats.org (Intergenerational strategies)
libertyridge.com (Spiritual retirement community)
mblackarchitect.com (Architect specializing in cohousing)
muircommons.org (Muir Commons Cohousing Community)
pbs.org/thoushalthonor/eden/ (Eldershire Communities)
saintjohnsmilw.org
sfgate.com/cgi-bin/article.cgi? (Senior frat house)
silversagevillage.com
swansway.com (Swan's Market Cohousing)
wikipedia.org/wiki/cohousing
WolfCreekCommons.net (Wolf Creek Commons Cohousing)

4. Assisted-Living and Continuing-Care Retirement Communities
retirement.org/ContinuingCareRetirementCommunity

"*The most powerful instrument in any health-care facility can be the facility itself. . . . Good design does more to support healing. And the sooner you call your architect, the better the design. Get your architect involved early.*"

—The American Institute of Architects

3

In Sickness and in Health
Assisted Living and Long-Term Nursing Care

OVERVIEW

The design of long-term-care facilities has responded to a paradigm shift in the philosophy behind long-term care. Long-term care is now seen less as a medical experience and more as a lifestyle experience. Advocates of this new approach emphasize the benefits of living in homelike environments where the *community* replaces the ward or geriatric wing.

The impact of this paradigm shift has been enormous. New ALFs, nursing homes, and dementia units are being configured as clusters of rooms around common areas that become communities of care.

Innovative design now includes indoor Main Street areas that encourage patients to reminisce about towns or villages where they grew up. Other design innovations include creative use of outdoor space and more effective pathways for wandering and way-finding.

The future design of long-term-care facilities will be shaped by at least two gerontological trends. One of these will be the increased ethnic diversity of the United States. Long-term-care facilities will be challenged to accommodate different ethnic communities, which will involve greater sensitivity to ethnic preferences for certain colors, lighting styles, and room sizes.

The other gerontological trend will be the increased reliance on assistive technologies, robotics, and telemedicine. The design of long-term facilities will have to accommodate robots that move from room to room and the interactive environment that comes from placing (or implanting) sensors on patients.

The most promising approach to the design of long-term-care facilities is humanistic design, which gathers input from elderly patients and not just from the owners or developers of the property. Humanistic design allows designers to modify their plans based on how elderly people respond.

Humanistic design will become more important as the baby-boom generation ages and needs long-term care. Preliminary research indicates that
Boomers will want different forms of senior housing when they reach their
eighties from what today's 80-year-olds want. There will be more demand for
single rooms, private baths, on-site health spas, and more interface with the
community. Boomers will expect to connect with their neighbors, both inside
and outside the facility.

There will also be an increase in urban housing for seniors because Boomers
are increasingly interested in living in or near urban areas. The nursing home
or assisted-living facility of tomorrow will be designed to be architecturally
compatible with the surrounding (urban) community, and the design of long-
term-care facilities will blend with the community by featuring retail spaces,
cyber-cafes, day-care facilities, and health spas at the street level.

ASSISTED LIVING: IT TAKES A VILLAGE

On September 11, 2001, the Hallmark in Manhattan evacuated residents
because of the terrorist attack on the World Trade Center, which was just a few
blocks away. Executive Director Ulrich Wahl recalls that the New York City
police and fire departments actually came into the Hallmark and set up a command post there (Ulrich Wahl, personal correspondence, 2001). Residents
were evacuated by bus shortly after the terrorist attack. The facility was not
damaged, and it eventually reopened. Not a single resident was injured during
the attack or the evacuation.

The Hallmark evacuation was extreme, and hopefully it will never be
repeated. But this event calls attention to how assisted living has changed and
what these changes mean to architects and interior designers. Now, more than
ever before, assisted living is becoming an urban phenomenon. The Hallmark
was not isolated from the neighborhood where it was located. On September
11, it became a command post and a refuge for others in the community. Far
from being isolated, the Hallmark was part of the citywide response to the
attacks on September 11.

PART OF THE NEIGHBORHOOD MIX

There has been a movement to integrate assisted-living facilities into the neighborhoods where they are located, and more attention is being given to the creation of home and community on site. In short, the emphasis is shifting from
"assisted" to "living," and to the fact that older people can be an asset and a
resource in the neighborhood where an ALF is located.

More than 1,000,000 Americans now live in ALFs. Another 600,000 live in continuing-care facilities that begin with assisted living and offer long-term nursing care when needed (Schwennsen 2006: 7). The typical resident of an ALF is a woman in her mid- to late eighties who does not need long-term nursing care but needs some assistance with the activities of daily living (Wikipedia, "assisted living:" 1).

There has been an important shift in the location and design of ALFs. Instead of building them in out-of-the-way places, efforts are being made to integrate the facility and its population into the neighborhood or community where it is located.

This perspective has been articulated in the AARP's "Global Report on Aging," by Wim Bakker of the Netherlands. Bakker explains that the Netherlands has made it a priority to integrate older and younger people and encourage people with disabilities to live in the community. The Dutch have translated this policy into the location and design of ALFs all over Holland. ALFs in Holland resemble apartment buildings, and tenants do as much as they can on their own. There are common areas on the ground floors, including Internet cafes and restaurants that are open to the public. The result is that "the building means something to the neighborhood" (Bakker, 2006: 2).

DESIGN THAT ENCOURAGES CONNECTION TO THE NEIGHBORHOOD

A growing number of ALFs in the United States are building on the Dutch approach to location and design of ALFs. AgeSong in San Francisco, for example, encourages interaction between residents of the ALF and the surrounding community. There are retail spaces that are operated by residents of the facility. Residents and members of the community get to know one another in these spaces.

AgeSong has been designed to be a "good architectural neighbor" (Glynn, 2006: 1) that adds to the mixed-use urban space where it is located. AgeSong offers its occupants dining rooms and lounges on every floor. The interior is constructed of materials—decorative tiles, cherry wood cabinets, and limestone flooring—that evoke a homelike setting. Windows are built lower so that residents can gaze out the windows while in bed or in a wheelchair (Glynn, 2006: 3).

The award-winning Avalon Square, in Waukesha, Wisconsin (AIA, 2004: 83), is another example of a good architectural neighbor. Avalon Square has integrated "commercial space, historic preservation, and clear urban-design language." It does so in a small-sized, Midwestern city. Village Care, in Manhattan, New York, offers the same mix of commercial space, historic preservation, and connection to the community. It is located in Manhattan's Greenwich Village and is becoming part of the neighborhood, both socially and architecturally.

The building's exterior "will be contextual with neighborhood architecture" (Anderson, 2006: 1) and has emerged as a result of a give-and-take with the community on everything from building design to neighbors' reactions to proposed rooftop gardens. A small percentage of the people who are attracted to urban assisted living, such as Village Care or the more upscale Esplanade, have relocated to Manhattan to be near their children, but the majority are "veteran New Yorkers who never left the city" (Green, 2005: 1). A similar dynamic is occurring in America's suburbs, where growing numbers of older people are choosing to relocate to nearby ALFs when they can no longer live independently (Figure 3.1).

ASSISTED LIVING COMES TO SUBURBIA

Even as recently as 15 years ago, the norm was to leave suburbia and relocate, sometimes hundreds of miles away. But in recent years, ALFs in suburban areas have been attracting local residents—a trend that is predicted to increase as Boomers reach their seventies.

The more successful of these ALFs provide "hotel-like touches" (Paquette, 2003: 6) that underscore the joys of "living" rather than the need for "assis-

Figure 3.1. Award-winning Avalon Square in Wisconsin is an ALF that has become a place where commercial space, historic preservation, and senior housing come together.

tance." This is being accomplished by doing away with double-loaded corridors and building homelike clusters of rooms. These clusters contain fewer units per floor, with common areas outside residents' bedrooms. The result is the feeling that this is closer to what residents had at home before moving to the ALF (Kepley, 2005: 2). The architecture, finishes, and interior design must also be homelike, rather than institutional, for these "hotel-like" touches to be effective.

The exterior of the more successful ALFs in suburban areas is decidedly homelike. There is a growing body of research on specifically welcoming exterior features that convey a sense of home (Marsden, 2006: 47–62). Familiar housing signals include smaller, more inviting porches and porte cocheres, rather than massive ones. A massive porte cochere is often intimidating and makes a facility look more like a hospital than a home (Figure 3.2). ALFs also look more homelike and approachable when they are surrounded by mature trees and attractive shrubbery.

Homelike attributes and hotel-like touches are consistent with the paradigm shift toward a social model of assisted living rather than a medical model. The

Figure 3.2. Avoid intimidating entryways; instead create more homelike entryways.

goal for designers is to create ALFs that house residents in small, homelike clusters and sometimes provide a continuum of care that offers different levels of assistance as residents become more frail.

The social model has transformed the assisted-living experience by accentuating connection to the community of residents inside the ALF and connection to the community at large (Kepley, 2005:3). Community outreach brings older people into the community and brings the community to the ALF. The goal is to alert the community to the valuable resource in its midst (Bakker, 2005: 2).

LONG-TERM CARE: FROM HOSPITAL TO HOMELIKE

There have been important shifts in the approach to designing nursing homes in the United States. During the past two decades, the paradigm for long-term care has shifted from a medical model to the idea that nursing homes should be homelike and therapeutic environments (AIA, 2006: 11; Schwarz, 1996: 73–78).

NURSING HOMES: A SHIFT IN DESIGN

There are currently 16,094 nursing homes in the United States (Nursing Home, Wikipedia.org, 2005). Most of these are classified as either intermediate or skilled nursing units, which has implications for architecture and design. Distinctions between intermediate and skilled nursing units are related to federal funding standards. Intermediate-care facilities provide just enough nursing care to qualify for Medicaid reimbursement. Skilled nursing units meet the more rigorous medical and epidemiological standards. As a result, they are covered under health-insurance plans that qualify them for Medicare reimbursement (Carr, 2005: 1). But the same medical and epidemiological standards that influence reimbursement decisions also influence the design of nursing homes.

Architects and designers are required to submit certificate of need applications that show that their plans are compliant with state regulations for nursing station locations and the number of rooms in a double-loaded corridor. The result is that nursing homes meet federal and state guidelines, but often have "not contribute[d] over the years to an environment that supported innovative design ideas" (Schwarz, 1996: 35).

There are now efforts to revise nursing home codes and create a new architectural paradigm for nursing home design. The original codes were restrictive. They were drawn from hospital codes and contained the implicit assumption that patients spend most of their time in bed and will be discharged in a relatively short time. Existing codes have also been criticized because they encourage residents to depend on caregivers for help and information.

There is now "a broadening movement to humanize care for elderly people with smaller, more domestic settings and a closer sense of community among residents" (Hamilton, 2005: 1). The challenge for architects and designers is now to make nursing homes more homelike by incorporating the social and psychological needs of residents, their families, and the staff of the nursing home. As Dr. William Thomas puts it, the goal should be to do away with "big boxes" and replace them with "green houses" (Thomas, 2006: 4). Recent nursing home design acknowledges long-term human needs that go far beyond the medical care available in big boxes and now tries to make life more meaningful for residents of nursing homes by creating designs that focus less on nursing and more on home.

DESIGNING HOMELIKE NURSING HOMES

Recent award-winning designs for skilled nursing facilities are homelike. Park Homes, for example, is a skilled nursing facility in Hillsboro, Kansas, which houses patients in households, or clusters, that are architecturally residential and feature single-family-home iconography (AIA, 2006). Staff is now assigned to one of these "households," and residents have more privacy. They also have more freedom when it comes to what they will eat, when they will wake or go to sleep, and how they will spend their days (Wikipedia.org, 2007: Nursing homes"). The design of residential households, or clusters (Krejci, 1994: 1), blurs the distinction between residents and staff and allows residents to continue living their lives, even as they require more skilled nursing care. Natural outdoor gathering spaces create spots where residents and members of the larger community can gather (AIA, 2006: 98). The design of the facility encourages residents' independence by making rooms and spaces easy to find and use and provides "traditional residential qualities of privacy, choice, [and] control" (Carr: 2005: 3).

The trend toward homelike nursing homes includes a variety of design strategies. One of these is "Edenizing," which means adding plants and allowing pets indoors and creating flower and vegetable gardens outside. By being involved with plants, pets, and gardening, residents recapture their connection to life; they have more of a stake in their household and the life around them. One of the most successful applications of "Edenizing" can be found at Traceway in Tupelo, Mississippi, which is home to the Green House Project (Israel, 2005: 1) (Figure 3.3). The Green House Project consists of "10 cozy cottages" where all residents live in households that are full of "sunlight, plants, pets, and access to outdoor spaces" (Israel, 2005:2). Plans are now under way for green house projects in 17 other states, which attests to the power of the green house concept.

Figure 3.3. The Green House paradigm makes this nursing home into a garden where residents are actively involved in the care and upkeep of their community.

The American Institute of Architects refers to Traceway, in Tupelo, Mississippi, as "the ultimate household concept" in nursing home design, "a journey toward a new paradigm of nursing care that included the client, the staff, and the designer" (AIA, 2004:2).

Another way to make nursing homes more homelike for residents is to make rooms more ergonomically comfortable. This can include installing folding doors for ease of wheelchair movement and low-mounted towel racks and medicine cabinets to encourage residents to function more independently (Krejci, 1994:2). In addition to lowering towel racks and medicine cabinets, it is important to lower bathroom mirrors. Unless mirrors are hung lower, people in wheelchairs cannot see into any of them (Weinstein, 2006: 6).

There is growing interest in designing resident-room furniture according to universal design principles. Chairs and beds, for example, can be designed for people with different needs, which can make resident rooms more comfortable and homelike. And even shared rooms can be zoned for territorial privacy by placing beds in opposite corners of the room (Figure 3.4).

The shift from hospital to homelike is also reflected in the design of corridors and doorways. Hospital corridors are long and double loaded, with rooms on either side of a long hallway. Homelike design focuses instead on the creation of more intimate and personalized spaces—recessed alcoves or vestibules containing two or three bedrooms, architectural detailing such as archways and hallway window seating, and corridors filled with plants, fish tanks, and birdcages. In the newer nursing homes, corridors become turf where friendships and activities can be nurtured. For example, some designers now personalize doorways by creating different wall treatments around doors. In some cases the wall treatment is bounded by a molding. The goal is to personalize the entry to a resident's apartment or room. In addition to the colored borders around the door, it is possible to personalize the entry with a memory box and shelf. The memory box becomes a marker that is filled with personal mementos that identify the person living in the room. The shelf can serve the same purpose, and in addition, becomes a place to rest a purse, the day's mail, or flyers, while a resident reaches for the key and unlocks the door.

Many nursing homes now allow—and even encourage—residents to decorate their own rooms. For example, some facilities allow residents to select the color their room will be painted from a choice of five or six different colors (Weinstein, 2006:1). In addition to personalizing the color of the walls, residents and staff members at the more progressive facilities are being encouraged to personalize the walls with family photos—not only photos of residents' families but also photos of caregivers' families (Weinstein, 2006: 7) (Figure 3.5). The intent is to reinforce the idea that everyone in a household—patients and caregivers alike—is family.

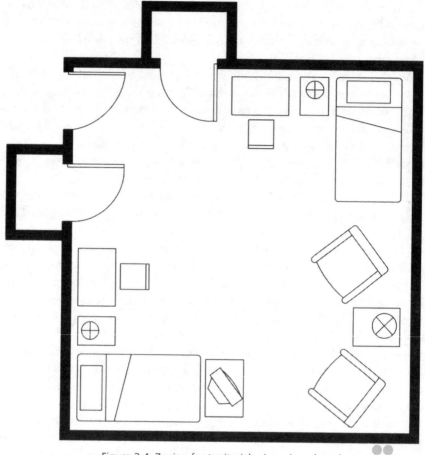

Figure 3.4. Zoning for territorial privacy in a shared nursing home bedroom.

HOMELIKE NURSING HOMES IN A CHANGING SOCIETY

The great challenge for the future is to design nursing homes that will be homelike for the new racial and ethnic groups who will be living there. Culture shapes color meaning (Guerin, 2002: 3), and this will impact the interior design of nursing homes as the ethnicity of patients begins to change. There is already evidence that more ethnic groups, especially Asian Americans, are now turning to nursing homes as their family members age. Indeed, nursing homes have already been challenged to meet the dietary and social norms of the Muslim community in Minnesota (Clemetson, 2006: 1), the Chinese

Figure 3.5. The walls around the doorways in this nursing home are painted a different color from the walls in the corridor. There is also a shelf next to and a light above each door.

community in Chicago (Babwin, 2004: 2), and Indian and Pakistani communities in New Jersey (AlamedaCenter.com/indian_program.htm). The Resort Nursing Home in Far Rockaway, New York, now has two entire Russian wings to house aging Russian immigrants who lived in Little Odessa, the nearby Russian community.

The challenge for designers in years to come will be to create therapeutic environments that respond to the needs of different ethnic groups. Research on color, meaning, and culture indicates that ethnic groups resonate differently to different color palettes and different spatial arrangements. For example, research on color-palette preference shows that the Japanese respond more to color palettes that include neutral or cool hues, while Koreans respond to color palettes including neutral hues and middle values. American clients are more comfortable with color palettes that include warm hues and middle values (Park and Guerin, 2002: 27–34.). Research indicates that different ethnic groups not only *prefer* different color palettes but also react differently to color. Mood and feeling vis-a-vis the same color can be different across ethnic groups. Comparisons of mood and feeling in response to the very same color were quite different for British and Chinese subjects (Ou, et al., 2004: 239), which is similar to the fact that housing design must be sensitive to ethnic differences (Guerin, Hadjiyanni, 2004: 1). This is an important fact to bring to the design of nursing homes and dementia units.

DIFFERENT ETHNIC DECORS IN THE SAME FACILITY

Therapeutic environments must employ colors that will be therapeutic for the people who are living there. For example, Arista Care at Alameda Center nursing home in Perth Amboy, New Jersey, is an example of a nursing home that has redecorated two wings so that the color palette and design would be therapeutic for two very different ethnic groups. In Arista Care Alameda Center, one entire wing has been designated for patients from the nearby Indian community and another for Latino patients. The color palette for each of the floors is different and distinctive. The Latino wing is decorated in tropical, Caribbean tones and is reinforced with Caribbean plants and fabrics. The Indian wing contains a small Hindu temple and images of Hindu gods and goddesses (Figure 3.6). There is also the distinctive sound of temple bells and the aroma of incense. Each floor has its own kitchen, and there is the distinctive aroma of Indian cooking on one wing and Latino cooking on the other. Administrator Michael Nieman says that there are waiting lists for places on both of these floors because they are so popular, and he is happy to be filling an important need in the community (Michael Nieman, personal correspondence, 2007).

The great challenge for architects and designers across the United States will be to create therapeutic and homelike environments for an increasingly diverse range of ethnic groups. Where possible, many nursing homes and dementia units now include a Main Street where patients can stroll or interact (AIA, 2006). But a stroll down Main Street will mean something very different to an aging woman who grew up in the Ukraine and an elderly man who spent his boyhood in Mumbai. The design of Main Street will need to take this into account.

ENVIRONMENTS FOR PEOPLE WITH DEMENTIA

Architecture and interior design can reduce anxiety and help people with Alzheimer's disease to be more engaged, and to feel that they are more in control of their environment. Like Main Streets everywhere, the one in the Village in

Figure 3.6. This nursing home in New Jersey has created a distinctive wing for patients who were originally from India.

Connecticut has storefronts, streetlights, and a clock tower. The difference is that the 175-foot length of Main Street at the Village is indoors. And it's not a movie set. This is a replica of downtown New Canaan, Connecticut. It forms the hub of the health-care facility, where most of the residents come from that nearby suburb (Baldwin, 2002:F1). The Village is at the architectural cutting edge because it has re-created a memory of downtown New Canaan for people who have lost the ability to recall it for themselves. The Village has other features that are now becoming the standard for Alzheimer's care: homelike settings, circular walkways, multiple kitchen areas, and smaller common areas. They call attention to the fact that architecture and interior design, everything from lighting cues to color schemes, impact people with Alzheimer's disease.

The paradox of Alzheimer's is that it creates the psychological need for stimulation, but at the same time "the stimulation [that people with Alzheimer's seek] is the one thing they cannot handle" (Gladwell, 1997: 139). The need for stimulation prompts endless wandering, and people with Alzheimer's almost always say they are looking for "home." The challenge, both architecturally and in terms of interior design, is to create environments where people can wander but where they will not be shocked or frightened by the discoveries they make.

For this reason, Alzheimer's requires homelike, and not medical- or hospital-based, design. The more successful Alzheimer's units house people in smaller residential units that often resemble households (Cohen and Day, 1993: 183), not hospital wards. At the more innovative facilities, residents are now grouped, or housed, according to ethnicity (AlamedaCenter.com, 2007; Clemetson, 2006; Babwin, 2004) or cognitive disability (Schwarz et al, 2005; Gladwell, 1997). Taliesin Architects, formed in 1959 after the death of Frank Lloyd Wright, has designed Alzheimer's facilities that are organized around continuum of care issues. Taliesin's Sun Health Residence for Alzheimer's care in Arizona contains a design unit, or household, that repeats itself for each level of care (Figure 3.7). Residents begin in a high-functioning household and move to different households as their functioning diminishes (Hensler, 1997).

Figure 3.7. The molecular concept: This design unit at Taliesin's Sun Health Residence for Alzheimer's care repeats itself for each level of care so that moving from one to the next is less traumatic.

TRENDS IN THE ARCHITECTURE AND DESIGN OF ALZHEIMERS' UNITS

Alzheimer's units work best when they create environments that reduce anxiety and confusion. The architecture and interior design of Alzheimer's units accomplish these goals in a variety of ways. They provide the following:

- Culturally supportive environments
- Way-finding (in halls and rooms) and wandering paths
- Technology and smart dementia units
- Opportunities for community-building and not so much patient care

Culturally Supportive Environments

The most gerontologically interesting approach is to create "culturally specific design supports" for dementia patients (Day and Cohen, 2000: 363–65). For this reason, the use of a Main Street design is becoming common in continuing care environments. The CCRC's Main Street provides a variety of cues that stimulate memory and encourage exploration and social activity. Main Street often has retail stores, restaurants, and hair salons. Figure 3.8 depicts the Main Street at the Forest at Duke, a 16-year-old CCRC in Durham, North Carolina.

Figure 3.8. Night view of Main Street at this CCRC in Durham, North Carolina.

Day and Cohen (2000: 365–67) describe facilities in Milwaukee, Wisconsin, and West Hollywood, California, that were home to Russian-Jewish immigrants with dementia. Cohen and Day created environments that supported a "culturally based sense of identity" (2000: 369) and built on the residents' "cultural competence" (Day and Cohen, 2000: 366). Building on Russian-Jewish social norms, Day and Cohen created space for residents to dress up and promenade, which is an important behavior in Russia. They provided space for a veterans' club, which appealed to men who had served in the Russian armies of World Wars I and II. The facilities in Milwaukee and West Hollywood also had feast halls where residents could eat and drink Russian-style meals (Day and Cohen, 2000: 380–388). The Alameda Center, in Perth Amboy, New Jersey, accommodates residents from India, from Central America, and from China (AlamedaCenter.com).

Way-finding and Wandering Paths

Apart from building on cultural heritage, successful Alzheimer's units make way finding a less confusing and more intuitive process (Passini et al., 1998: 136–43; Gladwell, 1997: 139; Hensler, 1977) (Figure 3.9). Way-finding is the action to reach a specific destination that includes the decision to go someplace, the gathering of information that facilitates the move, and the level of satisfaction with the move (Passini, et al., 1998: 147). People with Alzheimer's do not refer to cognitive maps when they walk from place to place. They refer to visual cues instead—things they see as they are walking.

The challenge in the design of dementia units is to reinforce visual connections to destinations, such as a bedroom, bathroom, or dining area.

People with dementia may be unaware that they are even searching for something, but they will enter a room if they can see and recognize it. It has been said of people with dementia that they realize where they are going "when they arrive there" (Hoglund and Ledewitz, 1999: 244). The two goals of way-finding must be 1) to empower patients and reduce stress or physical discomfort and 2) decrease residents' reliance on staff (Bane, 2006: 3).

Standard cues, such as changes in color or texture or lighting, do not necessarily work well for people with dementia. Even something as specific and personal as the memory or history box near a patient's bedroom may not help that patient recognize the bedroom and may only be helpful if that bedroom is the destination. The better strategy is to create clear sight lines and visual connections so that patients can see their options and then choose a path (Passini, et al., 1998: 142; Day and Cohen, 2000: 380).

It has been said that people with Alzheimer's are always searching for familiar places, but don't know them until they have found them. This constant

Figure 3.9. The indoor walking paths at this Alzheimer's day center in Memphis, Tennessee, consist of interconnected activity centers to provide walking spaces.

searching takes the form of rummaging and wandering. Most dementia units now create wandering paths where patients can walk whenever they wish. The traditional approach was to create ovals—indoor or outdoor—where the wandering could occur. Critics of the oval design have referred to them as "psychiatric racetracks" (Gladwell, 1997: 138), and there have been efforts to innovate such wandering paths. Hogelund and Ledewitz (1999: 242) speak of "engaged wandering," which means wandering (either indoor or outdoor) can include many areas in the dementia unit. It does not have to be restricted to corridors. The path can weave through various rooms and can also have places where people socialize.

The goal for the design of wandering paths is to avoid dead ends (Hogelund and Ledewitz, 1999: 243) because patients get angry, confused, and frustrated when they reach dead ends. Residents typically watch the floor when they wander, and patterns in flooring tile or carpeting can become distracting or confusing to them. Wandering paths should include seating and visual cues so that patients can occasionally rest and orient themselves while they are wandering. The innovative design for Croftspar Place, in Glasgow, Scotland, features a cloistered courtyard with "an external, semi-covered space outside of each housing unit that defines a continuous loop path" (Figure 3.10).

Common Courtyards and Garden Area

Common courtyards and garden areas are becoming important components of dementia units. The creation of wandering paths now includes pathways through courtyards and carefully landscaped gardens. In some dementia units, the gardens become an extension of Main Street and contain cultural cues, such as familiar street signs, lampposts, and park benches that evoke "the good old days." There are also sensory gardens where patients can stroll amid aromatic flowers and herbs. A recent, award-winning dementia unit contained a butterfly garden and also a bird garden (AIA, 2006: 124). Strategic use of garden and

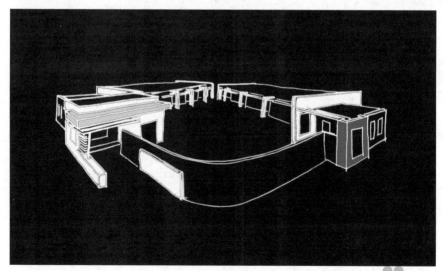

Figure 3.10. Croftspar Place, in Glasgow Scottland, features homes for each of the residents. The homes are arranged into two groups around a common courtyard. The wandering path circles the courtyard.

outdoor areas adds diversion to the wandering path and makes the act of wandering more therapeutic (Hoover, 1995: 3).

Assistive Technologies and Smart Alzheimer's Units

Dementia units are increasingly "intelligent environments" where assistive devices help patients to be more independent (Wikipedia.org, "assistive_ technology"). Assistive technologies are already available to "unobtrusively monitor activities of daily living (ADL) for adults on dementia units and prompt them with verbal and visual cues when necessary" (agingtech.org, 2007). One such system is called COACH (Cognitive Orthosis for Assisting Activities in the Home) (ncbi.nlm.nih.gov, 2007). COACH uses artificial intelligence to cue patients when they are washing their hands (Figure 3.11). For example,

Figure 3.11. The COACH system helps patients in a dementia unit wash their hands through the use of assistive technology, which prompts them through the hand-washing sequence.

COACH prompts patients to turn on and turn off the water and then dry their hands. The COACH system contains computerized modules to track the position of hands at the sink, to plan the hand-washing sequence (i.e., to wet the hands before putting soap on them), and to prompt the patient when activities are done out of sequence.

Dementia units already depend on telecare, an assistive technology that uses electronic sensors connected to an alarm system to prevent patients from wandering out of the dementia unit. The future will bring even more wearable and implantable sensors (fastuk.org). In addition to technologies that help with ADLs, there will also be assistive technologies that help with cognition. Neuropage, for example, is an external memory aid for adults in the early stages of dementia. Neuropage is an automated system that reminds people to do or complete specific tasks (Neuropage.uk.nhl). It is one more technological aid that is making dementia units more effective at caring for Alzheimer's patients.

Community-Building

There is now a trend toward the creation of households that house 8 to 12 patients in clusters around a common courtyard (AIA, The Gables at Westminster-Canterbury, 2006: 122). The goal is to create smaller, more homelike communities where patient care can be low-key and personal. Homelike communities almost always include a family kitchen that becomes the social hub of the household (AIA, 2006: 122). The American Institute of Architects identifies the house, household, or living community as the emerging residential model for dementia care as an "evident trend in senior living" (AIA, 2006: 11). The cluster has become an important design feature of special-needs dementia units. This usually takes the form of smaller residential areas, or communities, where residents' rooms are clustered around a spacious living room (Krejci, 1994; AIA, "Special Care Facilities," 2006).

Residential clusters are designed to enhance overall safety and quality of life for the people who live there (Schwarz, Chuadhury et al, 2005: 61) (Figure 3.12). The design must serve two purposes. Clusters must lead to common areas that are open to all residents, and for that reason, there has to be unobstructed access to the kitchen and parlor area(s). But each cluster must also be visually separated from other clusters so that residents will not be distracted by residents from other clusters.

The intent is to make the cluster less institutional and more homelike. This includes shorter corridors, public spaces with direct access to gardens or outdoor areas, and architecture that echoes home, for example, by creating peaked roofs over each cluster (Weisman et al, 2001: 87; AIA, 2004: 126). People are more likely to stay active in an atmosphere that reflects "real life and

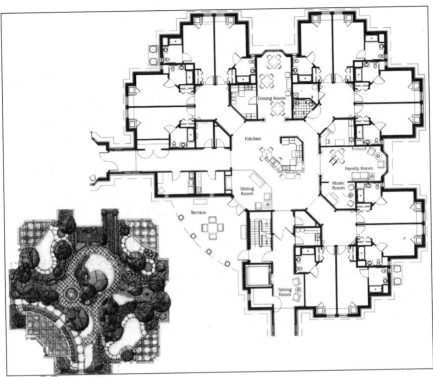

Figure 3.12. Residences are clustered in groups called "households," designed to provide interaction without sacrificing comfort and privacy. A restorative courtyard with gardens is central to the memory support center.

not hospital life" (Krejci, 1994: 1). Clusters should house no more than 10 to 12 people (Hoglund and Ledewitz, 1999: 238).

The American Institute of Architects reminds architects and laypeople alike that the goal of the design of Alzheimer's units should be therapeutic, and that architects and interior designers alike should create environments that allow patients to feel "reassured, comfortable, unthreatened, and interested" (Hoglund and Ledewitz, 1999: 260).

THE FUTURE

The design of long-term-care facilities—be they ALFs, nursing homes, or dementia units—will be shaped by larger, more comprehensive changes in American society.

RACIAL AND ETHNIC DIVERSITY WILL POSE DESIGN CHALLENGES

Longevity and diversity are intersecting to create more communities with elderly people from diverse ethnic backgrounds. The challenge for architects and designers will be to create long-term-care facilities that resonate with ethnic differences in color, light, fabric, and floor covering preferences. Preliminary experience with Russian (Day and Cohen, 2000), Japanese (Kershaw, 2003), and Muslim (Clemetson, 2006) ethnicities indicates that architecture and design will be challenged to design long-term-care facilities that are appropriate for each of these groups.

BOOMER TASTES AND LIFESTYLE WILL IMPACT ON DESIGN OF LONG-TERM-CARE FACILITIES

Architects and designers will also need to respond to the needs and wants of Boomers. Preliminary research indicates that Boomers will want single rooms, fitness centers, indoor pools, and privacy. Long-term-care facilities will also create more intergenerational linkages by incorporating child-care and day-care facilities on site, along with retail space and cyber-cafes that are open to the general public (Weinstein, 2006: 6; Anderson, 2006:4).

ALTERNATIVES TO LONG-TERM-CARE FACILITIES WILL EMERGE

The aging of Boomers and the trend toward healthier aging will lead to new long-term-care arrangements. Perhaps the most provocative idea is to make some cruise ships into nursing homes. It has been said that cruise ships are ALFs waiting to happen, that the very same people who today choose to live in ALFs might someday prefer to live on cruise ships. The estimated cost for a year aboard a cruise ship was only about $6,000 higher than the cost of living in an ALF: $40,000 for a year in a Chicago nursing home, as compared to $33,260 for a year aboard Royal Caribbean's *Majesty of the Seas* (Parker, 2004: 1).

There is growing interest in another form of long-term care—the Virtual Retirement Community (Belkin, 2006: 1). The virtual retirement community is a nursing home without walls—a network of friends who agree to look out for one another by staying connected through e-mail, telephone, and home visits. The virtual retirement home is a social contract entered into by people who want to age in place—usually in their own homes—but who want the peace of mind of knowing they can call or e-mail friends for help when they need to.

MORE ASSISTIVE TECHNOLOGIES, ROBOTICS, AND TELECARE

Long-term-care facilities will see an increased reliance on robotics, telecare (electronic sensors connected to alarm systems), and assistive technologies. These will be increasingly interactive, requiring patients or residents to respond to voice reminders to complete such tasks as taking medications or turning off lights.

MORE HUMANISTIC DESIGN

The previous section predicted that more elderly patients or residents will be expected to respond to electronic voice-prompts that tell them to do everything from taking medications to hand-washing. The question is this: Whose voice should it be? Humanistic research is based on client-centered data—that means that the voice and the opinions of elderly patients or residents will be sought after. Interviews and focus groups with older people will show exactly what they will accept or tolerate, which can then be used to decide which technologies will be introduced at a nursing home or dementia unit and which will not.

NEW DESIGN ELEMENTS

The American Institute of Architects (AIA, 2006: 127) predicts that more long-term-care facilities will feature Main Street designs, smart technologies, community-based services, and better landscaping as elements for organizing design.

NOW THAT YOU'VE READ CHAPTER 3

KEY TERMS AND CONCEPTS

ALF (ALF)
COACH sensory system
color palette
community outreach model of assisted living
culturally supportive environments
dementia unit
humanistic design
intelligent environments
Neuropage

social model and medical model of assisted living
telecare
virtual retirement community
wandering paths
way-finding

QUESTIONS FOR STUDY AND DISCUSSION

1. How is humanistic design different from the more traditional approaches to designing nursing homes and ALFs?
2. What are some advantages of designing long-term-care facilities that have retail spaces or cafes that are open to the general public? In your opinion, how do residents benefit from this? And how does the general public benefit?
3. Many nursing homes and dementia units are now creating a Main Street area for the residents who live there. How can Main Street be designed to be therapeutic and fun for older people?
4. What can designers learn from talking with elderly people before designing a Main Street area?
5. One important trend in the design of long-term-care facilities is the growing attention to the design of gardens and outdoor spaces. How can designers make gardens and outdoor spaces safer and more therapeutic?
6. The transition from hospital-like to homelike has impacted on the design of corridors and doorways leading to residents' rooms. How are corridors and doorways being designed in the more homelike nursing homes?
7. It has been said that the focus in assisted living has gone from "assisted" to "living." How does this impact the design of ALFs?
8. There is growing interest in the design of entryways at nursing homes and ALFs. What are some of the messages that are conveyed by a pitched roof?
9. How can designers create more homelike environments in dementia units when dementia care is becoming more technological and robotic?
10. The "Eden" alternative makes a nursing home or dementia unit into a green house or Garden of Eden where residents are actively involved. How can the design of a facility contribute to this approach for long-term care?

HELPFUL WEBSITES

aahsa.org/advocacy/housing (AAHSA/housing site)

activeandable.com (Active & Able: Products with Age-Friendly Features)

adaptiveenvironments.org (Adaptive Environments)

AgingBeautifully.org (Design secrets for aging beautifully)

aging.state.ny.us/explore/housing (Housing alternatives for seniors in New York State)

agingtech.org/browsemain.aspxCAST Clearinghouse [CAST (Center for Aging Services Technologies) Intelligent environment for older adults with dementia]

aia.org/architect/thisweek06/117 (AIA, Design for Aging Review)

aia.org/dfa_news_citations (AIA architectural jury on a variety of long-term-care facilities)

AlamedaCenter.com (Multiethnic nursing home)

EdenAlt.com (What is Eden? The Eden Alternative)

EGA.net/projects (EGA Architects: ALFs and Long-term care facilities)

ElderCareLink.com (Directory of local ElderCare services)

ElderWeb.com (Choosing a nursing home)

elite-care.com (Extended Family Residences: An Alternative to Assisted Living)

Retirement.org (Continuing Care: Specialized Services, Support, & Security)

Saintjohnsmilw.org (Supportive living with assisted care, skilled nursing care, and in-home supportive care)

Seniors-site.com (CCRCs)

en.wikipedia.org/wiki/nursing_home (Nursing home)

PART II
LEARNING FROM
OTHER CULTURES

"*Yasukichi knows that an old folks' home is in his future. He becomes obsessed with the legend of Obasuteyama . . . where the elderly are supposedly left to die in the mountains. Yasukihi soon starts to see the nursing home and Obasuteyama as being roughly the same.*"

Excerpt from the review of the
Japanese film *Ikinai* (1999)

Japan
The Future Is Robotic

OVERVIEW

Japan's rapidly aging population has posed exciting challenges to home-design professionals. Now, more than ever before, Japan's elders want to live independently, to live *near* but not *with* their children. The desire for independence is complicated by Japan's lack of caregivers. More Japanese women are now entering the workforce instead of remaining at home as dutiful wives and daughters-in-law. And government restrictions on immigration restrict the numbers of non-Japanese people who can migrate to Japan and become home-health workers. In response, the care and housing of elderly people in Japan has become more high-tech. Nursing homes, assisted-living facilities, and other forms of senior housing now rely more on robotics, networked appliances, and other information technologies. Although Japan's senior housing is looking toward the technological future, most senior housing continues to maintain traditional Japanese touches: a rock garden or tea ceremony room. The future will be even more robotic, and Japan is now beginning to explore corporate retirement communities and ocean liners that serve as either floating group homes or assisted-living facilities.

FUTURISTIC HOME

Tokyo's winters are snowy and long, and winter is the time when elderly people worry about falling on icy ground. But the elderly couple who are moving into a futuristic home on the outskirts of Tokyo will worry a lot less about falling on ice. Their home will have a self-heating sidewalk that activates at the first hint of snow and automatically melts it away. This is just one example of how this "House of the Future" will actively collaborate with that elderly couple to keep them safe and comfortable. The house will also help them to navigate from room to room. For example, once one of the couple says, "I am going to the bathroom," the lights in the hallway leading to that bathroom are switched on. And, according to Japan Information Network, "in winter, the heated toilet seat is automatically switched on as well" (Japan Information Network, 2002: 1).

It will not be long before households all over Japan are relying on networked technologies that allow people to "talk" with their appliances, and allow appliances to "talk" with one another. Toshiba, for example, has developed a new oven that is linked to a central computer in the house and automatically downloads software that "adjusts cooking temperature to the food being cooked" (Japan Information Network, 2002: 3)[1]. Japan is at the cutting edge of networked technologies, and the Japanese are hopeful that these and other technological breakthroughs will help older people avoid accidents. These very same technologies will allow them to be independent.

CHOUJUKOKU: THE LAND OF LONGEVITY

Independence and safety are real concerns in Japan today, which is now, statistically speaking, the oldest nation in the world. The Japanese call their nation "*Choujukoku*," or the Land of Longevity. Average life expectancy for Japanese women in 2002 was 85.23—the oldest life expectancy in the world—and the average life expectancy for Japanese men in that same year was 78.32. More than 20,000 Japanese people are already aged 100+ years and the birth rate continues to fall (*Trends in Japan*, 2003: 1).[2]

Just as Japan is *Choujukoku*, it is also the land of declining fertility (Hall, 2005: 6). It is no wonder that the Japanese are now investing so heavily in product design and innovative housing for older people. With its population rapidly aging and a caregiver shortage that will only grow worse as family size decreases, the future of senior home design has to be robotic.

LIVING WITH OR NEAR CHILDREN:
SENIOR HOUSING IN JAPAN

Japan now has the lowest percentage of people aged 15 or younger of any industrialized nation: 14 percent as compared with 20 percent in the United States and 19 percent in Britain (Hall, 2005: 6; Ogawa, 1997: 1).

With the number of elderly people steadily increasing, Japan now has more frail or dependent elderly people than ever before, but unfortunately, there are fewer family members or home-health aides available to take care of them (Hewitt, 2005: 1). These changes are transforming the ways that older people

TABLE 4.1 PERCENTAGE OF PEOPLE AGED 65 OR OLDER IN JAPAN'S PREFECTURES

PREFECTURES	PERCENT	PREFECTURES	PERCENT
Kagoshima	22.5	Hukuoka	12.9
Kochi	20.4	Yamanashi	12.6
Yamaguchi	18.1	Hukui	12.1
Wakayama	17.9	Hukushima	12.0
Miyazaki	17.4	Nara	11.8
Shimane	17.2	Niigata	11.6
Ehime	17.1	Okinawa	11.6
Hiroshima	16.2	Iwate	11.5
Oita	16.1	Yamagata	11.5
Nagasaki	15.7	Ishikawa	11.5
Tottori	15.5	Aomori	11.1
Kumamoto	15.2	Toyama	11.1
Okayama	15.0	Gihu	10.1
Kyoto	14.9	Shizuoka	10.0
Kagawa	14.7	Ibaraki	9.8
Hokkaido	14.5	Gunma	9.8
Osaka	14.4	Kanagawa	9.8
Tokushima	14.1	Shiga	9.5
Tokyo	14.0	Aichi	9.4
Nagano	14.0	Tochigi	9.2
Mie	13.8	Miyagi	8.9
Hyogo	13.3	Chiba	8.5
Saga	13.2	Saitama	8.1
Akita	12.9		

Households consisting of people aged 65 or older by city. Data are grouped so that prefectures (analogous to the states in the United States) with the oldest households are listed first.
(Source: Ministry of Health, Labor, and Welfare, 2000.)

are housed and cared for. A study done in 1999 shows that 65 percent of elderly people who need care are still living with or near their children (Ishii-Kuntz, 1999: 67; *Japan Statistical Yearbook*, 2003: 123, Table 9). It is still unusual in Japan for older people to live in nursing homes or assisted-living facilities. The world around them is rapidly changing, but Japanese people still want to spend their final years at home, with their families. In fact, there is a Japanese saying that captures this desire. "To die on tatami" is what the Japanese say: to live a long life and then die a "pokkuri death," without being a caregiving burden (Takahashi, 2003). Decades ago, that would have happened in the home of the oldest son. But today it is just as likely to occur in an apartment, a single-family home, or a multigenerational dwelling.

AT HOME IN THE *MINKA*

The word in Japanese for a traditional house, or country house, is *minka* (Figure 4.1). This word literally translates as "household" or "family." As recently as 1990, almost half of all elderly people in Japan were living with their children in homes very much like this (Traphagan, 2003: 7). The clasic *minka* would contain a series of sliding panels, known as *fusuma*. By adjusting the *fusuma*, it is possible to make a room larger or smaller. In addition, the sliding *fusuma* panels transform space from public to private, or vice versa, as needed. Bedding, called *futon* in Japanese, can be placed on the *tatami*-covered floor when it is time to sleep or rest. Otherwise, that bedding is rolled-up and stored out of sight, in closets or cabinets (Ishimoto and Ishimoto, 1963: 7; Takeshi, 2002: 76). In other words, there is no designated bedroom in the *minka*. A room may be a small space where one or two people sleep at night, but can become a

Figure 4.1. The traditional Japanese country house, or *minka*.

larger dining space for the entire family. This is accomplished by opening *fusuma* to make the space larger and public.

FUSUMA CONSTRUCTION

Although the *minka* might be a small structure, it is flexible enough to accommodate the household living there. This is how two Japanese interior designers put it: "Here the family live and entertain. Here they dine and, often, the family [or some members of it] also sleep" (Ishimoto and Ishimoto, 1963: 6).

The genius of *fusuma* construction is that it creates multipurpose space, and this has implications for elderly people who live in traditional Japanese homes.

Room design in most Western nursing homes is not flexible, as form and function are specialized. The nursing home is more like a hospital than anything else. "A double-loaded corridor with a nurses' station located to allow good observation of the patients' rooms makes considerable sense in an acute-care setting, but is much less desirable in a place where people live for extended periods in life" (Schwarz, 1996: 31). Residents in an American nursing home like the one described here by Schwarz are required to go from place to place when they need meals, recreation, physical therapy, and other activities. But the *minka* is different. It can be reconfigured as needs and situations arise, which makes it an ideal space for caregiving.

In the traditional country house, older people would typically have their choice of sleeping spots. It was only necessary to slide the *fusuma*, and an elderly person or couple would have a private alcove for sleep or rest. And although there was no emergency chord or panic button, help was never far away. Architect Nakagawa Takeshi (2003: 77) reminisces about his boyhood in a *minka* with *tatami* floors and *fusuma*. There were visual barriers, recalls Takeshi, but he could always hear the sounds of the other people in the house. He knew they were nearby, and he could call out to them anytime he wanted (Takeshi, 2003: 80). An older person living in a clasic *minka* never had to worry about being unattended. Help was always just on the other side of the *fusuma*.

THE NORM OF CORESIDENCE

As far back as the eighth century A.D., there is evidence that older people were supposed to be looked after by their grown children. The norm of coresidence was that "parents were never to be left alone by themselves" (Sano, 1958: 33). Home design in Japan has not only been shaped by that ancient social norm but also by the fact that there is now a shortage of caregivers to look after the world's most rapidly aging population. Interestingly, a growing number of

Japan's elderly people are not interested in coresidence. And this has impacted home design in Japan as much as the caregiver shortage has.[3]

A JAPANESE EXPERIMENT IN SENIOR HOME DESIGN

A nationwide survey of Japanese people done online in 2002 (*Japanese Attitudes on Aging: Online Survey.* 2002: 1) found that more than half of respondents aged 65 or older were not interested in living with their children so much as living near them. In fact, only 28 percent of people aged 65 or older surveyed said they wanted to live with their children. Fifty-four percent wanted to live near their children, and 18 percent dreamed of living in far-off places like Hawaii or Australia. Home design in Japan has begun to reflect these shifting priorities. No design shows this gerontological shift better than an experiment called *nisetai jutaku*, or multigenerational house, which first appeared in housing markets during the 1970s (Brown, 2003: 65).

Nisetai jukatu was an attempt to nurture the traditional, multigenerational household. The very short life of this architectural experiment and its failure to catch on with the Japanese public tell a great deal about home design in this aging nation.

The *nisetai jutaku* was meant to provide opportunities for coresidence even as older people and their adult offspring were beginning to demand more single-family housing. It was an attempt at what Hadjiyanni (2005: 5) calls "culturally sensitive" home design.

HOME DESIGN WITH A SOCIAL AGENDA

Home design can have a social agenda. The size of rooms or the availability of particular appliances can make relationships possible. Here, for example, is how home design in a Minnesota community, thousands of miles away from Japan, helped to maintain the norms and relationships of a particular group. When Hmong immigrants from Laos first settled in Minnesota in the 1970s, they had difficulty maintaining traditional Hmong culture in standard American homes. With the help of interior designers, culturally sensitive homes were built with extra-large sinks, stoves, and freezers. These appliances enabled the Hmong to cook their traditional foods "and store large quantities of meat from sacrificial animals" (Hadjiyanni, 2003: 5).

Hmong kitchens in Minnesota are far from the multigenerational homes that were built across Japan in the 1970s. But they illustrate the conditions necessary for home design to be culturally sensitive. First, there must be identifiable norms or behaviors (e.g., a style of cooking). Next, there must be an obstacle to that norm or set of behaviors (e.g., the galley kitchen, which made Hmong-style cooking impossible). And finally, there must be consensus that the norms or behaviors are worth maintaining (e.g., the Hmong love their cuisine and craved Hmong-style cooking in Minnesota).

Japanese real estate developers created the prototypes for *nisetai jutaku* in the 1970s, at a moment when there was concern that the norm of coresidence was weakening. Multigenerational homes usually contained two separate apartments but also had common space such as a kitchen. The idea was to allow the generations to live separately, but be together under the same roof. They may have been living under the same roof, but many families did not enjoy living there. Naomi Brown explains that the multigenerational home was a letdown to Japanese elders, and a source of friction to their *yome*, or daughters-in-law (Brown, 2003).

DESIGNING FOR INDEPENDENCE IN JAPAN TODAY

Older people did not want to give up their independence—or their single-family dwellings. More often than not, they felt they were being exploited in the *nisetai jutaku* (Brown, 2003: 57–64). There were complaints of exploitation, as when, for example, children used their elderly parents or in-laws as live-in babysitters, and the elderly tenant—who was typically the owner of the home—resented having to share it. The younger generation typically had to relocate to distant towns or villages and become tenants in houses owned by their parents, which made them unhappy. Wives, in particular, resented that they would now have to be subordinate to a mother-in-law. Instead of unifying the generations, the *nisetai jutaku* polarized them even further. For this reason, this first experiment in senior housing had failed within 10 years (Brown, 2003: 66–70; Leavitt, 1989: 221).[4]

But Japan's architects and interior designers learned from this mistake and went on to develop living arrangements that were indeed culturally sensitive. By the 1980s, developers had more or less abandoned the concept of the multigenerational home. They began instead to design high-tech homes that allow older people to live independently and age in place.

JAPANESE HOMES: TECHNOLOGIES ENCOURAGE AGING IN PLACE

The Japanese now refer to the growing number of elderly people in Japan as "the Silver Tsunami."[5] But unlike a real tsunami, this demographic one did not take the country by surprise. Japan, like Sweden (see Chapter 6) and Israel (see Chapter 8) has been preparing for this age wave.

Japanese homes are now built to be barrier free, with "fewer steps and obstacles for the elderly" (Wikipedia.org, "Housing in Japan," 2005: 5). This involves building homes with a zero-step entrance, wide doors, "and at least a half-bath on the first floor" (MacDonald, 2005: 1). It also involves positioning light switches at waist-level and placing outlets at waist-level on the wall. Newer homes are often designed for the needs and limitations of older people—paving and flooring materials that reduce the risk of falling and window coverings that reduce glare are often used (Bunker-Hellmich, 2001: 1).

PRESERVING THE ARCHITECTURAL PAST

In addition to designing specifically for older people, the Japanese also retrofit existing structures to make them safer and easier for older people to navigate. The Japanese are reverent about their architectural past; it is not unusual for them to retrofit homes for seniors rather than tearing them down. http://careful.jp (translated into English from the Japanese) is one of many websites that offer tips on how to make older homes safer and more senior-friendly. The website contains a series of before and after photos. In one of the before shots, there are traditional *tatami* mats on the floor, but they are not taped down and can cause people to trip or fall. In the after picture, the same room has a less slippery, wooden floor, and it is now free of obstacles. Another pair of images shows how to make the exterior driveway safer and senior-friendly. The before picture shows a driveway that is slick with ice. A small flight of stairs (also slick with ice) leads to the front door. The after image shows a carport that has been covered to prevent rain or snow from accumulating on the driveway, and the flight of stairs has been replaced by a ramp leading to the front door (Figure 4.2).

The website http://careful.jp focuses on areas of the house that are especially troublesome for older people: the kitchen, the stairs and, especially, the bathroom. The after photos of bathrooms show fixtures and appliances that help older people avoid slips or falls while showering, toileting, or washing. Sometimes older houses need more than appliances. They need structural overhauls as well.

Teaching Old Houses New Tricks in Kyoto

Old town houses (known in Japanese as *machiya*), for example, are made safer and more livable for older people in Kyoto while preserving "a taste of *machiya* architecture, like the posts and beams" (*Trends in Japan*, 2005: 2).

THE COLLABORATIVE HOME: HELPING SENIORS TO AGE IN PLACE

The Japanese now rely on a mix of technologies and human services to make buildings safer and more comfortable for older people. Figure 4.3 shows

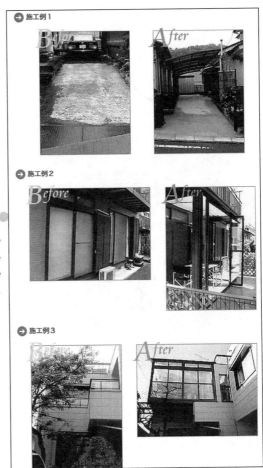

Figure 4.2. These images show Japanese readers how to make their homes safer and more navigable for older people.

SANYO Electric's Human In Roll-Lo Bathing (HIRB), which was designed to help bathe the elderly at retirement homes/centers (or nursing homes). It is a highly functional nursing bath tub, with both the operating nurse/aide operability and user's privacy in mind. The goal, for a growing number of Japanese architects and designers, is to create houses that "collaborate" to provide care and companionship for older people, not just to house them. Instead of the dutiful *yome*, or daughter-in-law, the caregiver(s) might now be a home-health worker, a system of networked appliances, and perhaps even a robot. The goal is for the senior to maintain dignity and independence, just as it is in many of the world's most rapidly aging nations (see Chapter 6, Sweden). But the idea of the collaborative home is uniquely Japanese.

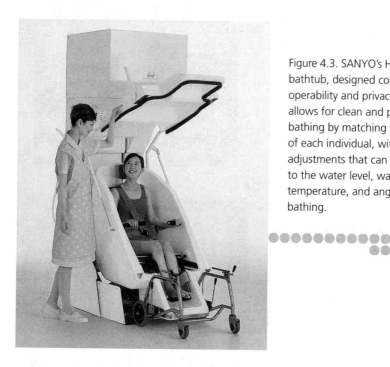

Figure 4.3. SANYO's HIRB nursing bathtub, designed considering operability and privacy. The bath allows for clean and pleasant bathing by matching the needs of each individual, with adjustments that can be made to the water level, water temperature, and angle of bathing.

HIGH-TECH, HIGH-TOUCH: JAPAN'S NEW SENIOR HOUSING

The Japanese are reinventing the relationship between older people and their homes. They are doing this by linking information-communication technologies, caregivers, and in some cases, the rooms of the house, making them into collaborative environments. This combination of technologies and personalized care has been called "high-tech, high-touch" (Almekinders, 2005). At the crux of high-tech, high-touch housing is the idea that home health care can and should be delivered in new and efficient ways. The soaring demand for health care and the fact that elderly people typically need more such care require new approaches to home health care. High-tech, high-touch allows the Japanese to provide health care to older people in the newer homes being designed especially for older people and in older homes where they still live with other family members. Indeed, Japan's new-age caregivers sometimes seem like characters from science fiction. Imagine a room full of sensors that remind the occupant of that room to turn off a light switch or take medication. Or imagine a toilet seat that warms up when activated far away from the bathroom.[6] Add to this mix a robotic caregiver that can take somebody's vital signs, play checkers, and make small talk. In Japan, the robotic future is happening right now (MSNBC, 2005: 1). Robotics, networked appliances, and telecommunications systems make this possible.

Robotics

Early in 2005, a Japanese company began marketing the robotic *Yori-soi ifbot*, which performs 15 functions, including conversing, calculating, advising, and medical checks (Figure 4.4). In addition, the *Yori-soi ifbot* has "108 LED lights built into its head so that it can express emotion" (*The Economist*, 2005: 59; *Akibalive*, 2004:1). A few years before the release of this robot, Mitsubishi Heavy Industries had developed another robot known as *Otoshiyori Tasukemasu*, which translates into English as "let me help senior citizen" (Pacific Research Consulting, 2003: 1). This robot is being marketed as a caretaker for people who live alone and also as a watchdog for the home. The robot's caretaking abilities include reminders to take medications, online reports to family members who live or work outside the home, and sharing of digital photos taken inside the home using the camera that is built into *Otoshiyori Tasukemasu* (Pacific Research Consulting, 2003).

Robotics is being heralded as a way to offer Japan's elderly population "a new lease on life" (MSNBC, 2005). This includes aging in place because robotic helpers can provide physical therapy to those who need that sort of care (i.e., they are rehab robots) or mental stimulation to people with Alzheimer's and other forms of dementia. Robotic wheelchairs or robotic Seeing Eye dogs (Kakuchi, 2002:1) move easily through the barrier-free environment in new Japanese homes, and they communicate online with health-care personnel or family members (MSNBC, 2005).

Figure 4.4. This robot is already an interactive caregiver for older people in some Japanese nursing homes.

Robots come in a variety of shapes, colors, and sizes. What they have in common, however, is that they work directly with older people as robotic companions, physical therapists, Seeing Eye dogs, and so forth.

Networked Appliances

Networked appliances make life safer and easier for older people by enhancing the environment around them. They create interactive environments where it is possible for people to regulate their appliances and for appliances to regulate one another. For example, Toshiba now markets a line of appliances—including ovens, refrigerators, and washing machines—with self-monitoring capabilities. Such appliances can automatically notify a repair company when problems arise. And Toshiba will soon offer a system that "wirelessly monitors the door/window opening/closing information, lighting ON/OFF, etc., in the house" (Toshiba, 2006: 1). The corporate giant Samsung asked, "How might connecting such devices to the Internet and to [one an]other make daily life and interpersonal communications more harmonious?" (Human Factors Research and Design, 2004). Networked appliances can help maintain the dignity and safety of older people and eliminate or simplify household tasks such as doing laundry or making sure that doors and windows are closed. These systems also bring assistance to the home, as when the police are summoned in an emergency. Japan Electronics and Information Technology Industries Association (JEITA) predicts that particular networked appliances will be especially useful for older people. JEITA points, for example, to voice-operated systems that would allow older people to open doors, turn lighting on or off, and operate appliances from a bed or lounge chair (*Japan Information Network*, 2002; Schadler, 2005: 1).

Telecommunications Systems

The television is more than a source of entertainment in the collaborative home. It is also the telecommunications hub of the home. In addition to being a television, new technology enables it to display a menu of domestic activities when it is activated by a remote control. Each of these activities can be (re)programmed. Somebody sitting in the living room can monitor the progress of the laundry, the cooking of a meal, temperature and light in the home, and so forth.

In addition to giving people these options, the telecommunications systems being developed in Japan also link appliances in new ways. In high-tech homes on the outskirts of Tokyo, there are telecommunication systems that allow the refrigerator to order food on its own. If the number of eggs runs low, for example, the refrigerator can send an e-mail to the grocery store to request that another dozen eggs be delivered (*Japan Information Network*, 2002, Schadler,

2002: 1). The very same system also allows for home-based teleconferencing. An older person, for example, can use this technology to schedule conferences with two or three doctors in different locations or to schedule conversations with grandchildren in various places.

Telecommunications systems give older people the capability to maintain their homes—and themselves—for much longer. The collaborative environment also includes home-health workers and aides. The rapid aging of Japan's population means that more people than ever before require assistance in the home. But Japanese families are often unable to provide such care because so many wives and daughters-in-law now have jobs and careers. Home-health workers, or what the Japanese call "home helpers," are taking the women's places. Many of these home-health workers are being paid by the government in an effort to keep older people in their homes and avoid expensive nursing care.

A revision in the nursing-care insurance law emphasizes the support and maintenance of older people in their homes. This means that more home-health workers are now available to assist older people with "light assistance," including housekeeping, meal preparation, nutritional counseling, and light exercise (*The Japan Times*, 15 July 2005: 1).

According to Japan's Ministry of Health and Welfare, the number of home helpers increased from about 23,000 in 1986 to about 180,000 in 2000 (Ministry of Health and Welfare, 2000: 1). This exponential increase reflects the fact that Japan's rapidly aging population needs home helpers for the seniors to maintain independence and age at home. But under the new system, home helpers are supposed to collaborate with elderly people in cooking, doing housework, and even taking in the laundry (*The Japan Times*, 15 July 2005: 2) instead of doing these tasks for them.

Bathing-Service Vans and Portable Hot Tubs

In addition to home helpers, Japan is seeing an increase in the number of businesses that help make homes more collaborative. For example, there are bathing-service vans that park in front of an older person's home (Figure 4.5). The elderly person is lifted into the van and enjoys a bath in the rear of the vehicle.

There are also personnel dispatch companies that conduct home visits and then give updates to family members who are living or working elsewhere.

In addition to the personnel dispatch companies, there are now more than 60 taxi companies that participate in an emergency-transit system. Older people sign up for this system by paying a fee and registering their medical information. In case of an emergency, the participating taxis take them to nearby doctors or emergency rooms (web-Japan.org, 1997: 2). Japan's Q.P. Corporation is now selling soft tableware made from silicon and nutritious boil-in-the-bag foods

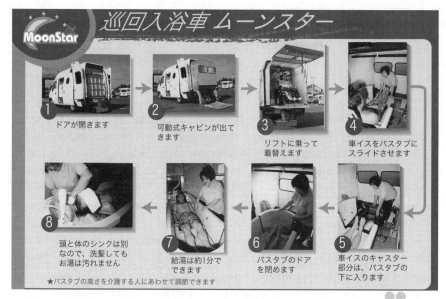

Figure 4.5. This van brings the bathtub to homes where older people cannot easily bathe.

whose target market is the elderly (*Trends in Japan*, 2000: 1). These services—and more—allow for collaborative homes and the independence that older people in Japan need and want.

Adult Day Center Design—Maintaining Health and Tradition

Part of Japan's effort to help older people age in place is to offer adult day centers and adult day care. There are currently 4,623 adult day centers and an additional 2,087 adult-day-care centers in Japan. A Japanese day center is a lot like an American senior center—someplace where well elderly can go for companionship and activity. In contrast, day-care centers provide medical, dental, and mental-health services, as well as health and nutrition counseling. The two functions are increasingly integrated into a single service center. For example, Fureaimura Syanoki Day Service Center (www.fureaimura.jp) offers not only therapeutic bathing, which is more of a health-care service, but also the traditional Japanese hot tub, which is more recreational. See Figure 4.6 for an example of a hot tub.

The exterior of Warashieko Day Service Center is another example of recreational and health-related services in a traditional setting. The exterior features clasic Japanese landscaping, including a garden, but the traditional garden footbridge has been replaced by a ramp with guard rails. The entry to the

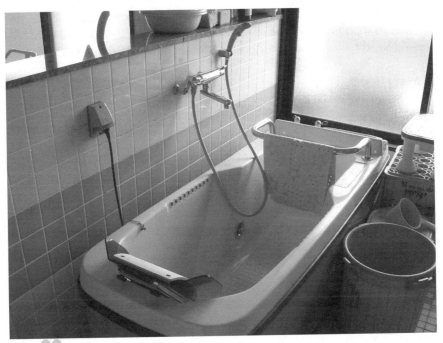

Figure 4.6. Access to the hot tub includes grab bars and nonskid flooring. The window behind the hot tub overlooks a traditional Japanese garden.

day service center is traditional, with a place to remove shoes, but the doors slide open automatically and there is a ramp for wheelchair access.

Architect Toshiaki Kawai brings the same love of tradition to the design of an adult-day-care center in Kyoto. Kawai recently created an adult-day-care center in an historic town house in Kyoto. This, according to the architect, honors both older people *and* older environments (Webb, 2003: 70). The project created a new, senior-friendly space in the Kamigyo district of Kyoto. The history of the building has been preserved, but it has been reconfigured to make it safer and easier to navigate for older people. The adult-day-care center is helping to turn Kamigyo, which was once a declining industrial district, into an age-integrated community where elderly people now have a place of their own to congregate. It provides supportive amenities such as a tea room, recreational space, and a place for contemplation. This adult-day-care center includes traditional Japanese elements such as sliding screens and an indoor garden. But it also has contemporary, senior-friendly features, including an elevator to help older people get from one level of the building to another, and it has a combination of colored and textured walls that make way-finding easier. In addition to these architectural details, this adult-day-care center in Kyoto will also feature a mix of teamwork and technologies designed to help avoid the move to a nursing home (Webb, 2003: 70).

Nursing Homes

When older people in Japan can no longer live independently, they will most likely move into assisted living or a nursing home. This pattern—a change in residence as health deteriorates—is very different from the Swedish pattern (see Chapter 6, Sweden).

Sweden has a government-sponsored care-at-home policy that brings a variety of services into the homes of older people. Sweden's care-at-home services include visiting homemakers, home nursing care, meals-on-wheels, and adult day care. As a result, "the large majority of Swedes manages their chores and lives independently in old age" (Hellner, 2005: 8). Compare this with Japan, where older people usually change residence when they can no longer live independently.

Japan's Ministry of Health and Welfare estimated in 1997 that 4 million elderly people would need nursing care by 2010 (web-Japan.org, 1997: 3), and that 100,000 elderly people every year would join the ranks of those who need nursing care or assistance with activities of daily living (web-Japan.org, 1997: 20). The estimate today is closer to 4.5 million (*The Japan Times*, 15 July 2005: 1). Most of them reside in nursing homes, either public or private.

There are three types of public nursing homes. The first is *tokubetsu yogo rojin*, or skilled nursing homes, for people aged 65 or older with severe physical or mental disabilities (Figure 4.7). There were 4,866 skilled nursing homes in 2005. These government-run *tokubetsu* are the most popular alternative to private, for-profit institutions. *Tokubetsu* nursing homes offer residents a shared room, including meals, nursing care, and a small allowance. Because they are reasonably priced (compared with private, for-profit nursing homes), they are in great demand. In 2003, there was a waiting list of 230,000 people nationwide for these publicly owned and operated *tokubetsu* (*The Japan Times*, 2 April 2003: 1–2).

The next category is *yogo rojin* for lower-income people who cannot live independently. To qualify for room and board in a *yogo rojin*, a person must fall below the official cutoff point for admission. Japan had 905 *yogo rojin* homes in 2005 (*The Japan Times*, 2 April 2003, 2–3).

Finally, there are *keihi rojin* for people aged 60 or older who come from abusive or dysfunctional homes and have nowhere else to live. Seventeen *keihi rojin* offer low-cost and emergency housing to older people who qualify to be there. Also included in the *keihi rojin* category are 47 specialized nursing homes for the blind or visually impaired.

Japan Nursing Home Network (www.r-home.jp) offers a comprehensive description of nursing homes throughout Japan. Most of these nursing homes

Figure 4.7. A *tokubetsu rojin*, or Japanese nursing home.

have standard Western features such as television, dining rooms, and recreation centers. But in addition, there are three distinctive Japanese design elements in Japan's public and private nursing homes: a traditional Japanese room, (rock) garden, and hot tub.

JAPANESE NURSING-HOME DESIGN ELEMENTS

For decades, the Japanese have tried to preserve their unique culture while becoming more Western. Even though many of today's Japanese homes have the most up-to-date technologies and appliances, they still also feature some clasic Japanese design elements.

JAPANESE ROOM AND/OR TEA CEREMONY HOUSE

In most Japanese homes, there is a traditional Japanese room, with *tatami* mats and *fusuma* screens. Brown (2003: 62), writing about the multigenerational house of the 1970s, mentions that the downstairs apartment—where the elderly member(s) of the family would live—always had a Japanese room with *tatami* mats. Many nursing homes also have a Japanese room and/or a tea ceremony house on the grounds. The Green Tokyo nursing home is a typical example. Green Tokyo features a Japanese room that overlooks a clasic Japanese rock garden (Figure 4.8).

Even if there is no space or budget for a full Japanese room, many facilities will have a traditional Japanese *tokonoma*. The *tokonoma* is a recessed alcove where important or significant items are proudly displayed. Some assisted-living facilities in Japan now provide *tokonoma* space for every resident, usually near the entry to each resident's room. The *tokonoma* helps to "maximize awareness and orientation" (Cohen and Moore, 1999: 106). Residents take pride in maintaining the *tokonoma*, and activities associated with maintenance are therapeutic for that reason. In a similar vein, Leng Leng Thang (2003: 73) describes a day-care facility for both elderly people and children that features a traditional altar in the midst of an experimental setting.

Figure 4.8. A Japanese room overlooking a clasic rock garden in Green Tokyo nursing home.

Figure 4.9. A Japanese tea ceremony house at Kamigyo in Kyoto.

Nursing homes sometimes have tea ceremony houses on the grounds. These are often popular spots for residents of nursing homes, who go there to relax and experience the ritualized tea ceremony. For example, the adult-day-care center in Kyoto, which was mentioned earlier in this chapter, also has a distinctive tea ceremony room (Figure 4.9). There is even space for the tea ceremony at a relatively inexpensive, one-story congregate-care facility built in 1973 called the Welfare Annuity Home. Although a low-budget facility, the Welfare Annuity Home features a tea ceremony house surrounded by a lush garden where residents can stroll, meditate, or tend the flowers (Shin'ichi Okada, 1997: 167).

THE GARDEN

Designs of Japanese nursing homes—even the ones that are publicly owned and operated—are attuned to the importance of the garden in Japanese life. The garden is a traditional and symbolic element in Japanese home design (Figure 4.10). Even in modestly priced *tokubetsu*, there is an effort to make this

Figure 4.10. A clasic Japanese garden at Green Tokyo nursing home.

piece of cultural heritage into a decorative and therapeutic piece of the nursing home. Schwarz (1999: 92; 1996: 258), for example, speaks of the need for nursing homes to become less focused on cure and more concerned with healing. "The new type [of nursing home] . . ." he writes, "should not induce, through its architecture, illusions of *curing*, but rather should focus on *healing* . . ." (Schwarz, 1999: 259). The Japanese nursing home, more than its American counterpart, has come to use gardens (and gardening) in this way. They are more than decorative; they are in fact healing gardens (Hoover, 1995: 1).

This calls attention to the different relationship between a nursing home and its garden(s) in China and in Japan. In China, the nursing home is often situated on the land according to principles of *feng shui* (see Chapter 5, "China"). The connection between the Chinese nursing home and its garden(s) is thought to be auspicious and a source of positive healing energy. In Japan, however, the connection is more about beauty than about energy. For example, the garden at the Group Home in Manazuru (built in 2002) is a strategic backdrop—something serene for residents to gaze at. The architect of this group home writes, "The glass facade opens up the building toward the forest, consisting of cherry, eucalyptus, and mandarin trees. Views of the faraway ocean dominate and define the internal space" (Jones, 2004: 10). Sun City Kashiwa, in Japan's Chiba Prefecture, is another good example of how Japanese nursing homes use gardens in therapeutic ways. Sun City Kashiwa is a congregate-care facility with independent housing, assisted living, and a skilled nursing unit (Sun City, Chiba, 2002: 84). All three of these residential units overlook a bamboo grove and *koi pond* and are surrounded by densely wooded land. The garden also contains looping walkways, and there is land set aside for community gardens. The garden provides a tranquil view for people who are bedridden. The looping walkways allow for exercise and, at the same time, provide a path that brings residents back to where they started. Residents with Alzheimer's tend to be forgetful, and the circular path brings them back to where they began their stroll. The community gardens allow residents to maintain their dexterity and engage in familiar gardening activities. And although there might be reference to *feng shui*, it is not the motivating principle behind the layout of this garden.

HOT TUBS

At the Warashiko Nursing Home an elderly man sits in a *yubune*, or cedar hot tub (Figure 4.11). The water comes up to his chin. He is staring into a mirror that is propped up on the side of the *yubune*—and he is shaving. This is a centuries-old ritual, but it is happening in a nursing home and not a *minka* or country inn. The hot tub is a traditional focus of family and community life

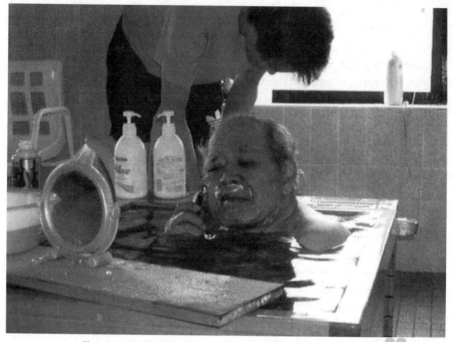

Figure 4.11. A nursing home patient shaving in a hot tub.

in Japan. Many nursing homes and assisted-living facilities have incorporated the hot tub into the design of the property, and they are an excellent example of how a traditional amenity has been updated for older people in congregate settings. The Green Tokyo nursing home, for example, offers hot tubs with grab bars and panic buttons, and there are separate hot tubs for women and men. By focusing on safety and the challenge of entering and leaving the hot tub, this traditional experience has been preserved.

FOR-PROFIT NURSING HOMES

Japan also has for-profit nursing homes, or *yuryo*. Japan's 334 *yuryo* are more exclusive than the publicly run facilities and draw their residents aged 60 or older from Japan's more affluent social classes. The monthly rent for rooms in a publicly owned *tokubetsu* is about 120,000 yen per month (or about $1,034). Luxury retirement homes for Japan's seniors, like Sincere Korien, can cost as much as 200,000 yen per month (or about $1,800). For that money, residents can also enjoy feedback from biosensors, robots, and information technologies.

Sincere Korien (Lytle, 2003: 1–2; Morikawa, 2002: 1) is perhaps Japan's most publicized digital nursing home. Sincere Korien was financed and constructed by Matsushita Electric in Neyagawa City. The 107 residents who live here are monitored by biosensors that track changes in heat or mass and inform the nursing staff if patients have wandered out of their rooms at night. Every resident at Sincere Korien has a robotic plush teddy bear that reminds them to take their medications and plays memory games with them (Lytle, 2003: 1). In addition, there are digital health-monitoring machines that allow residents at Sincere Korien to communicate with their doctors (Morikawa, 2002: 1).

GROUP HOMES

Japan must house a growing number of people with dementia and other cognitive disabilities. The number of people with dementia increased from 101,000 in 1990 to 189,000 in 2005, and it is projected to reach 292,000 in 2020. The increase in the number of dementia cases is complicated by Japan's shortage of caregivers and by the rising cost of home care.

In response to these changes, Japan modified its health-insurance system in 2000 to make living in group homes reimbursable. The result has been a steady increase in the number of group homes ever since that year. Japan had 266 group homes in 2000 when the insurance system changed. Four years later, there were 3,200—an increase of 400 percent (Yokohama, 2005: 3).

The design of group homes reflects urban and rural lifestyles in Japan today, and group homes located in Japan's cities are often indistinguishable from the houses and apartments around them. Green Tokyo, a Japanese "for-pay" nursing home, has a special dining room for residents with a variety of disabilities (Figure 4.12).

Many group homes incorporate familiar design elements from Japanese homes and gardens—for example, a traditional Japanese room with *tatami* mats, or a rock garden. In this way they make cultural heritage into a therapeutic resource in caring for people with dementia. The therapeutic value comes from the activities that occur in such traditional spaces and not from the traditional decor (Cohen and Day, 2000: 366). Decor and color scheme are less important than the activities that are possible in Japanese rooms and other

Figure 4.12. Green Tokyo's dining room is designed for residents with a variety of disabilities.

traditional spaces. In one group home, for example, the Japanese room is a place for arranging flowers and for listening to traditional Japanese music. The rock garden in another group home is a place to stroll and meditate. Research on Japanese group-home design also finds that there is a decrease both in agitated behaviors and physical aggression when traditional lighting reduced shadows on walls and floors in the group home (Schreiner, Yamamoto, and Shiotani, 2000: 4).

THE FUTURE

Home design in Japan is responding to the demands of an aging population. The newest challenge to home design is retirement. A growing number of Japanese men are anxious about severing their ties to the Japanese corporations where they work.

CORPORATE RETIREMENT VILLAGES

There are now a sizable number of retired people in Japan, but work is crucial to Japanese identity. Schneider and Silverman, writing about Japanese culture, insist that many Japanese workers see the work group as their family and strive to prove their loyalty, perseverance, and success at work (2006: 11–13). It comes as no surprise, then, that retirement is a crisis for the work-oriented Japanese. Some corporations are responding by designing communities where retired workers can live near one another (Wiejers-Hasegawa, 2003: 1). It remains to be seen if Japan's corporations will become even more involved with home design as members of the loyal workforce reach retirement age.

FLOATING HOTELS

The Japanese have also begun developing "floating hotels" aboard ocean liners. These are ships that are designed to accommodate people with Alzheimer's or those who require nursing care (*Trends in Japan*, 2004: 1). In *Choujukoku*, the Land of Longevity, sailing off into the sunset will be something you can do without leaving home!

NOW THAT YOU'VE READ CHAPTER 4

KEY TERMS AND CONCEPTS (JP=JAPANESE)

adult-day-care centers
adult day centers
Choujukoku (Jp: Land of Longevity)
collaborative housing
fusuma (Jp: sliding screen)
futon (Jp: sleeping pad)
minka (Jp: clasic country house)
networked technologies
nisetai jutaku (Jp: intergenerational house)
norm of coresidence
tatami (Jp: bamboo mat)
yome (Jp: daughter-in-Law)
yuryo rojin home (Jp: nursing Home)

QUESTIONS FOR STUDY AND DISCUSSION

1. Why is Japan called *Choujukoku*, or the Land of Longevity?
2. What are networked technologies, and how are they being used in Japan to make life easier for its aging population?

3. Why is the architecture of the *minka* so flexible? How did this make it easier to care for an aging family member?
4. How did the experimental *nisetai jukatu* contribute to the design of senior housing in Japan?
5. How do Japan's collaborative homes encourage aging in place?
6. What are some of the traditional design elements in most of Japan's modern nursing homes?

HELPFUL WEBSITES

bamo.com (Sun City Kashiwa)
koujuuzai.or.jp (Foundation for Senior Citizens' Housing)
nenrin.or.jp (Foundation of Social Development for Senior Citizens)
yuroko.or.jp (Japanese Association of Retirement Housing)

NOTES

1. The house was developed by JEITA (Japan Electronics & Information Technology Industries) as a prototype in 2002.
2. In Japan's Okinawa Prefecture, there are 31.19 centenarians for every 100,000 people, and in Amami Prefecture, there are an astounding 56.57 centenarians for every 100,000 people—the world's highest ratio. (*Trends In Japan*, 2003).
3. Naohiro Ogawa, "Demographic Trends and Their Implications for Japan's Future." Japan Information Center, 7 March 1997: 23–40. See especially, "Co-residence with Parents," pp. 5–7. Ogawa finds that the percentage of elderly people or couples living with a young married couple fell from 62 percent in 1965 to 30 percent today.
4. See Leavitt, "Two Prototypical Designs for Single Parents" (1989) for an account of why an American experiment in home design, a two-family home with an apartment for a single mother and one for a widowed woman, was also a failure.
5. The phrase "Silver Tsunami" is now being used in at least two ways. First, it has a demographic meaning: the rapid growth of the population aged 75 or older (*The Silver Tsunami: A Graphical Depiction,* 2004: 1). But it is also being used to capture the difference in technological aptitude between today's elderly people and the more techno-savvy Boomers (*The Silver Tsunami,* 2005: 1).
6. The Japanese now market a variety of products that make toileting a more comfortable experience. Toto, which is best known in this field, markets a "washlet" nozzle that extends from under the toilet seat and

shoots a stream of "soothing, gentle warm water for cleansing." Other products include a warm air dryer, deodorization, antibacterial protection for the commode, and soft seats to eliminate annoying "toilet slam" (Toto, 2005: 1). Elderly people are a prime market for these popular products.

We're going to take care of your parents for you.
—Loving Hearts Nursing Home,
Shenyang City, 2003

5

China
The New Revolution Is Gray, Not Red

OVERVIEW

For centuries, family life in China was based on the norm of filial piety: Parents could expect their sons to take care of them in their old age. Very often this involved moving into the home of a son and daughter-in-law, though sometimes it meant that a son and his family would move into a parent's home. But ever since the 1970s, China has successfully controlled population growth by only allowing families to have one child apiece. In addition, many young people do not feel obligated to take care of their aging parents or in-laws anymore. As a result, three decades after the one-child policy took effect, many elderly Chinese people have nobody to take care of them. In recent years, there has been an increase in the number of nursing homes and senior-day-care centers. But most seniors in China continue living with their children in crowded houses and apartments. Senior housing in China today is developing against this conflicted backdrop and in response to it.

CARING FOR AGING PARENTS

The ad was enticing. Loving Hearts Nursing Home (a pseudonym) had made an offer to the people of Shenyang City: Bring your aging mother or father to live there, and Loving Hearts Nursing Home would provide a comprehensive room with a private bath and shower, modern furnishings, a telephone, and an electronic intercom* for just 1,000 RMB[1] down and 900 RMB per month. Loving Hearts even promised to drive families to and from the nursing home so that an elderly mom or dad could personally tour the premises.

The ad appeared in local newspapers, on flyers, and even on the Internet in this bustling industrial city. And in less than a week, there was a long list of prospects waiting to tour the nursing home.

But some of the elderly people on that list had been added without their knowledge or consent. Their names had been put on that list by their children—mostly sons. In Chinese families, a son is responsible for the care of his aging parents. In fact, the Chinese have a saying: "I will raise a son to care for me when I am old." But filial piety cannot be taken for granted in China anymore. When they were questioned by the authorities in Shenyang City, the children from these families confessed that they did not want to take responsibility for their aging parents.[2]

The norm of filial piety is being challenged in China and not for the first time. During the 1960s, Mao Zedong encouraged young people in China to join the Cultural Revolution and remake Chinese life, which often involved challenging the authority of elders and forced young people to be reeducated while living in barracks. But the Cultural Revolution, with its militant Red Guards is long gone. The current revolution in senior home design is being fueled more by demographics and globalization than by politics (Jackson and Howe, 2004: 14). This time, the revolution is gray, not red.

SLEEPING CLOSEST TO THE STOVE: TRADITIONAL HOUSING FOR SENIORS IN CHINA

Until about 30 years ago, there were hardly any nursing homes in China. There were no senior-day-care centers and no apartment buildings just for seniors. Unlike Sweden (see Chapter 6), where independent living during old age is the norm, there are different expectations in China.

The social and demographic fact is that older people in China usually live with relatives, typically with their children. Research has shown that less than 10 percent of people aged 70 to 79 and just 2 percent of elderly people aged 80 or older ever lived on their own prior to 1990 (Saunders, Xiaoyuan et al., 2003: 3). And it is only since the 1990s that independent living has become an option for large numbers of older people.

Most Chinese peasant families still live in small farming villages, though the urban population has been growing rapidly ever since the 1980s (*China Statistical Yearbook*, 2003: 99). It is customary for everyone in a traditional peasant family to eat and sleep together in the same room.

Wealthier families, however, live in more elaborate houses that can be modified or added to as a family's circumstances change. But even in wealthier households, older people living in the home rarely eat or sleep very far from other family members.

To Western readers, the living conditions in peasant homes are unthinkable, especially the idea of different generations sleeping together in the same room, let alone the same bed. But domestic architecture and interior design in China were not shaped by Western norms or sensibilities. They were shaped by Confucian tradition, and Confucian tradition puts a premium on living with and for one's family.

Until recently, senior housing in China meant being housed and cared for by one's children. Architecturally and socially, this was the Confucian way. The Confucian ideal is that aging family members should occupy the honored spot in the family and in the home. According to architect and anthropologist Judy Schaff:

> [Chinese] houses and their sitings reflect the traditional "Confucian" sensibility, the value of construing the locally available elements, both human and material, to maximize their fit. It is for this reason that one way the story of China can be told is through the changing face of the architecture (Schaaf, 2001: 6).

The best descriptions of traditional home design for seniors in rural China come from Xiajia Village in China's Heilongjiang Province. Anthropologist Yunxiang Yan visited Xiajia Village seven times between 1989 and 1999. In *Private Life Under Socialism* (2003), he describes traditional housing arrangements for elderly people, which were based on Confucian guidelines. It was common for peasant families to live in houses consisting of two or three *jia*, or rooms, that were always arranged horizontally and in a row or straight line.[3] The peasant hut, or *majiazi*, would have an unheated west room for storage, a central room containing two stoves for cooking and the ancestral shrine, and an east room where family members ate meals and slept. Horizontal pipes starting at the base of the stoves would run underneath the two beds (known in Chinese as *kang*) on opposite walls in the east room. This is how the beds in the east room of the *majiazi* were heated. In addition to sleeping on these long, heated beds, families would also eat their meals on them. At mealtime, short-legged tables were placed on the beds and dinner was served (Yan, 2003: 116). The floor plan in Figure 5.1 depicts the three-*jian* unit in a twentieth-century peasant hut. It is surprisingly similar to the three-*jian* homes of northern and southern China built a century earlier.

The entire family would sleep in the east room at night. Sleeping arrangements reflected the hierarchical and patriarchal nature of Chinese families. The choicest spot (known in Chinese as *kangtou*, or near the stove) for sleeping, and for eating always went to the senior male in the family. His spouse would eat and sleep next to him, also close to the warmth from the stove. Children would typically sleep on the south bed, which was heated by pipes running from the second stove to underneath the south bed. Location on the *kangtou*

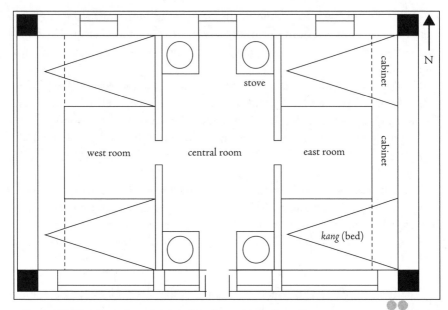

Figure 5.1. The floor plan of the twenty-first-century three-*jian* peasant hut in Xiajia Village, China.

reflected a person's importance in the hierarchy of their family (Schaaf, 2001: 166). The concept of privacy, especially when it separated one generation from another, was virtually unknown.

Aging family members fared a little better in the homes of wealthier families, but they still ate and slept close to their children and grandchildren. Chinese families who could afford to do so would add *jian* as needed. When they would expand the home, the Chinese always added odd-numbered multiples of *jian* because "odd numbers were considered lucky numbers." (Knapp, 2000: 22). For example, a three-*jian* home (the basic living unit) might be expanded to a five-*jian*, or a seven-*jian* home. According to tradition, the oldest members of the family would be entitled to the choicest spots to eat and sleep within the newly expanded home, or what Shen (2001: 87) refers to as "the most protected location" of the house.

Figure 5.2 shows what one of these elaborate Chinese homes would have looked like. It would have typically been a larger, rectangular dwelling with a central courtyard, a central hall, and then two longer bays (sets of *jian*) (Figure 5.3). Aging members of the family would sleep in one of the longer bays flanking the courtyard. The flexibility of *jian* construction allowed families to care

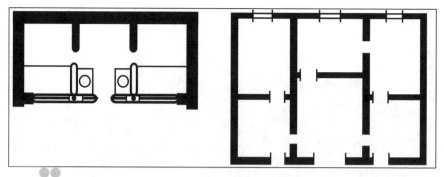

Figure 5.2. The three-*jian* floor plan of peasant huts in China today is very similar to this nineteenth-century design.

for aging parents or in-laws, or would give an aging couple the flexibility to allow children to move in and be caregivers in exchange for a place to live.

Most urban families in China now live in Western-style apartment buildings. But even in the densely populated cities, there was no specialized senior housing until the 1980s. In China's crowded cities, older people would move in with their children or would invite their children to move in with them. It would not be until the late 1980s, when China's economic and social policies began to change, that senior housing even became an option.

FROM CHARITY HOMES TO ALFS

Prior to the 1980s, the only housing options for elderly Chinese peasants— apart from living with children—were social welfare institutions and local charity homes. These were little more than state-run barracks for indigent older people. One writer described these places as "drab, dormitory-style warehouses for the penniless" (Beal, 2000: 2). During the 1980s, China began to build senior housing; however, this is still considered a new concept in China.

Shanghai is China's wealthiest city. Yet there were no nursing homes there until 1998. "People were not willing to enter nursing homes in the past," says the owner and operator of Minsheng House, Shanghai's first private nursing home. "They [i.e., nursing homes] were considered places for those without descendants" (French, 2006: 10). Today, however, that nursing home is 95 percent occupied.

Now an estimated 18 percent of older people in China are living in senior housing. Chinese economists estimate that the senior-housing industry is

Figure 5.3. Wealthier families would construct homes with a central courtyard and longer bays or sets of *jian*.

experiencing a growth rate of 15 percent per year (Daniels, 2004: 1), and recent surveys estimate that an additional 20 percent of elderly Chinese people would prefer to live in senior housing or nursing homes if they could afford to (*Financial Times*, 21 June 2004:1; *Shanghai Daily*, October 18, 2004: 1). Today, senior housing is becoming more popular and socially acceptable.

Senior housing no longer consists of charity homes for the penniless. It is true that some of China's nursing homes are overcrowded and understaffed (French, 2006: 10), but others are modern and attractive. And such places are attracting more affluent older people. This is how the director of an attractive, carefully landscaped nursing home in Chongqing City describes the seniors who are moving there: "Most are civil servants or professors who have pensions" (Daniels, 2004: 1). The director of a nursing home in Hong Kong echoes this point, saying that "there is a demand from the middle-class elderly, who want to find a place to enjoy their retirement" (Lee, 2003: 1).

There are now extremes in the cost and quality of senior housing in China. For example, Shanghai now boasts the $7.6 million Zhongren Nursing Home, which can provide medical, psychiatric, and rehabilitation services for about 400 elderly people (Xinhua General News Service, 23 October 2003: 1). But not far from the Zhongren are two other nursing homes that lack all but the most basic amenities. The Alzheimer's unit shown in Figure 5.4 still has bars on some of the doors and windows.

The medical capacity in most nursing homes is still minimal, reports China's Xinhua General News Service (*China View*, 5 April 2005:1):

> Resident doctors are only authorized to treat conditions no more complex than a common cold. Patients are transferred to hospitals for more complicated interventions and at their own expense.

The range of amenities available to seniors living independently is also widening. Low-rent senior housing and public housing offer the basics, but not much else. For example, in China's largest cities—Beijing, Shanghai, and Nanjing—the amenities for seniors living in state-controlled apartments

Figure 5.4. Even in China today, there are extremes based on economic backgrounds as to how Alzheimer's units are designed.

include little more than an emergency pull-chord above the bed so that an elderly resident can summon help (Xinhua General News Service, 25 September, 2004: 1). At the other extreme, Cheerful Court in Beijing will offer 247 studio apartments and 377 one-bedroom apartments that will feature "an indoor swimming pool, jacuzzi, gymnasium, library, grooming room, hair salon, Chinese music room, cafe, convenience shop, garden, and traditional Chinese and Western medical services" (*South China Morning Post*, 4 September, 2004: 1).

The gap will continue to widen between the poor and the wealthy as more private investors build housing and hospitals that target the small but affluent sector of China's senior population. In Liaoning Province, for example, the number of private nursing homes increased from 200 to more than 300 in 2003 (Yong, 2004: 1) and represents the fastest-growing sector of the nursing home industry in that province.

China is embarking on a campaign to encourage aging in place by making existing housing more senior-friendly. This includes installing handrails and larger bathrooms (*South China Morning Post*, 9 June 2001:1), assistance bells, nonskid tiles and flooring, and entrance ramps into existing structures. In addition to these renovations, many Chinese cities are increasing the number of services being offered to seniors who live alone. In Shanghai, this includes social workers who "monitor the city's older residents, paying regular house visits aimed at combating isolation and making sure that medical problems are attended to" (French, 2006: 10).

In addition to encouraging China's empty-nesters to age in place, there are now efforts to encourage families to take care of aging family members. Some Chinese cities are now experimenting with a plan that would pay family members 250 yuan ($12.33) per month to take care of aging parents at home. The policy is meant to appeal to family members who are unemployed or between jobs, and older people who might otherwise move into nursing homes (Qin, 2005: 1).

Senior housing is being shaped by more than just the increasing numbers of China's elderly people. It is also being shaped by the growing affluence of seniors and their families. Now, more than ever before, there is a class of seniors who want to live in more comfortable and attractive surroundings.

In response to the increasing numbers of affluent older people, there is now more variety in the financing of the construction and in the architectural design of senior housing. This includes seniors-only apartment buildings, ALFs, intergenerational houses where a percentage of apartments are set aside for people aged 60 and older, nursing homes, and geriatric hospitals. Senior housing ranges from small, residential, low-rise homes to high-tech apartment towers and residential complexes like the modernistic Li Chong Yuet Ming Nursing Home in Sheung Shui City. The Chinese god of longevity welcomes visitors to a nursing home in Tianjin City. The nursing homes in Figure 5.5 and 5.6 are "Western" by Chinese standards but have traditional architectural elements, such as red trim for good luck and feng shui seating.

Chloe Lai (2004: 1) says there is also a demand for intergenerational housing in urban areas. Typically, apartment buildings are designated as intergenerational buildings where seniors and their children and grandchildren will live in neighboring apartments. This is a specifically urban form that allows extended families to maintain traditional relationships in urban high-rise neighborhoods, illustrating that the old norm of filial piety may be weakening, but it has not disappeared entirely.

APARTMENT BUILDINGS

Apartment buildings also allow for other senior-housing arrangements. There have been high-rise apartment buildings dedicated entirely to the elderly and disabled people. Most of the apartments in these buildings are studio apartments outfitted with "elderly-friendly features such as nonslip floor tiles and support bars." When polled, 67 percent of the aging residents of

Figure 5.5. The Chinese god of longevity stands in front of this nursing home, which features traditional elements: red trim for good luck and *feng shui* seating.

Figure 5.6. Western-style senior housing is becoming more common in China today.

these high-rise buildings said they prefer to live on the 10th floor and below (Angus, 2003:22). Interestingly, both the elderly and the disabled residents of these specialized high-rise towers said they would prefer to live in buildings where their studios were integrated into a mix of specialized and regular apartments. Their hope was to achieve a better resident mix and to "encourage interaction between the elderly and younger families" (Angus, 2003: 24). Interaction with younger people is easier when apartment buildings reserve a percentage of apartments for seniors but scatter those apartments throughout the building instead of grouping them together in one wing or on specific floors of the buildings (*South China Morning Post*, 9 June 2004:2). In China today, surveys indicate that there is growing interest among seniors to be independent. For example, a 1999 survey by the *Liaoning Daily*, one of the largest newspapers in China's Liaoning Province, found that seniors who were surveyed prefer self-care to home care and preferred to live independently (*Liaoning Daily*, 23 June, 1999: 1). Liaoning has the largest percentage of elderly residents of any province in China. More than 10 percent of elderly people surveyed in Liaoning Province say that they would prefer to live in retirement homes or on their own rather than live with their children (*Financial Times*, 2004: 1). And one-sixth of seniors aged 65 or older in Shanghai say they would prefer to live in nursing homes rather than be a burden to their children (Xinhua General News Service, 25 September 2004: 2).

SERVICES AND RENOVATIONS

The Chinese government is beginning to respond to demands from seniors to be more autonomous. Public housing for empty-nesters in China's largest cities is being upgraded with services and renovations that will help seniors live independently. In Shanghai, for example, the Civil Affairs Bureau is adding medical nursing and psychological counseling to the "cooking, shopping, and emergency help" that are already available to older people who live alone (*Shanghai Daily*, 11 June 2004: 1). And many Chinese municipalities now install an assistance bell that an older person can ring if and when an emergency occurs (Xinhua News Agency, 25 September 2004: 3).

But just because Chinese seniors want to live independently, it does not mean they wish to be cut off from their families or from younger people. They want more housing options so that they can develop their own best way of maintaining contact with their family and community.

One way of maintaining contact with the community is through senio day care. Senior day care enables older people to spend most or part of the day with other seniors and return home at the end of the day. Senior day care is becoming more important in China as more elderly people choose to live alone or live with children who must work during the day. Rather than staying home alone, older Chinese people who enroll in senior day care have opportunities for daily physical checkups, breakfast, lunch, and recreational programs. In addition to senior day care, there is a growing number of senior recreational centers where residents can enroll in such activities as "shadowboxing, folk music, opera, chess, and handicrafts" ("Elderly Daycare," 12 October 2004: 1). Senior day care and senior recreational centers are becoming home away from home for countless seniors in China who spend mornings and afternoons there. Just as there is more variety in the types of senior housing available in China today, there is also a variety of financing and construction arrangements.

A MIX OF PUBLIC AND PRIVATE OWNERSHIP

Senior housing in China is owned and operated in at least three different ways. The largest landlord is the Chinese government. There are more than 36,000 nursing homes, ALFs, and senior-day-care centers in China today, and 15,700 of these are government run, usually at the municipal level. The remainder are privately owned and operated (China Statistical Yearbook, 2003: 837).

Within the private sector, housing options range from small and intimate to large and institutional. More than half of privately owned housing for seniors is family owned and operated. These are usually smaller facilities or apartment complexes, and they advertise themselves as offering the closest thing to filial piety. For example, Guangzhou City boasts an upscale, privately run, 15-bed home called East Wind Elderly Home, which charges an entrance fee of more than $1,000 and monthly rent of $90 (Eckholm, 1998: 1). More recently, there is the home page for a 20-bed assisted-living facility in Cheng Sheng City. The owner of this small assisted-living facility is a man in his early thirties. The home page shows him smiling, a carnation in his lapel, and his well-dressed wife by his side. Behind this young couple is a group of elderly residents. The image reinforces the message on the home page: "Come and be part of our family," reads the copy. This may not be filial piety, but it is the next best thing in a rapidly changing society.

The remainder of privately owned facilities are corporate and tend to be large and institutional. For example, Tian Jin Seniors Home, located in Tian Jin City, is a 550-bed facility. There are geriatric wards in this nursing home (including 120 beds) and independent and assisted-living units. Residents of Tian Jin live three to a room. The facility boasts a lecture hall, an exercise room, a library, and a computer room. Adjacent to the nursing home is the fully air-conditioned Tian Jin Senior Daycare Center. Another example, Jolly Place, a 243-unit facility in Hong Kong, offers "a sauna, reading room, gymnasium, and round-the-clock nursing care" (Lee, 2003: 1). Jolly Place has become so successful that the owners are now building a similar facility called Cheerful Court in another part of the city (Lai, 9 June 2004).

Data on corporately owned senior housing in China, though anecdotal, indicate that corporately owned facilities are beginning to merge and form chains consisting of two or more properties in a particular region or locale. These chains are then able to share staff, equipment, and advertising budgets. In Liaoning Province, for example, there are now 54 old-age care centers, as the Chinese sometimes call them. Half of these are owned and operated by the municipal government; the remainder are either family owned or corporately owned and operated. The corporately owned properties include a nursing-home chain comprised of three local properties (Hui, 2004: 2). One of these corporately owned properties, located in Sheng Cheng City, offers a continuum of care ranging from independent living to skilled nursing care.

Senior housing began as a governmental responsibility, but it is rapidly becoming a private-sector operation. Perhaps the future is the partnership of public and private investors that is now starting to happen in China's largest cities. Municipal-owned homes in Beijing, Shanghai, and Nanjing used to be charity homes that housed indigent and homeless elderly people. But even municipal-owned housing has become more entrepreneurial in China today. Many municipal homes will now accept "a mix of paying and welfare clients" (Eckholm, 1998: 4). This is also true of the Tian Jin Nursing Home in Tian Jin City[4], where there is free housing for the poor and monthly rental units for more affluent tenants. Years ago, it would have been unthinkable for elderly people from different social classes to live in such close proximity. But the new senior housing movement is more inclusive and makes older people from different social backgrounds neighbors.

Now, more than ever before, China's senior housing is being influenced by foreign design and foreign investment. For instance, Taiwan, China's longtime rival, has been an innovator in senior home design. Taiwanese innovations are now accessible to architects and interior designers in China and are beginning to shape the Chinese home-design market. For example, Yan (2003: 121) reports that homes throughout rural China are now adding Western features, such as a master bedroom, smaller and private bedrooms, and a family room. These additions are inspired by projects in Shanghai and now appear in magazines and websites on Mainland China. Investors are also bringing new architectural and design elements to China. For example, the Xinhua General News Service reports that an entrepreneur who had already built five "care homes for the elderly in Hong Kong" had just completed work on the Zhongren Nursing Home in Shanghai, which closely resembles its counterparts in Hong Kong (23 October, 2003: 1).

DESIGN ELEMENTS: A CHINESE AND WESTERN MIX

The architecture and interior design of the new senior housing in China is a mix of Chinese and Western sensibilities (Figure 5.7). Across China, nursing homes or ALFs will have traditional Chinese design elements and symbols along with Western technologies and circuitry. For example, Figure 5.8 shows a new, two-story assisted-living facility. The gateposts in front of the facility are topped with red trim, and the front door is framed in red and gold leaf, which are auspicious colors in China. The *feng shui* of gates and entrances has traditionally been a very important part of domestic architecture and design in China (Shen, 2001: 83). These clasic elements represent health and prosperity in Chinese culture. On the Sheng Cheng building, they are superimposed on a boxy, white concrete structure that has been built in the Bauhaus tradition. The resulting facade communicates two messages: the Confucian idea of vitality and the Western idea of efficiency. These are appropriate messages for a building that will be the new home for people who will now be living apart from their children. Chang Gung Cultural and Health Promotion Village is more Western in form and function than Sheng Cheng. Its curved, multicolored exteriors could

Figure 5.7. Senior home design in China is being influenced by aesthetics and design breakthroughs from Taiwan, Hong Kong, and western nations. These images illustrate assisted living in Taiwan.

be part of building in any part of the world, and the facility provides a continuum of care. Chang Gung Village offers residents billiards and a computer room along with traditional activities such as mahjong and tai chi (Figure 5.9).

Many Chinese nursing homes and ALFs now contain a mix of Chinese and Western design elements. This is especially true for exercise and activities rooms. Along with open areas for traditional Chinese tai chi exercise, some nursing homes and senior residences now have Western-style fitness rooms where residents can exercise with weights, barbells, and stationary bikes. Sometimes Chinese and Western design elements converge in the same room(s), as in this nursing home's television lounge (see Figure 5.10). Aging residents can

Figure 5.8. This ALF in Sheng Cheng City displays clasic Chinese design elements.

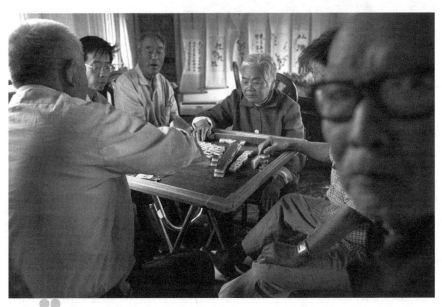

Figure 5.9. Elderly Chinese people playing mahjong in this nursing home.

Figure 5.10. This facility features an excercise room with a space for doing *tai chi* and a television lounge, which has a mixture of traditional Chinese *kang* seating and Western-style chairs.

watch television while sitting in chairs (the Western mode for doing this) or reclining on Chinese sofas, or *kang*.

INTERIOR DESIGN: TRADITIONAL ELEMENTS, NEW MESSAGES

China's Internet and advertising media are filled with scores of images of nursing homes, ALFs, and senior apartments. These are intended for Chinese audiences, and they give important messages about aging in the absence of filial piety. Typically, they show rooms and gardens filled with people—often from different social backgrounds—who are enjoying themselves despite the fact that they now live apart from their families. There are images of residents eating, sleeping, playing mahjong, or doing tai chi. These are important images in China today, where it is not yet entirely acceptable for older people to live apart from their children.

REMODELING AT HOME

Estimates vary, but the number of China's seniors in nursing homes, senior housing, and geriatric wards is a small percentage of the total. The majority of seniors in China are either living with their children or living alone in homes where they have been for years. This helps explain the rapid growth of China's home-health industry, which includes home-health aides and other caregivers (*Shanghai Daily*, 2 July 2004: 1; *Shanghai Daily*, 11 June 2004, French, 2006: 1). There is also an increase in the number of homes that are being retrofitted with guardrails, emergency pull chords, and nonskid floor products to make homes safer for aging residents (Daniels, 2004: 1). Perhaps the most detailed account of remodeling appears in the field notes of anthropologist Yunxiang Yan.

Yan mentions that many peasants in rural towns and villages can now afford to expand or remodel their homes. By the early 1990s the Chinese, even peasants living in remote villages like Xiajia Village in China's remote Heilongjiang Province, began experimenting with new construction materials (including brick, tile, and reinforced concrete). With the help of these materials, the peasants were able to build larger, more urbane homes (Yan, 2003: 121). This new domestic construction was influenced by urban home design, especially innovations from Shanghai, where the master bedroom and the family room were gaining popularity. The floor plan of a 1997 house in rural China was the first in Xiajia Village to include a Western-style master bedroom for the married couple who would live there. The traditional multipurpose east bedroom of the three-*jian* house has been replaced by a configuration that gives the married couple a private master bedroom, but may not be advantageous to the elderly (Figure 5.11). There are reports of elderly family members being relegated to small, drafty bedrooms far from the warmth of the heating stove (Yan, 2003:127). Even though they are still living with their children, they may be marginalized by the new, Western-style renovations.

PROSPERITY, CHANGE, AND SENIOR HOUSING IN CHINA TODAY

The prosperity of the late 1980s coincided with a number of social and demographic problems that impacted China's aging population and its housing arrangements. The norm of filial piety had begun to erode. More children were unable or unwilling to look after their parents. During the 1970s, China instituted a one-child policy: Married couples could only have one child and were penalized and shamed if they had any more than that. By the 1980s, this policy

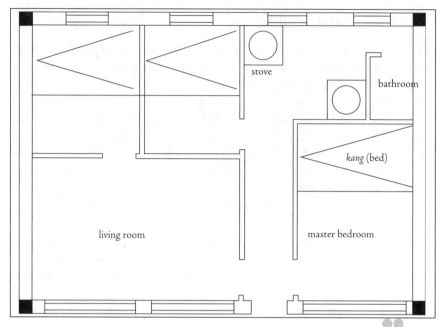

Figure 5.11. The three-*jian* floor plan has given way to a more Western
floor plan, with consequences for family dynamics.

started having unexpected repercussions (French, 2006: 1). The parents and
grandparents of these only children realized that they might be without caregivers when they became old and frail. In fact, by the late 1980s, the Chinese
had already begun calling this the 1-2-4 dilemma: one child might have to care
for two parents and four grandparents.

At the same time, a larger percentage of Chinese people are living to be 65
years or older. China's National Committee on Aging estimates that the number of Chinese aged 65 or older will increase from 100 million to 200 million
between 2000 and 2007 (Qin, 2005:1) (Table 5.1).

The percentage of elderly people in China will leap from 11 percent of the
Chinese population (in 2005) to 15 percent in 2015, 24 percent in 2030, and 28
percent in 2040. Jackson and Howe add that these figures probably "understate
the magnitude of China's age wave" (Jackson and Howe, 2004: 10). This follows from the fact that the aging of the population will be accompanied by
a decrease in fertility, which means that the actual percentage of older people
could be even higher (Jackson and Howe, 2004: 10–11).

The problem of a rapidly aging population is compounded by the fact that
men outnumber women in China's younger population. This phenomenon has

TABLE 5.1. WHERE TO FIND PEOPLE AGED 65 OR OLDER IN CHINA'S PROVINCES AND CITIES

NUMBER OF PEOPLE AGED 65+ IN 2000 BY PROVINCE

Total Number of People Aged 65+=88,110,000

Province	Number of People Aged 65+	Province	Number of People Aged 65+
Shandong	7,290,000	Jianxi	2,530,000
Jiansu	6,510,000	Fuken	2,270,000
Henan	6,440,000	Xianxi	2,140,000
Xichung	6,200,000	Guichung	2.040,000
Guangdon	5,230,000	Helongjian	2,000,000
Hunan	4,690,000	Jiling	1,600,000
Hebei	4,630,000	Gansu	1,280,000
Anhui	4,460,000	Inner Mongolia	1,270,000
Chejiang	4,140,000	Xinjiang	870,000
Hubei	3,800,000	Ninsha	250,000
Liaoning	3,320,000	Quinghai	220,000
Guangxi	3,200,000	Tibet	120,000
Yunan	2,570,000		

NUMBER OF PEOPLE AGED 65+ IN SELECT CHINESE CITIES IN YEAR 2000

City	Number of People Aged 65+
Shanghai	1,930,000
Beijing	1,160,000
Tinajing	830,000

been called China's "Bachelor Bomb," and it means that there will be fewer women (i.e., wives and daughters) available to care for an aging parent (Poston and Morrison, 2005: 1).

There has been internal migration from the rural countryside to China's big cities. The economic growth that began in the 1980s has attracted millions in search of work to China's urban centers. For example, Riley (2004: 28) speaks of a "floating population" that already numbers between 30 million and 100 million Chinese from rural areas who are now living in urban areas, often without having official permission to do so. These "floaters" have difficulty finding suitable housing and must often live as tenants or boarders in already crowded flats and boardinghouses. Under these circumstances, it is not possible for them to invite their parents to live with them, as they would have in the rural villages of China.

Finally, China's traditional and insular society is being influenced by external ideas and products. Neighboring Taiwan and Hong Kong are innovators in

TABLE 5.2 MEDIAN AGE OF CHINA'S POPULATION

MEDIAN AGE OF THE ELDERLY POPULATION IN YEAR 2000, BY PROVINCE AND IN SELECTED CITIES

Overall Median Age	70.15		
PROVINCE	*MEDIAN AGE*	*PROVINCE*	*MEDIAN AGE*
Helongjian	75.68	Xianxi	69.06
Jiling	75.19	Quinghai	69.05
Liaoning	74.49	Xinjiang	68.17
Inner Mongolia	73.37	Xianxi	68.00
Chejiang	73.09	Yunan	67.98
Jiansu	71.59	Jianxi	67.90
Hubei	70.82	Ninsha	67.15
Hunan	70.54	Anhui	67.03
Fuken	70.44	Guangxi	66.64
Hebei	70.32	Henan	65.95
Chungchin	70.17	Tibet	64.30
Xichung	69.90	Guichung	63.92
Guangdon	69.78		

MEDIAN AGE OF THE ELDERLY POPULATION IN YEAR 2000, SELECTED CHINESE CITIES

City	Median Age
Beijing	78.04
Shanghai	76.28
Tinajing	74.93

senior housing and interior design, and China's largest cities are now being seen as places where multinational corporations can invest. The Internet has also been bringing new ideas about senior home and product design to China for some time now. And just recently, bloggers have begun adding their own thoughts on everything from filial piety to nursing home design (The *New York Times*, 24 November 2005: 1).

THE FUTURE

The Chinese have an interesting way of warning their friends to be careful. "May you live in interesting times," they say. In China, where continuity and tradition are values above all else, this is a warning indeed.

MORE UPSCALE SENIOR HOUSING AHEAD

There are interesting times ahead for the design and construction of senior housing in China. The rapid aging of China's population, along with the fact that more affluent people are in the market for senior housing, will create demand for better and more attractively designed living space. For example, McMansions have recently come to China, as have gated communities (www.orangecounty.com.cn, 2006). This calls attention to the market potential of upscale housing—a fact that will impact senior design. In addition to more upscale living space, there will be more standardization across China's far-flung provinces. There are already local chains of nursing homes and ALFs.

MORE CORPORATELY FRANCHISED NURSING HOMES

The future will see the design and construction of similar housing within and across provinces. In fact, corporations such as the Hong Kong-based Health-Care Asia, Ltd. are planning to design and build internationally.

GROWTH OF A HOME-REPAIR INDUSTRY

The trend toward remodeling and renovation of existing housing will only expand and intensify. The vast majority of China's seniors is still aging in place and will continue living in the same homes where they currently reside or with their children. Indeed, China's newfound prosperity has given many households the resources to modernize their living space.

GROWING INTEREST IN INTERIOR DESIGN

In addition, Western values have begun to influence Chinese home design. There is, for example, a growing interest in having a private master bedroom. This will mean that older people are demoted to smaller, more remote rooms in the remodeled house. There will be another unexpected problem as well. The remodeling craze is now beginning to spawn con artists who try to get older homeowners in China to pay for home repairs that they do not really need and cannot really afford. The title of a recent news article is ominous: "Salesmen Pressure Elderly to Renovate Homes for Better Health" (*Mainchi Daily News*, 11 May 2004: 1). Along with China's remodeling boom, there will be more home-related frauds and rip-offs. There are now accounts of elderly Chinese people being conned into buying mosquito nets, under-floor ventilation fans, and humidity controllers that they did not need (*Mainichi Daily News*,

11 May 2004:1). But perhaps the most significant change of all is the weakening of the one-child policy.

WEAKENING OF THE ONE-CHILD POLICY

For the first time in China, there is talk of easing up and allowing urban families to have two children if they so desire. The Chinese may soon become a population of two-child families, which will have even more implications for older people and their living space. It is likely that they will be stretched even thinner financially if there are children to care for in addition to aging family members. These are interesting times indeed.

NOW THAT YOU'VE READ CHAPTER 5

KEY TERMS AND CONCEPTS (Ch=CHINESE)

demographics
feng shui
filial piety
floating population
jia, jian (Ch: rooms)
kangtou (Ch: "the place next to the stove")
modular design
social welfare institutions and charity homes

QUESTIONS FOR STUDY AND DISCUSSION

1. This chapter discusses some unanticipated consequences of the one-child policy. Briefly explain what the intended consequence was, and then explain why the one-child Policy created an unexpected crisis in senior care.
2. Identify some ways that the new senior housing tries to advertise that life goes on for older people, even if they are not living with their children.
3. Why has it been so important for the new senior housing to include a mix of Chinese and Western architecture and design elements?
4. Why did the remodeling and renovation of peasant homes make life more difficult for the older people who were living there with their families?

NOTES

1. RMB is Chinese currency. A down payment of 1000 RMB would be equivalent to about $115.
2. This is now a crime in China. In 1996, China's Peoples' Congress passed a law requiring children to support their aging parents. As a result, aging parents now have the right to sue and demand that children take better care of them. Examples of Chinese parents who sued their children for neglecting them can be found in Leslie Chang, "Confucius Said: Sons, Care for Your Elders; Elders Say: We Sue." The *New York Times*. 3 April 2000, p.1.
3. See also Ronald G. Knapp, *China's Old Dwellings*. Honolulu: University of Hawaii Press, 2000. Says Knapp, "The Chinese refer to the line of *jia* as *yitiao long*, or 'The Dragon'" (Knapp, 2000: 5) to emphasize that the rooms must be built in a straight line.
4. Home page for Tian Jin Nursing Home, 2004.

The myth is as old as Sweden itself. Attestupa—or walk-ing the plank—would supposedly be the fate of people who were too old to work. Early versions of this myth have the elderly person walking off a cliff. Later versions involve walking the plank and ending up in the ravine.

6

Sweden
Independence by Design

OVERVIEW

Along with China and Japan, Sweden has one of the world's most rapidly aging populations. But the experience of growing older in Sweden is quite different from that experience in Japan or China. China and Japan are societies where older people expect to live with or near their children. In terms of home design, this often means that older people will move into or nearby the home of a son or daughter. The norm is very different in Sweden, where 90 percent of older people live on their own and *not* with their children. Independence in old age is a fact of Swedish life. By law, every municipality in Sweden must help older people be independent and continue living on their own. This involves providing social services, community health centers, and health aides who assist older people in their homes. Sweden now provides such home assistance free of charge to almost 10 percent of people over the age of 65. Although there are nursing homes in Sweden, the more popular alternative is the *servicehus*, where older people are able to live independently while receiving care. Very often, the residents of *servicehus* will live in studio flats furnished with their own possessions so that they still feel that they are living on their own. Even Alzheimer's units in Sweden—which are more intensively monitored than the *servicehus*—are equipped with kitchenettes so that patients can cook and eat on their own if they so desire.

The Swedish government has actually closed hospitals and pulled back on the number of beds in nursing homes. At the same time, there is a government-sponsored increase in the number of home-health workers and aides who do light cooking, cleaning, and shopping with the elderly people in their care. Sweden's population appears to be satisfied with these arrangements. When surveyed in 2003, only 3 percent of elderly people complained about not having adequate home care, as compared to 30 percent of elderly people in the United States.

The future of home design for an aging Sweden is still unclear. Sweden is about to experience the aging of its baby-boom cohort, known as *Fyrtiotalisters*, or "Children of the 1940s." This generation will demand different forms of housing from the type that satisfies today's elderly population. In addition, there are now sizable numbers of ethnic minorities living in Sweden. Their housing needs will be shaped by different norms and values than those that have shaped the design of Sweden's adult communities and senior housing thus far.

LAND OF AGE EQUALITY

In the Stacken residential complex, there is one sauna.[1] Everyone who lives in this community is welcome to use it, and many residents do. On cold winter evenings, men and women of all ages mingle in the sauna. Stacken also has some housing units that pair older people in need of special care and younger people who are willing to live with them. And so the sauna will entice the able-bodied as well as the occasional person with a cane or walker. Home design in Sweden today is not much different from this sauna: inclusive, comfortable, and respectful of age.

Sweden is the land of equality, a fact that has been shaping home design for decades. *Statistics Sweden*, for example, claims that there is more age and gender equality in Sweden than anywhere else in the world (*Statistics Sweden*, 2004: 7). Apart from gender equality, there is a tradition of age equality, which means that age is less of an obstacle in the daily lives of the elderly in Sweden than in other rapidly aging nations. Here is how one group sees the future of age equality in Sweden:

> Our vision includes 80-year-old students, government ministers of 75, 25-year-old local government assembly chairs, and people of 30 working alongside their sexagenarian mentors. (*Senior Citizen Sweden*, 2005: 7)

Older people are valued members of society in Sweden. And they are welcomed in a variety of residential settings. Some older people live with or near their families, but many more are able to live alone. An estimated 40 percent of seniors in Sweden now live alone by choice, and 70 percent of Swedish women over the age of 70 are living by themselves (Wikipedia 2005: 1). As for the remainder, about 45 percent of older people in Sweden live in age-integrated communities. Sweden, more than most other nations, encourages home and community design that makes it easy for older and younger people to live near one another. And regardless of where they are living, Sweden's elders are content with their care and housing. Only 3 percent of Sweden's elders complained of having unmet housing needs, compared with 30 percent of American elders (Peck, 2006: 1).

SWEDEN'S ADULT COMMUNITIES

The newest trend in Sweden is the adult community that neither isolates older people nor segregates them in senior flats or nursing homes (Gullbring 2002: 62). Russinet Houses, built in 2002, are an excellent example of a Swedish adult community (Figure 6.1).

Russinet consists of 27 apartments surrounding a central courtyard in the historic district of Lund, a Swedish university town. Russinet is not exclusively

Figure 6.1. Russinet is an adult community where residents are aged 40 or older.

for old people. Instead, it has positioned itself as a community reserved entirely for adults aged 40 or older; nobody under the age of 40 can live there, but people in their seventies are on the waiting list for the rare vacancy in this adult community.

Architecturally, Russinet echoes the quadrangles of the nearby university. The 27 apartments overlook a central, enclosed yard. There are multipurpose rooms and a commons area where all residents can prepare meals and eat together. Part of the philosophy behind Russinet is that people of all ages should cooperate in doing daily housework. In this adult community, the younger residents typically do more of the manual labor—moving trash cans to the street and shopping for food—while older residents are the ones who tend the communal garden and serve as the watchful eyes and ears of the community. Those who are retired contribute in their way, as do those who are working (Gullbring, 2002: 62).

Russinet not only integrates but also depends on its aging residents. In this way, it is not much different from Sweden itself, which has one of the world's most rapidly aging populations and one of the most enlightened approaches to home design for aging populations.

A RAPIDLY AGING SWEDEN

Sweden has one of the highest proportions of older people to younger people in the world: 17.4 percent of Sweden's population is aged 65 or older, and 5.2 percent is aged 80 or older (*The World Factbook*, 2005: 5) (Table 6.1). It is estimated that every fourth person living in Sweden will be over the age of 65 by 2030 (*Senior Citizen Sweden*, 2005: 2). Swedish life expectancy has increased rapidly over the past 50 years. As of 2005, for example, a Swedish woman aged 65 could expect to reach the age of 82.7, and a Swedish man aged 65 could expect to reach the age of 78.1 (Ministry of Health and Social Affairs, Sweden, 2005: 1). This means that in Sweden, more people than ever before are living to be very old and in need of assistance. Yet very few of them live with their children. In 2005, only 2 to 3 percent of children were sharing their homes with their aging parents (Johansson, 2005: 1) (Figure 6.2).

DESIGNING FOR INDEPENDENCE

Like other rapidly aging nations, Sweden has had to grapple with issues of care and housing for the elderly. But the Swedish response has been different from that of Japan (see Chapter 4) or India (see Chapter 9). Both of those nations are also aging rapidly. Until recently, the Indian and Japanese response to senior housing was family focused. The care and housing of older people in India and

TABLE 6.1. PERCENTAGE OF PEOPLE AGED 66+ IN SWEDEN'S LÄN, OR REGIONS

HOUSEHOLDS CONSISTING OF PEOPLE AGED 65+, BY LÄN:		
Nationwide	554, 335	17.25%
Stockholm Län	263,630	14.07%
Uppsala Län	43,781	14.47%
Södermanlands Län	48,438	18.55%
Östergötlands Län	73,308	17.45%
Jönköpings Län	60,382	18.30%
Kronobergs Län	33,406	20.39%
Kalmar Län	47,818	20.39%
Gotlands Län	10,522	18.25%
Blekinge Län	29,996	19.95%
Skåne Län	203,761	17.55%
Hallands Län	50,365	17.75%
Västra Götalands Län	259,132	17.02%
Värmlands Län	55,113	20.14%
Örebro Län	49,698	18.14%
Västmanland Län	47,913	18.36%
Dalarnas Län	54,520	19.75%
Västernorrlands Län	49,609	20.31%
Gävleborgs Län	54,802	19.81%
Jämtlands Län	25,321	19.81%
Västerbottens Län	45,214	17.60%
Norrbottens Län	47,686	18.87%

(*Source:* www.infosveige.com/lanskartor.php?lang=sv, 2005.)

Japan is still the responsibility of the oldest son and his wife. This obligation is known as "the norm of filial piety." Especially in India, the oldest son and his wife will typically reside in the father's home, which is known as patrilocal residence (Liebig and Rajan, 2003: 121). Sweden does not deny the importance of family, but the gerontological goal in Sweden is to keep older people actively involved in the community and not sequestered with their families. As the Swedish group Senior Citizen 2005 puts it, the goal for Sweden is to enable the elderly "to play an active, influential part in working, political and cultural life, the social economy, and their everyday lives" (*Senior Citizen Sweden*, 2005: 3).

To achieve this goal, Sweden implemented a policy of care at home in 1998 whereby older people are entitled "to help of high quality" (Hellner, 2005: 7; Ministry of Health and Social Affairs, 2005: 1). Ever since that time, the Swedish government and its citizens have been committed to helping people to age in place and not move into nursing homes or ALFs. This home care

Figure 6.2. A single-family Swedish home. Only 3 percent of elderly people in Sweden live with their children.

requires home-health aides who will come to elderly residents' homes and help out when residents are too frail or sick to care for themselves. Indeed, Sweden's at-home care is now equated with contributing to the common good (Larsson, 2005:127) and has become the residential norm.

DESIGNING SENIOR-FRIENDLY ENVIRONMENTS

Home care requires structural changes in the home. For example, Helsing-borghem, a Swedish adult community, created a more senior-friendly environment by creating ramps and walking paths while removing as many stairs as possible. There are also special houses in Helsingborghem for people in wheelchairs. The community boasts easy access to the laundry room, the garbage area, and parking. All apartments in Helsingborghem have fire alarms, entrance-door peepholes, and emergency alarms—amenities that give older people peace of mind. In addition, shortly before the housing complex opened, it was tested by a group of elderly people in walkers who strolled the grounds looking for nooks and crannies where older people might trip, get disoriented, or feel trapped, and such spaces were then modified.

In Sweden today, 93 percent of elderly people live by themselves or with their spouses. Almost 10 percent of them receive some form of at-home care. Such assistance is very inexpensive—and sometimes free of charge. It is provided by the municipalities where older people live. The AARP, a leading advocacy group for older people in the United States, is so impressed with these policies that it is "looking toward Sweden for its best practices, such as its progressive approaches to long-term care" (Manteghi, 2005: 5). The progressive policies of Sweden today may well be the progressive policies of the United States tomorrow. Of special interest to the AARP is the Swedish attitude that older people should age independently and in their own homes or neighborhoods, as long as possible.

Ever since 1998, Sweden has taken other measures to encourage older people to age in place. The most significant of these is the fact that the Swedish government has actually cut back on the construction of geriatric wards and nursing homes. Between 2000 and 2003, 7,400 beds in special housing and institutional care were eliminated. During the same period of time, an additional 7,200 jobs for home-health workers were created (Johansson, 2005: 4). This calls attention to the fact that Sweden has been rethinking how older people will be housed.

HOME DESIGN FOR AN AGING POPULATION

The Swedes refer to senior housing as *aldreboende*, which is a general or generic term for a variety of design traditions. There are actually three design categories within *aldreboende*:

1. *Kvarboende*, the design and retrofitting of the ancestral home so that an older person can remain there and be cared for by family members
2. *Eget boende*, the design of housing and communities where older people can live independently, either on their own or in communal or collective housing
3. *Sarskilt boende*, or the design of housing for special-needs populations

KVARBOENDE *(THE ANCESTRAL HOME)*

Sweden is committed to retrofit people's homes so that they can continue living there as long as possible. Structurally, the idea of retrofitting the home goes back centuries. A series of developments known as the Adel Reform shifted the focus of senior care from institutions to home during the 1990s (Johansson, 2005: 2). But long before those reforms, there was a rural tradition of home

Figure 6.3. Often three-generations' worth of Swedish families lived in farmhouses.

care for seniors. For centuries, Swedish farmhouses had been modified to make room for children and aging family members (Figure 6.3). Apart from building multi-bedroom homes, there has also been the tradition of building a smaller house situated near the main house. This is similar to mother-daughter arrangements in many U.S. suburbs (Hayden, 2003: 203), and to the *grosdaddy* house in traditional Amish communities. The *grosdaddy* house would be built near the main house on an Amish farmstead and was the place where grandparents would live (Kephart, 1997: 119). The same tradition has also persisted on some farmsteads in Sweden's remote rural *läns*. The custom was to add on wings to the house as needed. The resulting configuration, or *läntgard*, would be a U-shaped compound similar to *Gamlebyen*, a farmhouse with parallel wings extending from the central housing unit.

Though there are variations in form, all three of these arrangements permit older people and their families to live together. *Kvarboende* is the oldest form of senior housing in Sweden. It is centered around the ideas of retrofitting and universal design. Swedish architects and interior designers are committed to

TABLE 6.2. GLOSSARY OF SENIOR HOUSING OPTIONS

Eldrebolig	Elderly condo
Omsorgsbolig	Care sanctuary
Eldreleillighet	Apartments for the elderly
Aldersbolig	Lodging for aging people
Sykehjem	Nursing home
Gamlehjem	Home for the aged
Alders-og sykehjem	Nursing home for aging people
Rehabiliteringssenter	Rehabilitation center
Eldres hus	The elderly [people's] house
Eldrescenter	Elderly center
Pleie-og Omsorgshjem	Care and service center
Boligstiftelse	Shared housing/collective

making older homes safer and more senior-friendly. The goal is to create "an environment that promotes health" (Dilani and Morelli, 2005: 17) if and when an older person wants to live with adult offspring.

EGET BOENDE *(INDEPENDENT HOUSING FOR OLDER PEOPLE)*

Government policy and the rapid aging of Sweden's population have made options other than *kvarboende* far more popular. Sweden has put most of its social and financial resources into developing independent housing for older people, and this form of senior housing known as *eget boende* has become the most popular and—indeed—the preferred form of senior housing in Sweden today.

Sweden has a history of collective housing—for office, factory (Lindvall and Plunger, 1992: 87), and iron workers (Caldenby, Lindvall and Wang, 1998: 172).

A Tradition of Senior Housing

The design of homes, villages, and barracks for elderly Swedish people dates back to the late nineteenth century. Apart from being an example of collective housing, senior-home design in Sweden resulted from other, more practical concerns. For instance, the development of senior housing in Sweden coincided with emigration from Sweden to the United States. Nearly a quarter of Sweden's population migrated to North America in the late-nineteenth and early-twentieth centuries (Sodersten, 2005: 1). Typically, Swedish immigrants to the United States were younger people, creating an acute shortage of caregivers in Sweden. The variety of home design that developed in Sweden (during the late-nineteenth and early-twentieth centuries) was a way of responding to this caregiver shortage.

Fristad, for example, which was built in the nineteenth century, was a home for elderly people, "a period specimen of palatial institutional Baroque design" (Andersson and Bedoire, 1994: 290). *Fristad* had dormitories for elderly men and women, who slept separately but took meals together in the commons area. There was also senior housing for men or women only. Borgarhemmett, built between the years of 1905 to 1907, was a home for elderly Swedish men, and Handelskarens Heimgard (built 1939) consisted of 50 single-room flats for retired saleswomen.

By the twentieth century, the Swedes had moved beyond institutional hotels or barracks and began creating communities for older people. Socially, this is well within the Swedish tradition of creating housing collectives or communities (Caldenby, Lindvall, and Wang, 1998: 125–26).

New Housing Based on Traditional Forms

Architecturally, the creation of senior housing in Sweden meant turning to traditional Swedish forms—the rural village and the urban courtyard—and creating new forms of senior housing based on these archetypes. *Stora Skondal*, built in 1905, was perhaps the first senior community with a variety of housing options. These ranged from apartment flats to detached houses and even hostels with communal dining. The housing in *Stora Skondal* varied in size and appearance and was built in small clusters—a radical departure from the more familiar barracks or hotel—because the goal was to create a sense of community. In fact, creating gerontological communities has been more important than the design of any single home in many Swedish housing projects (Caldenby, Lindvall, and Wang, 1998: 97–99). Another experimental community known as Alderdomshem (built in 1924) billed itself as a small town for elderly people. The ground plan includes winding streets and clustered homes, which give it the feel of a self-contained village. Pensionarshem, built from 1950 to 1952, is a collection of 20 houses, each containing three flats. All 20 of these houses are built to feel like traditional Swedish village homes. They have roofs with gables and appear to be separate homes instead of apartment flats. Architecturally, these communities reject institutional solutions in favor of design that echoes the traditional home. The Swedes refer to this look as *hemlikeht*, or homelikeness—and it has become an important goal in home design for Sweden's aging population.

In recent times, the concept of the town or village for elderly people has given way to the concept of a town or village for all adults. Russinet, mentioned earlier, is an excellent example of *eget boende* where adults aged 40 and over live in 27 apartment flats overlooking a central courtyard. Architecturally, Alderdomshem and Russinet create a sense of community by grouping homes or apartment flats in picturesque clusters and by locating them around a central courtyard.

DISABILITY-COMPATIBLE HOUSING

Swedish researchers have identified two factors that help older people live independently for much longer. The first of these relates to the design of the home. Older people can live on their own for much longer when their homes are disability-compatible. The second is the connection to a thriving community. Bellevue Park provides both.

BELLEVUE PARK: INDEPENDENCE AND SOCIAL CONNECTION

Bellevue Park, built in 1998, is typical of Swedish housing that is now being designed to enhance independent living through design and social connection (Figure 6.4). It consists of 128 flats for old-age pensioners in the Swedish city of Malmo, and residents have their own apartments and live independently. The

Figure 6.4. Bellevue Park is an example of successful housing for people of all ages.

apartments have wider entrances, which accommodate wheelchairs and skid-proof flooring. There is also a commons area for the social activities that are so important in communities for old-age pensioners: indoor gardening, crafts, discussion groups, and—increasingly—computer clubs. In the tradition of *eget boende*, each of the 128 kitchens has a special view. Each one looks out onto the common stairway so that people on the stairs can look into the kitchen and vice versa. The architects of this housing complex, Boje Lundgaard and Lene Tranberg, point with pride to this architectural detail. These windows provide elderly tenants with opportunities for contact with their neighbors. It is possible to look into the kitchen from the stairwell and possible to look out onto the world from the kitchen. In other words, the kitchen window gives older people an additional measure of connection and security (*Arkitektur*, 6, 1992: 71). A new generation of Swedish housing now adds technological supports to the architectural one.

VALLGOSSEN HOUSE: BUILDING ON INFORMATION TECHNOLOGY

Vallgossen is among the first apartment buildings to use information technology to promote the tradition of *eget boende* (Figure 6.5). Most recently, one of Sweden's major insurance companies—Svenska Enskilda Banken Trygg Liv—moved into the field of senior living, promising to use IT and architectural design to create "modern and high-quality housing units . . . for the elderly" (*Svenska Enskikilda Banken Trygg Liv*, 2005: 92).

Independent living is now being enhanced even more by IT and architectural design. In 1999, the Swedish research and development bureau known as JM AB built two prototypes—an apartment building known as Vallgossen House (completed in 2003) and a cluster of six smart homes that were constructed in a Stockholm suburb known as Hagaberg. Vallgossen House has the technology necessary to help people "stay longer in their homes as they grow older" (Sandstrom, 2003: 7). The apartment building consists of 126 flats ranging from studios to apartments with terraces and even a few penthouses. In addition to these residential units, Vallgossen House also has spaces for social activities, including a sauna, party room, laundry room, and guest room. More important, it gives older people three different residential options, each with its own IT package. Residents have the right and opportunity to use all of these amenities.

In addition to these common areas, residents of Vallgossen have access to three different IT packages that make apartment living more comfortable and empower residents by giving them direct control over their apartments and by enabling them to remain in the building even after their health begins to deteriorate.

Figure 6.5. Vallgossen House offers three different IT packages that provide residents with the technology they need to age in place.

THREE LEVELS OF TECHNOLOGY

Type 1 IT Package

Each of the 126 apartment flats has basic, or Type 1 IT, functions. At the heart of this IT package is the home network, controlled by a laptop in every apartment. The home network can perform the following five functions:

1. Measuring daily use of water, electricity, and gas and providing comparative data on daily energy usage for the building at large
2. Linking fire, leakage, and burglar alarm systems to Vallgossen's security desk
3. Coordinating daily and weekly activities in the apartment and community
4. E-mail and e-notes, which facilitate communication among members of the household and within the building
5. Reserving time in Vallgossen's sauna, party room, laundry room, and guest room

In addition to these electronic capabilities, every apartment also has an electronic key that provides personal access to the lobby, laundry room, and underground garage. An integrated system for computers and telephones gives residents the flexibility to (re)locate their telephones and computers in any room of their apartments.

Type 2 IT Packages

Vallgossen House contains special apartments equipped with Type 2 IT packages. These technologically enhanced packages are found in apartments that have been designed to help older people live independently. Type 2 IT packages add three features that are especially helpful to older people:

1. An intercom that connects the living room, kitchen, and bathrooms and allows members of the household to communicate without walking from room to room
2. A security camera at the front door of the apartment so that the resident can identify who is at the door without opening it
3. Reception boxes near the front door that enable sick or frail people to receive deliveries at home without getting out of bed or even opening the front door. A reception box outside the door to the apartment is a secure place to leave deliveries (Figure 6.6). Every vendor making

Figure 6.6. This is a reception box where deliveries can be left without disturbing the resident(s).

deliveries to Vallgossen House gets a temporary key code. The delivery is made, the temporary key is surrendered at the security desk, and the vendor leaves. Only the resident who placed the order has the key necessary to open the delivery box (Sandstrom, 2003: 9–11).

Type 3 IT Packages

Vallgossen House also has two flats with Type 3 IT packages that have been developed with input from a nearby hospital. These two flats will be prototypes for assisted living in Vallgossen House. Features in the Type 3 IT package include:

1. A bathroom light that automatically lights up when somebody enters.
2. Remote controls in the bedroom that lock and unlock the front door and switch lights on and off in the rest of the apartment.
3. A good-night function that turns off all the power to the stove, iron, and small kitchen appliances from the bedroom.
4. The Photo Messenger, a telephone combined with photographs of significant others in the resident's life. Photo Messengers allow cognitively impaired people to make phone calls without having to remember or dial telephone numbers. The Photo Messenger is a particularly useful technology for people suffering from Alzheimer's disease because it enables them to continue doing something familiar (i.e., talking on the telephone) even though they may have forgotten relevant phone numbers or other details about the person they are phoning. Phone calls to significant others in the family are made by touching their photos. When making a phone call to a particular person, his or her photo lights up. If that person makes an incoming phone call to the apartment, his or her photo blinks on and off.

Vallgossen House will also use IT to link residents to their health-care providers, which is known as telemedicine (Sandstrom, 2003: 13). Telemedicine allows people in assisted living to remain in touch with their health-care providers without leaving their apartments. A package involving a telephone, webcam, and laptop computer allows for regular contact with doctors in other parts of the city. Apart from the medical applications, Vallgossen House is also developing financial and economic IT packages to help aging residents.

The success of independent living is based, in part, on the availability of home-health workers who provide elderly residents with help and social services. In 2003, home-health workers made home visits to more than 128,000 elderly people across Sweden. An estimated 20 percent of the elderly received intensive home-health care averaging 50+ hours per month (Socialstyrelsen,

2005: 3). In addition to these municipal home-health workers, there is a growing number of for-profit providers and producers of care, including private companies, cooperative associations, and even some of Sweden's largest insurance companies. The result is a wider and more diverse home-care system. In addition to working in apartment buildings, home-health workers also visit older people living independently in detached and semidetached houses. However, in one of Stockholm's suburbs, there is now a cluster of smart houses that may change how home-care workers visit aging homeowners—and why.

SMART HOUSES

In addition to apartment flats, the Swedish research-and-development program also constructed a cluster of six smart homes, which would promote *eget boende*, or independent aging, on a wider scale by bringing it to homeowners as well as apartment dwellers (Figure 6.7). This cluster of six smart houses was built in a suburb of Stockholm. Each of the houses has been angled to capture a maximum of solar radiation, and the houses are heavily insulated to reduce energy use. Every house features a small greenhouse near the kitchen and an upstairs "spa" that includes a whirlpool, sauna, and sink with double basins. Apart from modernistic architecture and design, each of the houses has IT designs to enhance quality of life and encourage aging in place. The technology includes the following features:

1. There is a central control panel that monitors the use of water, electricity, and gas. There are home and away programs to monitor

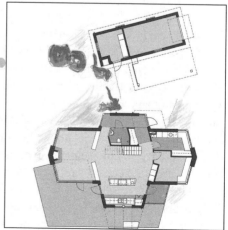

Figure 6.7. An example of an IT-designed smart house.

these commodities. The home program allows for control from inside when the house is occupied, while the away system allows for the remote control of gas, water, and electricity.

2. Every house has a weather station atop the garage. In addition to providing the household with updates on the weather, this weather station has sensors (sun sensors and wind sensors) that automatically control the house's sunblind (Sandstrom, 2003: 13).

3. Lighting in the hallway automatically goes on when people come home, and a good-night switch in the master bedroom shuts off lights throughout the house when people go to bed.

4. The house is heated with geothermal energy, and all rooms have under-floor heating.

5. The house is wired for intercoms in every room and outlets that accommodate telephones, computers, and televisions. This gives residents the opportunity to move their computers, telephones, and televisions around the house when necessary.

6. The house also has a central vacuum-cleaning system with the receptacle placed in the garage.

Smart houses will soon be another option for older people in Sweden.

MORE THAN A NURSING HOME: THE SWEDISH *SERVICEHUS*

Soren Nordin, a resident at the Gillbogarden nursing home, has let all of his newspaper subscriptions lapse. Newspapers have become quite unimportant to Mr. Nordin because, as he puts it, "I now read them online" (*Sollentuna Journal*, 2006: 1). Like many of the residents at Gillbogarden, he remains connected to family and friends through e-mail and the Internet. And when he needs to sharpen his Internet skills, he can refer to "Surftips-Seniorer" or "Tips on Surfing the Internet for Seniors" (Surftips, blogspot 2006: 1). Soren Nordin also enjoys a remarkable amount of privacy, choice, and independence because he is living in a Swedish-style *servicehus* and not a standard, medical-model nursing home (Hagfors, 2006: 4).

Gillbogarden is a Swedish-style *servicehus* dedicated to treating elders exactly as they would want to be treated and maintaining a familiar and homelike environment. The *servicehus* concept dates back 20 years, to a time when Sweden developed alternatives to the nursing home. The *servicehus* replaces hospital routine with social spontaneity and responds to the particular needs of the residents who live there (Figure 6.8).

Figure 6.8. Residents in a *servicehus* receive care but are encouraged to maintain their freedom and individuality.

THE SERVICEHUS*: MORE HOMELIKE THAN A NURSING HOME*

Instead of private or semiprivate bedrooms, the *servicehus* provides every resident with a studio apartment, which allows for privacy but requires very little upkeep. In addition to private apartments, there are common areas where residents can mingle. This includes the dining room, sitting room, and laundry room that are shared by all residents. Conspicuously absent are the familiar landmarks of the nursing home: the nurses' stations, semiprivate rooms, and the long institutional corridors that typically connect them.

The idea behind the *servicehus* is that every resident should be empowered to live independently—and not be regimented into the routines of a hospital or nursing home. Residents typically move to a *servicehus* when they can no longer live independently in their own homes, but they do not give up their independence as a result of moving into the *servicehus*. The living space is merely scaled down from an apartment or detached home to a studio flat, and it is intentionally homelike.

A visitor from Japan was impressed by the homelike feeling of the *servicehus*. Instead of living in institutional rooms, as they might in Japan, the residents of the Swedish-style *servicehus* lived in "private rooms . . . furnished with the residents' personal furniture" (Yasujiro, 2005: 2). This Japanese visitor was especially taken by the fact that every room had its own kitchen and that many of these kitchens had levers that "raised and lowered the sinks and cupboards." Most important, this visitor appreciated that there was a gerontological reason for the design of this kitchen: The kitchen was not coincidental. It was there to encourage independence. (Isayama, 2005: 3).

Residents in a Swedish-style *servicehus* continue to have control over decisions of their daily lives: when they will eat, sleep, do laundry, and clean house. And even though there is a common dining room in the *servicehus*, residents are free to cook meals in their own apartments—and most of them do so. On any given day, residents in a *servicehus* will prepare breakfast and dinner in their own apartments—typically with help from staff or family members. And they enjoy lunch together in the common dining room. But true to *servicehus* philosophy, the food is served as a buffet, or smorgasbord. It would be too regimented if residents sat at tables and waited to be served dinner or breakfast on a tray.

Unlike the hospital or nursing home, Sweden's *servicehus* encourages residents to dress, eat, and behave independently. In so doing, the service facilitates the process of aging in place. This requires continual staff training because the first impulse of many nurses or home-health aides is to pitch in and help.

DESIGNED FOR DEMENTIA

Sweden is also pioneering the design of living space for people with Alzheimer's and other cognitive disabilities. There are currently about 22,000 beds in group-housing environments for people with dementia.[2] But the greater effort is to enable people with dementia to live independently as long as they can. For this reason, the Swedish government recently developed three test homes that would allow people with Alzheimer's or other dementia to "stay longer at home while maintaining their independence" (Lundberg, et al., 2005: 1).[3] The project is called "At Home with IT" and relies on a variety of information technologies to make home safer and more manageable for people with cognitive impairments.

The three test homes employ information technologies to reduce mishaps and confusion in the home. For example, there is a go-away lock that turns off electricity connected to appliances, such as the toaster, stove, iron, and so on. As a result of using go-away locks, there is less of a chance that the stove, iron, or toaster will be accidentally left on. Every test home also has an intelligent key that knows if a door should be locked or not. As a result of these technologies, people with Alzheimer's are able to remain at home, living independently for much longer (Lundberg, et al, 2005: 3).

THE FUTURE

The future of home design in Sweden will be shaped, first and foremost, by the aging of Sweden's Boomers, or *Fyrtiotalister*. The *Fyrtiotalister* will come to senior housing with distinctive needs and wants. They will be more technologically sophisticated than today's elderly Swedish people. And the *Fyrtiotalister's* passion for technology will impact how and where they live.

SWEDEN'S BOOMERS WILL WANT MORE TECHNOLOGY

Some of Sweden's futurists predict that senior housing will be segmented along technological lines, with the very old living in low-tech housing while *Fyrtiotalister* move into high-tech housing (Browall, et al., 2002: 13). A report called *IT Sweden 2002* predicts that many of Sweden's Boomers will be urban nomads who want to control their homes even when they are far away from them. This will translate into more homes with remotely controlled kitchens, housekeeping activity, and entertainment centers.

MORE GATED COMMUNITIES

Gated communities are rare in Sweden today but surveys also find that the gated-community concept appeals to Sweden's *Fyrtiotalister* and may become more common in the near future.

HOME-HEALTH CARE IN SWEDEN

In addition to the aging of the *Fyrtiotalister*, home design in Sweden will also be shaped by the policy of home care for elderly people (Figure 6.9). Homes will be made more compatible with the needs of people who are either barely ambulatory or confined to bed. There will be more variations on information technologies that allow bedridden people to open or close doors, turn lights on or off, and accept deliveries. Unlike Japan (see Chapter 4, "Japan: The Future Is Robotic")—where robotic helpers are becoming a familiar part of senior care—the Swedish approach (relies on home-health workers). The problem, according to *Socialstyrelsen*, Sweden's bureau of social statistics, is that there is already a shortage of home-health workers, and it promises to get even worse in years to come (Socialstyrelsen, 2005: 11).

Figure 6.9. Home-health care has become a for-profit business in Sweden as the number of very old people continues to skyrocket.

NATURALLY OCCURRING RETIREMENT COMMUNITIES

The future of home design for older people who are living independently will include housing that is more accessible to home-health workers. Given the fact that entire apartment buildings are beginning to age in place, there might need to be new forms of security because home-health aides will be going from flat to neighboring flat as they care for the elderly people living on the same floor (Sandstrom, 2003: 15). This is already happening in many cities in the United States, and Sweden will need to turn to the United States for pointers on how to retrofit these buildings for increasingly frail populations.

The Swedish insurance giant SEB Trygg Liv has already entered the senior-living market. More of Sweden's corporate giants will soon follow. The result will be not only a greater variety in senior housing but also a widening gap between the more modest housing constructed with public money and the more upscale and technologically advanced housing that will come from corporate developers.

MORE RACIALLY AND ETHNICALLY DIVERSE POPULATION OF SENIORS

Sweden is being reshaped by the arrival of ethnic minorities. Once a very homogeneous society, Sweden has become "a multiethnic, multicultural, and

Figure 6.10. As Sweden's population becomes more diverse, there will need to be even more senior-housing options.

racially divided country" (Caldwell, 5 February 2006: 56; Aldrecentrum, 2005: 11).

Public housing will soon be pressed to enable members of these multiracial and ethnic groups to age in place; this may require new forms of design to accommodate their spatial and social norms (Figure 6.10).

NOW THAT YOU'VE READ CHAPTER 6

KEY TERMS AND CONCEPTS (Sw=SWEDISH)

acceptera (Sw: Influential pamphlet about architecture, published in 1930)
Aldreboende (Sw: Senior housing)
eget boende (Sw: Independent living)
Fyrtiotalister (Sweden's Boomers)
hemlikhet (Sw: Feeling like home)
kvarboende (Sw: Staying in the ancestral home)
servicehus (Sw: Nursing home)

QUESTIONS FOR STUDY AND DISCUSSION

1. Only 3 percent of elderly people in Sweden live with their children. Why is this, and how does it affect the design of homes and apartments in Sweden?
2. Sweden is now exploring new information technologies that will make it easier for older people to age in place. What are some of these technologies, and why will they be more important than ever in a country like Sweden?
3. If and when older people need nursing care, they often end up in *servicehus*. How are *servicehus* different from North American nursing homes?
4. Sweden has had great success in designing adult communities for people aged 40 or older. How can a residential community benefit from having people who are younger adults (and also older adults)? Would this experiment work in your city or town?
5. In what ways is home design for the elderly in Sweden different from home design for the elderly in Japan?

HELPFUL WEBSITES

aldrecentrum.se/eng.html (Stockholm Gerontology Center)
arkitekt.se/lankar (Swedish architects' website)
spfpension.fi/ [Svenska Pensionarsforbundet (Helsingfors)]
Stockholm.se/templates/template (Knuten, a meeting place for seniors)
sweden.gov.se (Housing policy)

NOTES

1. Special thanks to Greger Sandstrom and his paper, "Future Houses in Sweden," published by the Royal Institute of Technology, The Architectural School, Stockholm, Sweden. Sandstrom's information on plans for future apartment buildings and smart houses is gratefully acknowledged.
2. We want to thank Professor Stig Berg, at Jonkoping University's Institute of Gerontology, for data on numbers of people with Alzheimer's and other dementias who live in "special" or group housing.
3. The project was initiated by the Swedish Ministry of Social Affairs, directed by the Swedish Handicap Institute, and evaluated by the Royal Institute of Technology.

"Behind each mountain is still another mountain."
—Brazilian adage, *The Brazilians*

7

Brazil
*Senior Housing in the Land
of Youth and Beauty*

OVERVIEW

Brazil is one of the world's most rapidly aging nations. It has traditionally been a youth-obsessed culture, but there is now greater appreciation of aging and of the various lifestyles that older people can have. Brazilians are also experiencing changes in family life as more women enter the workforce. These factors together—the age wave, the shifts in public opinion, and changes in family life—have impacted senior housing in Brazil.

The norm in Brazil was that older people would live with or near their families. Their only other option was to live in a nursing home, or *clinica geriatrica*. However, ever since the 1990s, the range of housing possibilities has increased. Assisted living (the *casa de repouso*) has become increasingly common and more acceptable. In fact, there are now four times as many ALFs as nursing homes in Brazil. In recent years, a new and expensive form of senior housing has also become quite popular—at least with Brazil's elite families. This is the *residencial*, or senior residence, which often resembles a high-rise hotel and offers similar amenities.

Only a small percentage of Brazil's elderly live in specialized senior housing. The majority of older Brazilians either live with family members or are aging in place in their homes or apartments. As a result, Brazil's Accessible Institute (BAI) is raising awareness about universal design in hopes that more older people in Brazil will make their homes barrier-free and adaptable. To achieve this goal, BAI has built a prototype, the Universal Home, which is already influencing home design in Brazil.

The future of senior housing in Brazil will be shaped by the aging of Brazil's Boomers. The baby-boom generation will bring its own needs and lifestyles (more singles, smaller families, better health, and so on) to the housing market. The future will also see more specialty *residencials*, such as *Solardomarque* in São Paulo, which caters to wealthy older travelers. Other specialized *residencials* will develop to meet the needs of older people and their increasingly diverse lifestyles.

ATTITUDES TOWARD AGING IN BRAZIL ·

There is an old Brazilian adage that may as well have been written about senior housing in Brazil today: "Behind every mountain is still another mountain." Older people in Brazil should be able to live anywhere and everywhere they want; discrimination on the basis of age is illegal in Brazil. But there is "still another mountain" to scale—a mountain that has slowed the development of senior housing in this South American nation. This mountain is attitudes toward aging within Brazilian culture (Medeiros, 2004: 2).

It may be illegal in Brazil to discriminate on the basis of age, but there are powerful social norms dictating where and how elderly people should live. First, there is the norm that older people should not expect better housing and they should not speak up for their rights to safe and navigable living space. Survey research by BAI found that older people still show "overt, but misplaced, satisfaction in relation to their homes" (Perito et al., 2006: 1). Older people often assume that they must accept substandard housing because there are no alternatives in Brazil, and so they often resign themselves to living in unsafe or unsuitable environments.

Until the 1990s, there was no senior housing to speak of in Brazil and only two socially acceptable housing options for seniors. They could live with or near their children, or they could live in *asilos para idosos* (a pejorative term for "nursing homes"). Conditions have changed during the past 15 years, but there are still not enough options for older people who want to live on their own. *Residencials*, which are senior residences for older people who are independent and in good health, are only now becoming widely available.

In addition to this new housing option, there has been a shift in public opinion about aging. As Brazil's influential Boomers grow older, the Brazilian society is becoming more receptive to old age. This is a major change for a society that has been so obsessed with youth and beauty (Page, 1995: 440), and it has implications for the future of senior housing in this South American nation.

Brazilian culture has become more receptive to the idea that older people can live independent lives (Garcez-Leme, Luiz, and Espino, 2005: 2020). As a result, it is now more socially acceptable for older people to age in place or relocate to Brazil's new *residencials* and savor an independence that was unheard of even 20 years ago.

THE RESIDENCIAL

The *residencial* has become a new option for older people in Brazil, and it is now becoming competitive with aging in place at one's own home or apartment. Older people who are more affluent can now work with companies that will retrofit and renovate homes, making it safer and easier to age in place (Medeiros, 2004:1). The affluent can also hire home-health workers through agencies such as the São Paulo-based GeroCare Corporation (www.GeroCare. com.br). Older people who are financially needy can qualify for home-health aides and meals-on-wheels through government programs (Mazenotti, 2005: 1). The result is that senior housing has gone from being an unpopular last resort to a modern lifestyle. Brazilians of all social classes are now beginning to have housing options.

HOUSING OPTIONS FOR SENIORS

Senior housing in Brazil is even beginning to create niches in response to specific senior lifestyles. Residencial Solardomarques in São Paulo is a good example of a new housing niche. In addition to being a *residencial* with full-time residents, Solardomarques also welcomes older travelers and provides services and amenities that are geared toward travelers aged 60 or older—such as lists of tours, guides, and information on accessibility and (Solardomarques@Solardo-marques.com.br, 2006). This calls attention to how much senior housing has begun to change in this largest of all South American nations.

Until the 1990s, "senior housing" only meant geriatric care in a hospital or nursing home. At the present time, there are approximately 212 *clinicas geriatrica* and 663 *casas de repouso* in Brazil (www.GuiaMais.com.br, 2006; www. ListasOESP.com.br, 2006). Most of these are located in Brazil's largest cities. The hinterland has very little in the way of senior housing. According to industry insiders, there are three housing options for older Brazilians who want to relocate to specialized senior housing.

The first, and most familiar, is the nursing home, or *clinica geriatrica*. *Clinicas geriatrica* provide geriatric nursing care in hospital-like settings.

Next, there are *casas de repouso*, which are analogous to ALFs. These are settings where people can live independently, but they require help dressing or bathing and receive reminders to take medication or make appointments for physical therapy. In Brazil, there are 663 of these residences.

Newer and more architecturally significant are the *residencials*. Ever since the 1990s, these have become more popular in Brazil's larger cities. They are often well-designed apartment buildings that are more reminiscent of Miami's South Beach than Brazilian *clinicas geriatrica*. As of now, there are no Brazilian statistics on the number of *residencials*, though they are by far the most significant new option. This is because *residencials* are a new form of senior housing that appeals most to Brazil's wealthy retirees.

The meaning of "home" is often shaped by upper-class attitudes that then travel down the social ladder (Rybczynski, 1986: 1–12). This is most certainly true of senior housing in Brazil, which is being shaped by the attitudes and actions of Brazilian elites. Most of Brazil's new senior housing is expensive and attracts older people who tend to be white, wealthy, and female (de Vos and Andrade, 2005: 569–81). They, in turn, move to *residencials*, such as Santa Catarina in São Paulo (Figure 7.1).

The trickle-down of this concept has already begun. Some lower-income neighborhoods of Rio de Janeiro are now developing their own versions of the *residencial* and the senior center (Fallender, 2006: 3). Brazil's lower-income populations do not have easy access to the same media where more affluent people look for information about senior housing (i.e., television and the Internet) and so the marketing mix for senior housing in lower-income areas is different. In addition to advertisements in local newspapers, there is also guerrilla marketing. People walking down the street in one of the *favelas* that dot Rio de Janeiro or São Paulo are likely to see advertising for senior housing pasted to lamp-posts, walls, and doorways.

São Paulo's Permanent Commission on Accessibility (CPA) has gone a step further than guerilla marketing on lampposts and doorways. CPA now actively reaches out to older people and solicits their input for the design of new senior housing in lower-income neighborhoods (Passafaro and Williams, 2006: 1). As a result, the perceptions and needs of lower-income seniors will actually begin to trickle *up* and impact the design of senior housing in the *favelas* of São Paulo.

A RAPIDLY AGING BRAZIL

Brazil's age wave is responsible for the coming of the *residencial* and the proliferation of *casas de repouso* today. Brazil's age wave began in the late 1990s—at the same time that there was a decrease in fertility (Pravda, 2006: 1)—and it continues to shape Brazilian culture. Today's senior housing is a response to the growing numbers of older people in Brazil—people with a variety of needs and lifestyles. And it will not be long before more of Brazil's Boomers begin making their own demands on the senior housing industry (Sharovsky and Frank, 2006: 1).

Brazil has the fifth-largest population in the world and, although it is a developing nation, it will have the world's seventh-largest elderly population by 2020 (United Nations, 2001: 2). This means that Brazil has one of the fastest-growing elderly populations anywhere. For the first time ever, the oldest segment

Figure 7.1. *Residencials*, such as Santa Catarina, are an attractive new option for older people in Brazil.

of Brazil's population is growing more rapidly than the youthful segment (ages 1 to 12).

Brazil's elderly population will increase by 3.25 percent per year over the next 50 years, compared with an overall Brazilian population growth of less than 1 percent annually (Andrade and De Vos, 2002: 2). Today, 8 percent of all Brazilians are aged 65 or older. It will not be long before Brazil has the same percentage of elderly people as China and Japan. The *gerontological* impact is also worth considering because it ultimately impacts the architecture and design of housing for older people. Despite the Brazilian passion and quest for youth (Page, 1995: 441), Brazil is on its way to becoming a *gerontocracy*.

NEW ATTITUDES TOWARD AGING IN BRAZIL

There is a new, more upbeat attitude toward aging in Brazil. For example, Brazilian newspapers and magazines are now encouraging reporters to use the word *idoso* (Portuguese for "experienced" and "wise") instead of *velho* (Portuguese for "old person") (McLaughlin, 2006: 1). This linguistic change reflects the fact that Brazilians now have more positive attitudes about growing older. Old age in Brazil is being redefined as a time in life to be independent. In fact, Brazil has recently been called a "geroculture" (Garcez-Leme, Luiz, and Espino, 2005: 2022). This is paradoxical because Brazil is the plastic-surgery capital of the world, a place where youthful beauty is god (Page, 1995: 440; Hopgood, 2003: 2). Nevertheless, older people in cities like Rio de Janeiro, Curitiba, and São Paulo are beginning to enjoy a higher social status, more power, and more influence in the local community than the elderly who came before them. The growing popularity of *residencials* is a reflection of this gerontological shift.

THE SIGNIFICANCE OF *RESIDENCIALS*

Recent surveys of Brazil's older population (Perito et al., 2005: 1) indicate that those who can afford to live independently are now considering this option. Eighty percent of elderly people surveyed by BAI in 2004 said that they wanted to live independently if they could (A House for a Lifetime, 2005: 2). They no longer automatically live with a child or invite a child to live with them. In fact, fewer daughters are available to be caregivers to an aging parent or in-law.

Women have been entering Brazil's labor market in record numbers and are less available as caregivers.[1] This has contributed to the development of *residencials* and other living arrangements that do not place any demands on working daughters or daughters-in-law (Figure 7.2). There are parallels to what hap-

Figure 7.2. The popularity of *residencials* reflects the growing acceptability of independence in old age.

pened residentially in Japan (see Chapter 4, "Japan: The Future Is Robotic"). Senior housing markets in Japan developed, in part, because married women had entered Japanese labor markets in record numbers and were not available to be caregivers.

There has always been a history of nursing homes (*clinicas geriatrica*) in Brazil; they have served the population of frail and impaired elderly people. But in recent years, a number of new, architecturally interesting senior residences (*residencials*) have also been built.

These modern, high-rise *residencials* look more like apartments than ALFs. Most of them are in Rio de Janeiro, Curitiba, and São Paulo, Brazil's largest cities. That this is a gerontological facelift can be appreciated by looking back to the traditional and time-honored norms of senior housing in Brazil. It was not too long ago that an older person would move into the *barraca* of a son or daughter or invite one or more of the children to move in with him or her.

AGING IN THE *CASA*

An older woman traditionally lived with one or more of her children in her *casa*—her own household. This form of caregiving was possible because

Brazilian families are typically large and close-knit. There would usually be daughters available to help (Andrade and De Vos, 2002: 21). The alternative was to live near one's children or move into a *dormitoria* (bedroom) in a child's home.

All children in the traditional Brazilian family, or *parentela*, were supposed to bear equal responsibility for caregiving. This is different from the norm of filial piety in China, India, or Japan.[2] In all three of those societies, it is expected that children will take care of their aging parents. The difference is in deciding which child becomes the caregiver and why. Filial piety means that a particular child, usually the oldest son, will be responsible for the care of an aging parent. By contrast, Brazilian families display a more fluid set of responsibilities.

In Brazilian families, it is the norm that parents and children will all care for one another. "When the children were young," writes Lasky (2005: 1), "the parents would take care of all their children. When the children reached adulthood, they were not so quick to run away." Traditionally, one or more children were available to take care of an aging parent, whether it meant taking that parent in or moving into the parent's home.

THE BARRACA, OR FARMHOUSE

In rural areas of Brazil, older people lived with family members in a *barraca* (Figure 7.3). As in India (see Chapter 9, "India: The Karma of Senior Housing"), accommodations for an elderly parent would vary according to the wealth and social standing of the family.

However, it was understood that family members were responsible for one another and that the most desirable arrangement was to live with an aging parent or in-law.[3]

VERTICALIZACAO: HIGH-RISE LIVING

Accommodations for older people began to change when Brazil began urbanizing in the 1970s. The construction of high-rise apartment buildings in Rio de Janeiro and São Paulo in the 1970s constrained sleeping arrangements and altered the reciprocities owed by one generation to another (Camargo, 2004: 6). In fact, Perito (2005: 2) refers to the *verticalizacao*, or verticalization, of the cities that reshaped family life in Brazil because it was no longer possible to add on a room or a hammock, as was possible in the *barraca*. The apartments that became available in the 1970s typically had only two bedrooms and possibly an additional, smaller bedroom for a servant.

As high-rises began to dominate São Paulo, Curitiba, and Rio de Janeiro, it became more difficult for families to house an aging parent or in-law. Shifting

Figure 7.3. Brazilian *barraca*

family arrangements began changing the clasic conception of family in Brazil (-www.country-data.com, 1997: 3). The design of Brazil's new high-rise apartment towers encouraged conjugal rather than extended families. Inside these high-rise apartment towers, family life became more individualized (de Camargo, 2004: 10) (Figure 7.4). Instead of socializing and interacting as a group, family members now retreated to bedrooms to watch television or listen to the radio.

Beginning in the 1980s, more older people began living by themselves. The percentage of older women living alone went from 9.4 percent in 1980 to 16 percent in 1990 and increased from 6 percent to 8 percent for older Brazilian men during the same period of time (Berquo, 1996: 23; Ramos, Santos, et al, 1991: 34).

During the 1980s, older people who lived on their own were living in apartments that were "not in great repair" (Perito, 2005: 1). It would not be until the 1990s—and the start of Brazil's age wave—that senior housing would develop a social and architectural presence. With help from BAI, that presence has been both attractive and accessible (*Mercado*, 2004: 2).

Figure 7.4. High-rise-apartment living has changed patterns of caregiving in Brazil.

BRAZIL'S UNIVERSAL HOME: A PROTOTYPE

The BAI was formally launched in 2004, after nine years of providing informal support to architects and interior designers in São Paulo (Medeiros, 2004: 1; Paloma, 2006: 1). The institute has developed a prototype for a universal home that already has had an impact on the design of senior housing in Brazil. In fact, there are now efforts to implement the idea of universal design in five major Brazilian cities: Porto Alegre, Curitiba, São Paulo, Rio de Janeiro, and Belo Horizonte. Architects and designers from those five cities are now meeting on a regular basis to evaluate efforts at making Brazilian housing barrier-free and adaptable (Williams, 2006: 1).

ACCESSIBLE AND ADAPTABLE HOMES

According to architect Sandra Perito (Mercado.com, 2005: 1), the goal is to design homes that are accessible and adaptable. By accessible, Perito means that homes should be designed to be barrier-free. *Adaptable* means that these homes last a lifetime—they are designed in such a way that they can meet the changing needs of residents as they grow older. The prototype of the Universal Home was built in the city of Taubate in 2004 and has influenced senior-housing design in Brazil ever since (Mercado, 2005: 1–5).

Perito observes that most people in Brazil are aging in the homes where they lived when they were younger. The problem is that the homes have been designed with the needs of younger people in mind and have become less habitable and more dangerous as the occupants age. BAI insists that "the greatest challenge [in senior-home design] is the prevention of domestic accidents, which can cause traumas and limit the independence of the resident" (Perito, 2005: 1). The great advantage of the Universal Home is that it is designed to anticipate the physical and cognitive limitations of old age. The Universal Home includes the following design elements:

- Table on the front porch: A built-in table on the front porch is nothing more than porch furniture for occupants who are young and strong. However, it is a place for an older person to put heavy packages or bundles while he or she reaches for his or her house keys (Gomes, 2004: 2).
- Senior-friendly bathroom(s): Bathrooms in the Universal Home have been designed with the needs of older people in mind. Perito had interviewed 257 people aged 60 and older and asked them to share their housing needs. According to the survey, respondents were least satisfied with their bathrooms, and so Perito put time and effort into designing accessible and adaptable bathrooms (*Harmonia*, 2004: 2). For example, there is open space under every sink. This makes no difference to occupants who are young and healthy, but such space means something very different to residents who are wheelchair-bound because it enables them to get close to the basin without bumping into pipes below the sink (Social Responsibility in Brazilian Architecture, 2006: 1). There is also a stall-shower with antiskid flooring (in tile with different color and texture). This is merely decorative for younger occupants, but it helps older people avoid slipping in the shower (*Harmonia*, 2004: 3). Lastly, grab bars near the commode and in the shower help reduce slips and falls for everybody (Figure 7.5).
- Stairs: The stairs in the Universal Home are made of dark wood, which contrasts with the lighter wooden floors and makes the stairs easier to see. This is an important design element because older people often stumble on the stairs at the very top and very bottom. The color contrast between stairs and flooring is intended to minimize such falls. There are also bands of illumination beneath and

Figure 7.5. Universal Home: The stall shower is tiled in a different color and contains grab bars for added safety.

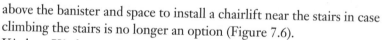

above the banister and space to install a chairlift near the stairs in case climbing the stairs is no longer an option (Figure 7.6).
- Kitchen: Kitchen appliances and cabinets are at waist level to reduce the need for stretching or bending. There are heat-resistant countertops on both sides of the stove. This permits the chef to remove a heavy pot from the stovetop or oven and quickly place it down—thus avoiding spills and burns. Kitchen counters are edged in tile of a different color so that it is easier to see where the countertop ends. The kitchen has smoke and gas detectors. The kitchen also has timers that automatically turn appliances off after a given time period. Automatic timers and smoke and gas detectors make the home adaptable for residents who are cognitively impaired or forgetful.
- Bedroom(s): Perito has designed headboards with built-in lighting and telephone/intercom connections. Bedroom closets are also illuminated, which makes it easier to locate clothing and avoid slipping or falling in the closet. Bedroom windows are easy to open and close, with latches at waist-level. Perito also replaces bedroom chairs with low banquettes that double as storage.

Figure 7.6. The staircase in the universal home is designed to minimize slips or falls. Notice that the wooden staircase is a different color than the wooden floors at the top and the foot of the stairs.

- The Garden: The Universal Home features waist-high gardens in boxes that stand three to four feet high. This allows residents to cultivate flowers and vegetables more easily—they can do so standing up, without having to kneel on the ground to do their gardening. Intercoms make it easier for somebody outdoors to communicate with people who are inside the house. Patio areas are covered in nonskid tile, and there is outdoor lighting that is automatically timed to go on at nightfall.

According to Perito, the cost of the Universal Home is only slightly higher than the cost of a conventional home (Gomes, 2004: 1), which should make it more appealing to people of all incomes. In fact, Perito insists that the Universal Home can have social impact because:

1. It is relatively inexpensive and can bring the advantages of accessibility and adaptability to people who have less money.
2. It allows people to age in place and thus helps keep communities intact. A survey by BAI finds that 80 percent of seniors surveyed in 2004 said that they want to remain where they were living and would do so for as long as they could ("A House for a Lifetime," 2005: 2).
3. It minimizes the falls and injuries that can be so debilitating to older people. Perito worries that 5 to 10 percent of Brazil's population aged 60+ are seriously injured and/or hospitalized because of domestic accidents ("A House For A Lifetime," 2005:3).

The message coming out of Brazil is that universal design can eliminate barriers, and make homes safer and more accessible as people grow older. Perito (Mulheratual, 20 September 2005:1) recommends that older people in Brazil strive to make the following changes in their homes so that they can live in—and enjoy their homes—for decades:

1. Indoors
   a. Install emergency lights that go on if there is a blackout.
   b. Install a telephone and an intercom in every bathroom.
   c. Add lighting in closets.
   d. Install automatic rolling blinds on windows.
   e. Install antiskid floors in bathroom(s), the kitchen, and the laundry room.
2. Bedrooms
   a. Install lighting in closets for better illumination.
   b. Eliminate shelves at floor level (too much bending).
   c. Install telephone in headboard of bed for easier communication.
   d. Tape scatter rugs to floor to minimize the risk of slipping.
3. Kitchen
   a. Install sensors that detect smoke and gas and automatically turn off burners on the stove.

b. Avoid spills and burns by locating the stove and oven at waist-level and by having heat-resistant countertops on either side of the stove. This allows the cook to take a heavy pot off the stove or oven and quickly place it down.
c. Install an intercom in the kitchen.
d. Install skid-proof flooring, and minimize the space between stove, sink, and refrigerator.

NURSING-HOME RENOVATION: A MULTIDISCIPLINARY APPROACH

There are currently 34 *clinicas geriatrica* in São Paulo (www.Listas OESP.com.br, 2006). Most of them have been designed in traditional ways that "medicalize, institutionalize, and professionalize long-term care" (Schwarz and Brent, 1999: xviii).

PROJECT VOVO: REDESIGNING BRAZILIAN NURSING HOMES

There have recently been efforts to rethink the architecture and design of *clinicas geriatrica* in Brazil. For instance, BAI has launched Project Vovo to assess the condition of senior housing—especially long-term nursing care—in São Paulo. This research effort on the part of BAI translates into English as the Deserving Grandparents Project ("The Renovation of a Nursing Home," *Sentidos*, 20 July 2004:1; "Project Vovo," Brasilacessivel.org.br, 2006:1). Project Vovo will be the first in a series of projects aimed at making Brazil's nursing homes more accessible and adaptable.

Project Vovo is a work in progress at a *clinica geriatrica* known as the Association Home for the Aging. The nursing home is located in the southern city of Jose Bonifacio, and it continues to be modified based on input from residents and from the multidisciplinary group of designers and gerontologists who oversee the project. There are currently 39 elderly people (15 women and 24 men) living there.

BARRIER-FREE NURSING HOMES

Project Vovo has reconfigured the residents' living space by converting some of the 9.6-square-meter bedrooms into new, specialized bathrooms and dressing rooms that are both accessible (barrier-free) and adaptable as residents become frail or cognitively impaired (Perito, 2006: 1). Renovations will continue to occur in response to the changing physical and psychological needs of the residents, and these renovations will be a prototype for future senior housing in Brazil (Perito, 2006:1). The goal of this project is to create an environment that is homelike, rather than institutional (Schwarz, 1996: 65–66).

CASAS DE REPOUSO

Casas de repouso are the single most common form of senior housing in Brazil today. As of 2006, there were 663 *casas de repouso* in Brazil (Guia Mais.com.br, 2006:5). They range from basic to luxurious.

The advertising for the typical *casa de repouso* focuses on available medical services and rehabilitation. Advertising for the typical *residencial* downplays health care even though the health-care support system featured in the residence is usually top-notch. There is a gerontological reason for this. The *residencial* offers seniors a new lifestyle and often downplays the caregiving function. The *casa de repouso*, however, provides care and rehabilitation and downplays lifestyle issues.

For example, the home page for Casa de Repouso Dr. Menotti Parolari shows images of hospital beds or twin beds and one hospital-like bedroom (Figure 7.7). This contrasts with advertising for *residencials*, which often feature king-sized beds. The hospital bed conveys the unmistakable message that the *casa de repouso* is a place for frail or chronically ill people. Also, the home page for Recanto Monte Alegre features an elderly woman in a wheelchair (Recantomontealegre.com.br, 2006), which underscores the medical and rehabilitative function of *casa de repouso*.

The home page for Casa de Repouso Nossa Casa shows an elderly woman being spoon-fed by a nurse's aide. The home page for Casa de Repouso Dr. Menotti Parolari advertises music therapy, physical therapy, an attending physician, and an infirmary that is open 24 hours/day. Photos of activities at Nossa Casa in the city of Curitiba show a therapy group being led by a nurse or nurse's aide who wears a white uniform. There are also references to the gardens on these properties and to meals, but these are of secondary importance.

Figure 7.7. Assisted living has become increasingly popular for middle- and upper-class Brazilians aged 60-plus.

Now, more than ever before, middle- and upper-class families rely on ALFs. This is consistent with the fact that more Brazilian women are working full-time and do not have time to be caregivers (Karsch and Karsch, 1999: 152; www.country-data.com, 1997: 2) (Figure 7.8).

THE *RESIDENCIAL*: SENIOR HOUSING AS A STATUS SYMBOL

Assisted living would be even more popular were it not for a new form of senior living—the *residencial*—which has rapidly become a status symbol for Brazil's elites (de Vos and Andrade, 2005: 567–68). The coming of the new and expensive *residencials* calls attention to an interesting development in senior housing both in Brazil and in other rapidly changing nations: Instead of being a demotion, senior housing is becoming a status symbol for the elite. The entry of women into the workforce in rapidly aging nations has created a crisis in caregiving. Expensive senior housing—Brazil's *residencials* or India's retirement resort communities, for example—becomes very desirable under these circumstances.

The *residencial* appeals to Brazil's elites because it positions itself as an extension of upper-class life, not an alternative to it. The decor of many *residencials* is tasteful and elegant; the gardens and outdoor spaces are lush and well tended. Perhaps the most significant image of luxury in this type of housing is the

Figure 7.8. This *casa de repouso* features services catering to medical and rehabilitative functions as well as offering daily masses and expert nutrition help.

king-size bed in the model apartments, on both the Santa Catarina and the Lar Sant'Ana websites.

Unlike the *casa de repousa*, with its hospital beds or twin beds, the images on the *residencial* websites typically include a king-size bed. This image connotes comfort, sexuality, and good health in ways that a hospital bed never could (Figure 7.9). Another image of the model apartment at Santa Catarina shows a kitchen with a coffeemaker. These photos of the model apartment imply that life will go on as it did before relocating to this *residencial*.

The typical advertising for *residencials* promotes the housing complex's amenities first and only mentions medical or health-care options toward the end of the advertisement. The home page for the Lar Sant'Ana website is a good example of amenities-first advertising. Lar Sant'Ana is a *residencial* on the outskirts of São Paulo. The home page mentions the expansive gardens ("8,000 meters of tropical garden"), spacious apartments, the *residencial's* party room, fitness room, coffee shop (open all day), home theater, lecture hall, patios, and more (larsantana .com.br, 2006). It is also true that this *residencial* offers medical services, physical therapy, acupuncture, and spiritual and psychological counseling. The medical and psychological services are all first-rate, but these are not the primary focus of the advertising; the primary focus on the home page is the amenities.

Figure 7.9. The king-size bed conveys the image that the older people who live in this *residencial* are still independent and sexual.

This is also true of advertising for the *residencial* Santa Catarina in São Paulo. Its home page shows a bedroom with a king-size bed, a state-of-the-art fitness center, a view of the tasteful lobby with chandeliers and a winding staircase, and a view of the *residencial's* facade, which is at least 15 stories tall. The advertising copy on the home page for Santa Catarina announces that this is a senior residence with the comfort of a hotel. The home page mentions that there is a spa, private club, and rooftop swimming pool on the premises.

These amenities give residents many options. Residents can continue to live traditional family-oriented lives if they wish, or they can pursue other goals and interests.

THE FUTURE

Brazil's senior housing will become more specialized in years to come. The full-range of Brazilian housing for seniors—from the private home to the *clinica geriatrica*—will adapt to the changing needs of older people.

The Accessible Homes movement already has had an impact on the design and redesign of senior housing, and this will continue to create more homes that are safe and accessible for seniors. Also, the Brazilian government is already beginning to train and subsidize home-health aides and other caregivers (Mazenotti, 2005: 41), which will make it possible for more seniors to age in place. There are also proposals to give seniors tax rebates and other benefits for making their homes barrier-free (Mazenotti, 2005: 41).

A HEALTHIER OLD AGE

The future will see a greater variety of housing options to meet the needs of this aging, frail population. This will include more nursing homes, hospices, and facilities for the cognitively impaired.

Apart from this increase in frail and impaired populations, there will be more people experiencing a vibrant, healthy old age. Brazil's *residencials* will begin to specialize in responding to the needs and lifestyles of these older people. There are already *residencials* that have specializations (such as the Residencial Solardomarques, which attracts older travelers). The future will see more chains of *residencials* that will attract travelers, people with particular hobbies or interests, or people making religious pilgrimages.

THE AGING OF BRAZIL'S BABY BOOM

Finally, Brazil's baby-boom contemporaries are on the verge of turning 60 and will soon need senior housing of their own. This generation of people is better educated, more diverse, and in better health than today's elderly population and will come to senior housing with a very different set of needs. The Boomer market will be yet another "mountain" behind the current "mountain" of age wave seniors.

NOW THAT YOU'VE READ CHAPTER 7

KEY TERMS AND CONCEPTS (Pt = PORTUGUESE)

accessible
adaptable
casa (Pt: house)
casa de repouso (Pt: ALF)
clinica geriatrica (Pt: nursing home)
conjugal and extended family
dormitoria (Pt: bedroom)
favelas (Pt: slums)
gerontocracy
idoso, velho (Pt: wise, old)
parentela (Pt: extended family)
residencial (Pt: senior residence)
verticalizacao (Pt: verticalization or high-rise apartment life)

QUESTIONS FOR STUDY AND DISCUSSION

1. What were the traditional housing options for older people in Brazil prior to the 1990s?
2. Explain why the *residencial* is a new and important alternative for older people in Brazil.
3. When did Brazil's age wave begin, and how has it impacted the Brazilian population?
4. How did the coming of high-rise apartment buildings impact the traditional *parentela*, or Brazilian extended family?
5. Project Vovo is experimenting with ways to make *clinicas geriatricas* less institutional and more homelike. What exactly is Project Vovo trying to do?
6. In what ways is the *residencial* different from *casas de repouso*? And why do *residencials* now appeal to Brazil's elite?
7. What are one or two factors that will shape the future of senior housing in Brazil?

HELPFUL WEBSITES

brazzilmag.com
country-data.com/cgi-bin/query/r-1712
designfor21st.org/proceedings
gerocare.com.br (advertising for Brazilian for-profit home-health
  providers)
globalenvision.org/library/5/1066
gringoes.com
guiamais.com.br
larsantana.com.br
www.Listas OESP.com.br
mercado.com
mulheratual.com.br.
nossaCasa.com.br (Website for Casa de Repouso Nossa Casa.)
recantomontealegre.com.br (Website for Casa de Repouso Recanto
  Monte Alegre).
revistasim.com.br
solardomarques.com.br (This *residencial* also caters to elderly travelers.)
universalhome.com.br.

NOTES

1. (Karsch and Karsch, 1999: 144–45). Between 1980 and 1995, the labor-
   force participation of women aged 40–60 (the women most likely and
   able to be caregivers) went from 20.5 percent to 43 percent (Karsch and
   Karsch, 1999: 144). The result was that traditional reciprocities weakened. Older people could no longer expect to live with or be taken care
   of by family members.
2. See in this book Chapter 4, "Japan: The Future Is Robotic," Chapter 5,
   "China: The New Revolution Is Gray, Not Red," and Chapter 9,
   "India: The Karma Of Senior Housing."
3. These reciprocities have weakened because families are smaller and
   cannot take care of aging parents or in-laws as easily (Karsch and
   Karsch, 1999: 149-52). Nevertheless, a recent survey by HSBC Bank
   ("The Future of Retirement," HSBC 2004: 6) finds that older Brazilians—more than people from any of the other 10 nations surveyed—
   still view their family as their major source of happiness and security
   (82 percent). In 2004, 94 percent of elderly Brazilians surveyed said
   that they expected their children to care for them in old age.

"Bringing my elderly and infirm mother from two of Boston's best nursing homes to Gilpaz was truly coming to the Promised Land."

—Testimonial by grateful American daughter, 2000

"Beth Protea is an exemplary senior citizen facility founded by the South African community in Israel and worldwide."

—Advertisement for Beth Protea, 2006

8

Israel

From Kibbutzim to Naturally Occurring Retirement Communities

OVERVIEW

Israel is one of the world's most rapidly aging nations, but its population is aging differently than other nations. For example, in the United States, Sweden, China, Brazil, and Japan, the population is aging because of increased life expectancy. However, Israel's age wave is the result of not only increased life expectancy but also the migration of elderly people to the Holy Land. This has important implications for housing and home design. On one hand, one group of these aging immigrants is affluent and choose to retire in style. Many of Israel's retirement communities and luxury high-rise apartment building are designed to appeal to these affluent immigrants. On the other hand, there are also many elderly immigrants who arrive in Israel with little money and no social support. Israel's response to this group of immigrants has been to design and construct sheltered communities and absorption centers that serve as self-contained communities for immigrant populations.

In addition to immigration, home design in Israel has been shaped by the internal dynamics of this complex society. Many of Israel's 267 kibbutzim are becoming NORCs because the residents have lived together for 30-plus years and are now aging in place. The result is kibbutzim that began as farms being redesigned to meet the needs of their aging residents.

There is also the challenge of housing Israel's aging Palestinians, who depend now more than ever on the Jewish state for housing and health care. To answer this challenge, Israel has begun to offer a variety of housing options and social services to Palestinians. Israel is helping older people to age in place by providing a range of volunteer services. This is seen in residency nursing homes and ALFs. For example, Yad Sarah has a fleet of vans, operated by volunteers, that makes emergency repairs, such as electrical repairs and the replacement of broken locks, in the homes of older people. The result is a volunteer service that helps older people remain in their homes and age in place. Israel's future will be shaped by baby-boom migration, and there is already the beginning signs of housing that will offer the amenities and activities that appeal to Boomers.

EFFECTS OF ISRAEL'S AGE WAVE

Feyga, an 82-year-old Ukrainian woman, is preparing to move away from Tulchin, the town where she has lived most of her life. Her grandson Gregory has flown all the way from New York City to help his ailing grandmother pack and ship her belongings to Israel. Feyga, who is elderly, widowed, and a Holocaust survivor, is about to relocate. Her health is failing, and she can barely live on her own anymore, but she has decided to migrate to Israel, where she will live out her final years. In the end, she also wants to be buried in the Holy Land.[1]

Feyga is part of a mass migration from the former USSR that began in the 1990s and is characterized by the relatively old age of the immigrants (hw .Haifa.Gero, 2006: 1). An estimated 130,000 elderly immigrants from the former USSR had arrived in Israel by 2001, and they now constitute 20 percent of all the elderly people living there (*Mashav: Planning for the Elderly*, 2003: 2). Hundreds of elderly people still relocate and establish residence in Israel every year.

Feyga will settle in one of the world's most rapidly aging nations. She will probably live in one of the absorption centers being built for Soviet émigrés. There, she will live with other Russian-speaking immigrants and begin the process of adjusting to life in the Holy Land.

Israel's construction boom has been shaped by this geriatric immigration from other nations. Many of these newcomers, like 82-year-old Feyga from the Ukraine, are actually elderly when they arrive (Be'er, 2001: 43), and their advanced age impacts how and where in Israel they will be housed. Nursing homes are the only possibility for many of these new immigrants. Yet, along with nursing homes and ALFs, Israel is now designing sheltered communities and absorption centers where older immigrants can live near people who migrated from the same part of the world as they did. These elderly immigrants usually live on their own in Israel's sheltered communities, but the community becomes a place where they can mingle with others who speak their language and understand their needs. Even though these immigrants are new to Israel, many of them are aging in the very same way as Israel's own population: at home and with the care and support of family and friends.

Immigration has added thousands of people to Israel's age wave, but Israel's age wave is actually the result of two demographic changes. The first is immigration, but the second is the increased life expectancy of Israel's native population.

The rate of increase for Israel's elderly population is twice that of its general population (*Mashav: Planning for the Elderly*, 2003: 2). More than 16 percent of Israel's population is aged 60 or older (AARP.org/research/international, 2006: 1). According to Israel's Central Bureau of Statistics, between 1996 and 2000, the number of Israeli residents aged 65 or older increased by 32 percent, and the percentage of those aged 75 or older increased by 50 percent (hw .Haifa.Gero.2006: 2). In fact, a significant percentage of Israel's elderly people are now aged 75 or older—the oldest of the old. The oldest old now comprise 43 percent of all elderly Israelis (health.families.com/isreal). This demographic fact is part of the explanation for the rapid construction of senior housing, nursing homes, and long-term-care facilities in Israel today.

A TRADITION OF HOME CARE IN ISRAEL

Despite rapid changes in Israeli society, most elderly people still rely on their families for social support. Connections can be financial, but they can also be social. Social connections take the form of caregiving, shopping, babysitting, and companionship (Litwin, 2004: 212). One Israeli woman, for example, reminisces about the housing arrangement for her grandmother while she was growing up in Holon, on the outskirts of Tel Aviv in the 1980s: Originally, her grandparents lived apart from the family. But after her grandfather died, her parents built a second story onto their house, gave the first floor to the grandmother, and moved the rest of the family upstairs.

Another woman, who grew up in Haifa, tells a similar story about home care:

> Our grandmother moved in with us shortly after our grandfather died. My mother was the oldest child. She had three sisters and one brother. Her brother and three sisters all lived in Israel, and they worked out an arrangement to take care of our grandmother. Grandma lived with us in Haifa, in the home of her oldest daughter. Our apartment had four bedrooms. Grandma got her own bedroom—it was the smallest of the three. Mom and Dad had their own bedroom. Me and my siblings shared the other two bedrooms. Grandma would spend a few weeks with each of her other daughters. She would live with them for a few weeks here, a few weeks there. But it was understood that her "real" home was with her oldest daughter. She would visit her son and his wife, but never stayed with them. She didn't feel at home with her daughter-in-law (*The Diary of Miriam Herzog*, 2006).

Figure 8.1. Older people once moved in with one of their children in houses much like the one shown here.

It is no longer common for older people to live with their families, but many of Israel's elderly people have informal support systems that include at least one child. Indeed, surveys show that there are still strong connections between the generations in Israeli families (Brodsky and Morginstin, 1999; Central Bureau of Statistics, 1997: 123; Mashau, 2003: 3).

Some older people in Israel are beginning to substitute peer supports for family (Figure 8.2). Retirement communities offer this option. At communities like Protea village it is possible to enjoy the company of neighbors and friends. Israel provides more housing options to older people than most other rapidly aging nations.

AGING IN PLACE

There are different options for older people who are frail or who cannot afford to live in retirement communities. An estimated 13 percent of elderly people who live at home need assistance with at least one activity of daily

Figure 8.2. Older people can live independently and tend to rely on peers in retirement communities.

living (JDC-ESHEL, 2003:2). In most cases, it is a family member—usually the spouse or a daughter—who assumes the role of primary caregiver (Health.Families.com/Israel). The ideal situation is for an elderly person to remain at home as long as possible and rely on informal supports from family members, in addition to support from home-care professionals, homemaking services, and adult-day-care centers (Brodsky and Morginstin, 1999: 77–78; Health.Families.com/Israel).

Volunteers Who Make Home Repairs

Israel sponsors a number of organizations that send volunteers to the homes of elderly people in need of assistance. The largest of Israel's volunteer organizations is Yad Sarah, which provides emergency services for the homebound elderly. Yad Sarah helps older people to maintain the safety and integrity of their homes. If not for Yad Sarah's volunteers, many elderly people would be living in dangerous or uninhabitable homes. Elderly people all over Israel can phone Yad Sarah for emergency home repair. This includes plumbing or electrical emergencies—the two most common emergency visits—and appliance and furniture repairs (Figure 8.3). Yad Sarah has a fleet of mobile vans that transport plumbers, electricians, and other mechanics or tradesmen to the

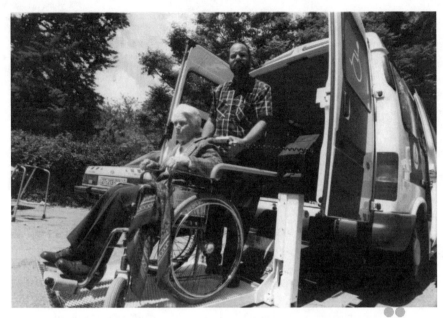

Figure 8.3. This is an example of a home-repair service van that makes emergency repairs for lower-income older people.

apartments of homebound elderly. The repairs are done either free of charge or for a nominal fee.

In addition to doing emergency home repairs, Yad Sarah will upgrade home safety for frail older people. It is common for elderly people to move to nursing homes because they are afraid that they will be victims of robberies or assaults. Yad Sarah routinely makes the kinds of repairs and installations that improve home security and hopefully make older people feel safer about where they live. For example, volunteers will install peepholes and new locks on the front door of an elderly person's apartment for just a nominal charge. This gives many older people the peace of mind they need to remain in their apartments and their neighborhoods, especially if they are living alone. Yad Sarah also provides a home-emergency alarm system that currently connects "thousands of older Israelis" to a computerized communication center in Jerusalem (yadsarah.org, 2006: 3).

Home Health Care and Products

Israel also has an extensive system of home-health workers, who will assist in home care and are paid to do so.[2] The goal of this system is to create the social and medical supports necessary to keep people living in their own homes or apartments.

Home-health care also involves assistive technologies and products to help people remain at home longer, and Israel is a world leader in this area..[3] Israeli companies such as GeronTech and Tzora Active Systems offer products to improve seniors' mobility in and around the home (Figure 8.4). There is even a line of Israeli home furnishings designed to make homes safer and more comfortable for the elderly. One of the most interesting of these home-furnishing products is the Israeli-made Homecare Bed. The Homecare Bed operates like any hospital bed would, but it has the appearance of bedroom furniture. Wooden panels (these panels come in a variety of woods) camouflage the metal frame of the Homecare Bed to make it look more domestic (yadsarah.org, 2006: 8, "Homecare Bed"). The idea behind this product is to maximize the care and comfort of the patient without compromising the domestic feel of the bedroom.

Figure 8.4. Companies like Israel's GeronTech are developing assistive technologies such as this Easy Mover Person Transfer System to help older people age in place.

Israeli companies such as GeronTech and Tzora Active Systems have developed products that enhance mobility in and around the home (tzora.com; GeronTech.com). In addition to developing assistive technologies, GeronTech has also pioneered the CogniFit series of software programs, which are designed to strengthen seniors' cognitive abilities. Thus far, target markets for CogniFit include people who worry about becoming forgetful or who want to continue to drive an automobile (cognifit.com 2006:1). Israeli devices and cognitive software are helping older people to live independently and not move into nursing homes.

There is now an Israeli company called Golden Computers that markets a line of assistive technology called Considerate Computer. This technology helps older people become more comfortable with computer technology. Considerate Computer has an "easy-to-use menu-driven interface" that allows seniors to go directly to favorite computer games, e-mail, or shopping websites (davrez@zahav.net.il, 2006: 1). Assistive technologies like Considerate Computer allow older people to maximize their chances of aging in place by creating strong, reliable links to the community at large.

Aging in place is often exhausting—both mentally and physically—to the family members and friends who provide informal care. Israeli-based Geron-Tech is now marketing a device intended for family members and informal caregivers. The EasyMover Person-Transfer System allows caregivers to lift patients off beds easily, avoiding injuries or sprains on both the caregivers' and patients' parts, and enables patients to live at home longer.

THE KIBBUTZ AS NATURALLY OCCURRING RETIREMENT COMMUNITY

Seventy-five of Israel's 267 communal settlements have become retirement communities, complete with geriatric health centers and assisted living (Figure 8.5). Many others are heading in this direction. The architecture of many Israeli kibbutzim has been modified in response to the fact that the population is aging in place. Some of these communities, like Kibbutz Ramat Yohanan, have built on-site Alzheimer's units and nursing homes for aging residents.

KIBBUTZ ARCHITECTURE AND SOCIAL CHANGE

The addition of Alzheimer's units, nursing homes, and ALFs on the grounds of kibbutzim is a current example of the interplay between kibbutz architecture and social change in Israel. However, kibbutz architecture has responded to social and political changes before. During the first 50 to 60 years of the kibbutz movement, for example, kibbutz architecture was much more political. During the early years, the architecture expressed three fundamental values of the kibbutz movement: frugality, equality, and the rejection of private property (Amir et al., 2005: 147). This translated into communal settings for meals, communal nurseries for children, and barracks-like housing for everybody else. However, kibbutz architecture began to change during the 1980s and 1990s, reflecting the growing privatization of Israeli life. Sociologically, this was a moment when nuclear families gained status and power, even in the social world of the kibbutz. There was greater tolerance of private property, and this translated into more individualized housing for families, including conspicuous displays of status in the form of landscaping, gates, fences, and home renovation. Architecturally, these are expressions of the fact that the original ideology had weakened (Amir et al, 2005: 160–63). Today, many kibbutzim are trying to attract younger families by offering a mix of communal dining, playgrounds, and attractive private homes.

NORCS

Today's kibbutzim are responding to Israel's age wave in new architectural ways. At least 75 of Israel's 267 kibbutzim are NORCs (Miles, 2005: 3; Sykes, J.T. and Hunt, M. 1997: 17). The original settlers are now well into their seventies or eighties, and they require a variety of medical, social, and psychological services. This age wave has produced at least three architectural responses.

The first of these is architectural specialization: Communities such as Beth Protea have added subdivisions for independent living (Protea Village), for assisted living (Keren Beth Protea), and for long-term nursing care (Protea Plus). Beth Protea is accessible to residents from all three of these areas.

The second response is architectural adaptation. Instead of developing new subdivisions or tracts, adaptation involves retrofitting an existing town or community to make it more appropriate for elderly people. At Kibbutz Heftziba, for example, this has involved adding ramps for wheelchairs, installing grab bars in showers, and color-coding sidewalks to make way-finding easier for elderly persons. Apart from these physical changes, there is a staffing component to adaptation: A town or community also adapts by providing appropriate staff. The weekly newsletter at Kibbutz Heftziba contains contact information for the geriatric social workers, nurses, and physiotherapists on site. This kibbutz has also contracted for the services of a geriatric physician.

The architectural response to the aging of the kibbutz population also includes the design and construction of Alzheimer's units. Kibbutz Ramat

Figure 8.5. The Geriatric Division at the Sheba Medical Center was built
to care for the particular needs and demands of the elderly
while striving to optimize the individual's functional
integration into family life and society.

Yohanan, for example, built Hemdat Avot for aging residents who had special cognitive needs, and the facility is also accepting a limited number of patients from outside the kibbutz. Hemdat Avot is a nursing facility with a secure Alzheimer's unit. There are 24-hour medical supervision and a staff that includes social workers, physical therapists, and recreational therapists.

In addition to these geriatric conversions, some of Israel's kibbutzim are offering amenities that attract young families (Kershna, 2007: 1–4). As a result, there are new, "suburbanized" kibbutzim, which are attracting young families. Architecturally, there will be more specialization ahead.

NURSING HOMES: NEW CONSTRUCTION AND NEW POPULATIONS

Apart from transforming kibbutzim into retirement communities, Israel's age wave has also led to more nursing-home construction. In Israel today, 4.4 percent of elderly people reside in long-term-care institutions (JDC-ESHEL, 2003:2). There are now approximately 400 state-licensed nursing homes in

Figure 8.6. This modern nursing home is located in Haifa.

Israel; of which 110 are public, 200 are private, 8 are government-run, and 75 are on kibbutzim (Sinai, 2005: 1). This represents an increase in the number of nursing homes of about 18 percent over the past 10 years. In addition to the 13,000 beds available in Israel's nursing homes, another 3,000 beds are available for geriatric care—both rehabilitative and acute—throughout Israel (hw.Haifa. Gero.2006: 3).

PRIVATE-SECTOR NURSING HOMES

Traditionally, the financing and regulation of nursing homes has been a government monopoly in Israel (Menirav, 2000: 1). However, the sector is gradually being deregulated, and much of the new nursing home construction is now coming from the private, for-profit sector.

Until around the 1970s, Israeli nursing-home populations reflected the ethnic stratification in the larger society. Early in Israel's history, there were separate old-age homes for Sephardic and Ashkenazi Jews. For example, in 1948, the Sephardic old-age home was a landmark on Jerusalem's Jaffa Road (Kroyanken, 2006:3). And even today, there are nursing homes and kibbutzim that cater more to one of these groups than the other.

A NURSING HOME FOR THE ARAB COMMUNITY

Arabs make up 20 percent of Israel's population, but only 3 percent of them are elderly. This is because the life expectancy of Arabs is often shorter than that of Jews in Israel. Furthermore, elderly Arabs have less income and education than elderly Jews (Health.Families.com). Elderly Arabs are also less likely to visit senior-day-care centers or employ home-health aides. Israel's small Arab community relies more on family support, even though the traditional authority of Arab elders is waning. In recent years, elderly Arabs have lost power and status in their families because their traditional power is being undermined by the increased education of younger men and the decline of the extended family. As a result, a small but growing number of elderly Arabs are now living in nursing homes. This would have been unheard of a decade ago, but this reflects the changing dynamics of Arab communities within Israel. Dabouriya Home for the Aged now advertises itself as "the first publicly funded, culturally adapted nursing home for Israeli citizens of Arab descent" (Suleiman and Walter-Ginzburg, 2005: 1). The design of Dabouriya Home

Figure 8.7. Beth Protea now offers different levels of care.

reflects traditional Islamic values, such as separating the sexes and including rooms or areas for prayer, and reflects the interplay of culture and housing design (Rapoport, 2001: 150).

ASSISTED LIVING

Many Israelis age in place in Israel's towns and cities, but there are also other forms of senior housing for elderly people who are in relatively good health. The first of these is assisted living, which is becoming increasingly popular in Israel. The construction of ALFs typically comes from the private sector, sometimes from the community itself.

Beth Protea, for example, is a privately owned retirement community that recently added on an ALF. In addition to assisted living, the residents of this facility have access to hydrotherapy, physiotherapy, and occupational therapy (Figure 8.7). Until about 10 years ago, most ALFs in Israel were small, privately owned operations. But these self-contained ALFs are being eclipsed by a new form of ownership and organization: the ALF chain.

ALFS CHAINS

Mishkenot Clal is one of the leading Israeli chains of ALFs for senior citizens (Figure 8.8). Mishkenot Clal locates ALFs in or near population centers. It is a private sector response that draws on the local workforce to provide home-health workers, waitstaff, and administrators for their facilities.

Cresthaven, another chain of ALFs, is located outside of the busy, bustling cities of Israel. At Cresthaven's Shomron property, for example, residents are housed in their own detached, two-bedroom houses, which they can furnish to suit their individual tastes. (See also Chapter 6, "Sweden: Independence by Design." The Swedish *servicehus* also gives residents the opportunity to bring some of their home furnishings with them when they move in.) Cresthaven provides common areas for dining and recreation, but it gives residents a sense of autonomy through the housing arrangements.

The Amigour construction of ALFs in Israel is twice what it was just 10 years ago (Amigour/2006) and will continue to reflect the growth of the for-profit sector in senior housing.

ASSISTED LIVING FOR IMMIGRANT POPULATIONS

In recent years, the Israeli government has stepped in to build ALFs to meet the needs of elderly immigrants, especially immigrants from the former Soviet

Figure 8.8. An ALF owned by Mishkenot Clal Ltd.

Union (Brodsky and Morginstin, 1999: 79). These ALFs have evolved into supportive neighborhoods where older people with similar ethnic backgrounds can learn the skills necessary to assimilate into Israeli society. By living in supportive or sheltered neighborhoods, the immigrants interact with others who speak the same language, and they have access to their homeland's activities, cuisine, and social supports. This has become such a priority that Israel recently converted a number of absorption centers and hostels into 2,000 additional housing units for elderly people (jafi.org.il/hous-ing_for_the_elderly). Sheltered-housing communities usually have a part-time housemother or housefather who speaks the same language as the immigrants who live there and who help them access social services. The goal of these communities is to help these aging immigrants assimilate into Israeli life (Brodsky and Morginstin, 1999: 80). There are currently 4,750 housing units in 46 sheltered-housing facilities. These housing units are typically equipped with emergency call systems, grab bars in showers, and nonskid surfaces on floors. Some of these supportive neighborhoods are located in Israel's urban centers, but most of them are located in developing towns on Israel's periphery (Amigour.co.il/2006: 1).

Figure 8.9. The sheltered-housing community at Ezrat Avot will be expanded to include more low-rent housing and a community center for elderly people living nearby.

SHELTERED HOUSING AND ABSORPTION CENTERS

The Israeli government has been building a number of low-rental sheltered-housing settlements for elderly immigrants from other parts of the world (Meyers, 2001: 2) (Figure 8.9). Many of them migrate to Israel with no savings or social support. Amigour, which is Israel's largest provider of housing for the elderly, is one of the agencies dedicated to provide housing and other forms of shelter for such people. Another agency is Mishan.

SHELTERED HOUSING AND SUPPORTIVE COMMUNITIES

There are now supportive communities for elderly people in most Israeli cities (Brodsky and Morginstin, 1999: 78–79). By 2005, Amigour had converted 23 absorption centers into senior citizen homes where elderly immigrants make the transition to Israeli life (Amigour.co.il 2006: 1). It provides apartments and also lodging in senior citizen homes, and, in fact, now operates 53 senior citizen homes in Israel. But the most interesting of Amigour's efforts is the

Figure 8.10. Amigour's Tel Aviv expansion will create more low-rent housing for older people and space for community events.

supportive community, which houses people and also provides services for the surrounding community. The sheltered-housing community in Kiryat Ono is an excellent example of the community-outreach concept. The Kiryat Ono complex includes a senior center and 79 low-rent housing units. The property is being expanded so that it will include an additional 80 housing units and a community center that will serve older people in the surrounding community. There will also be protected areas on every floor of the residential tower that will be for community use.

The expansion of Amigour's sheltered-housing community in Jerusalem will be even more comprehensive. The current structure contains 128 low-rent units, each with a single room, kitchenette, and bathroom (Figure 8.10). The ground floor contains a lobby, lecture hall, and synagogue. The expansion will add 155 more low-rent housing units, each with protected space for community events.

A final example of a supportive Amigour community is the Seniors' Mall in the Upper Nazareth area of Israel's Galilee region. The mall includes a combination of low-rent senior housing and a shopping mall staffed entirely by seniors who live nearby. The Seniors' Mall caters to the needs and wants of older people in a variety of ways. In addition to shops, there is an adult-day-care center, meeting rooms for activities, and even a local post office. The Seniors' Mall is a social and architectural response to the rapid aging of Galilee's population.

Mishan has built housing for older people in 10 of Israel's urban centers (www.ihf.net/index.asp?id=63, 2006). There are currently 4,850 older people living in Mishan housing. The Mishan site at Ramat Efal is a continuum-of-care community, where 1,000-plus residents can live independently or find a place in the community's four wards or in the community's nursing ward. The Mishan site at Be'er Sheba is a seven-story building that includes a dining hall, cultural center, mini-market, and bank in addition to 180 living units.

ACTIVE RETIREMENT LIVING

Retirement is now seen as an opportunity to actively pursue hobbies and dreams, not the time to withdraw. The proportion of men aged 55 to 64 in the labor force has declined from 80 percent in 1961 to about 66 percent in 1998, while the proportion of women in the same age group increased from 17 percent in 1961 to 34 percent in 1998 (Central Bureau of Statistics, 2000). Senior housing in Israel is adapting to this change. In addition to such traditional senior communities, there are now upscale resorts and kibbutzim, such as Ahuzat Rishconim or Ein-Gedi, where older adults can hike, play sports, and pursue a variety of active lifestyles.

Kibbutz Lohamei Hagetaot, for example, has invested nearly three million dollars in a luxury spa that will include lavish guest houses and sports facilities (ynetnews.com, 2005: Kibbutz Lohamei Hagetaot). It joins the ranks of other activity-oriented kibbutzim such as Ein Gedi (Figure 8.11). Baby-boom retirees and visitors already flock there for its wellness center, its desert safari excursions, and the Ein Gedi spa. There is also a botanical garden and upscale restaurants. These amenities are especially appealing to Boomers who are already seeking experiential travel and will soon be seeking experiential retirement experiences.

The active-retirement lifestyle is similar to what is being developed in the United States at Del Webb's Sun City Festival, where the focus is on self-development and social connection through activity. Israel's new active retirement is a step in this direction—and many worlds away from traditional home care in the Holy Land.

THE FUTURE

The future of senior housing in Israel will be shaped by far-reaching changes in the Israeli family, and the larger society.

Figure 8.11. A public building at Kibbutz Ein Gedi.

FAMILY STRUCTURE WILL CONTINUE TO CHANGE

There are predictions that the number of children per family in Israel will decrease. In this respect, Israel is demographically similar to China. It will be a nation where fewer children are available to be caregivers to their aging parents. In addition to this change in family structure, there will be more women who find themselves sandwiched between the needs of their children and the needs of their aging parents or in-laws. Such cross-pressures were minimal when there were two or three daughters per family. In 1999, for example, about 10 percent of Israel's population was caring for an elderly parent, and 42 percent of them took care of aging parents on a daily basis. Yet, there will be fewer caregivers available as fertility decreases and as more Israeli women begin working outside the home.

MORE KIBBUTZIM WILL BECOME NORCS

Israel can expect to have more kibbutzim becoming NORCs and is already anticipating the immigration of elderly people who come to the Holy Land without their families. Overlaid on these changes is the growing political activism of Israel's elderly population. As of 2006, there has been a vocal Pensioners' Party, which advocates for pensioners' rights and housing opportunities. What elderly people are losing because of demographic shifts they may regain through voting and political activism.

NOW THAT YOU'VE READ CHAPTER 8

KEY TERMS AND CONCEPTS

geriatric immigration
kibbutz, kibbutzim
sheltered neighborhoods

QUESTIONS FOR STUDY AND DISCUSSION

1. Why do elderly people migrate to Israel, and how does this make Israel's aging population different from the aging populations of China, India, Brazil, or Japan?
2. Why and how are some of Israel's collective villages, known also as kibbutzim, becoming NORCs?

3. Why has senior housing in Israel been influenced by technological and architectural developments in the United States?
4. Why is it accurate to say that assisted living is becoming the most popular form of senior housing in Israel?

HELPFUL WEBSITES

aarp.org (2006:1)

amigour.co.il (2006:1)

bethprotea.org.il (Beth Protea Retirement Facility)

cognifit.com (Cognitive-solutions software from GeronTech)

cresthaven.homestead.com (Cresthaven: An ALF)

davrez@zahav.net.il (Considerate Computer, 2006)

eg@ein-gedi.org.il (Kibbutz Ein Gedi, 2006)

gerontech.org.il (GeronTech: Israeli Center for Assistive Technology and Aging)

gilpaz.co.il (Gilpaz ALF)

health.families.com/Israel

hw.haya.gero (University of Haya Gerontology Department, 2006)

ihf.net.index.asp (2006)

jafi.org.il/housing for elderly (Amigour owns 46 sheltered-housing facilities, 2004)

jdc.org (Nazareth Seniors' Mall, 2006)

jointnet.org.il/gerontech (GeronTech: The Israeli Center for Assistive Technology and Aging)

Matityahu.org

Mishkenot-clal.co.il (Mishkenot ALFs)

tzora.com (Tzora Active Systems, Ltd.)

savion.co.il (Savion Ltd., Homecare Bed)

yadsarah.org (Israeli Home Health-Care Innovations, health and fitness center for the frail elderly, and mobile repair unit)

ynetnews.com (Kibbutz Lahome: Hageteat, 2005)

NOTES

1. Feyga's migration to Israel is not unusual. The rapid aging of Israel's population reflects, in part, the fact that many elderly people from other nations migrate to Israel so that they will be buried in the Holy Land (Meyers, 2001: 1).

2. See also Chapter 6, "Sweden: Independence by Design."
3. The Yad Sara Exhibition and Training Center displays a wide range of Israeli-made home-health-care innovations that are intended to help older people remain in their homes.

"*When the afternoon post brought another letter from Sagar, 'Mother, you really should come and live with us, we worry about you all alone . . . especially when you're sick like this,' she wrote back the same day, with fingers that shook a little, 'You're right, my place is with you, and the grandchildren.'*"

—Chitra Banerjee Divakaruni,
Mrs. Duta Writes a Letter

India
The Karma of Home Design

OVERVIEW

India has been transformed by two decades of economic prosperity. The nation has gone from being an economic backwater to being one of the world's most important economies. All of this growth has brought new careers and opportunities to younger people throughout India. Yet the impact on India's aging population is less clear-cut. Indian family life is being strained by migration and new career patterns. The old norm of filial piety is being weakened because younger people are migrating to other parts of India and emigrating in record numbers to other parts of the world. India's old-age homes have always been seen as a last resort, the place where older people would live if their families were unwilling or unable to take them in. But one result of the new economic order is an increase in the numbers of people moving into old-age homes.

In addition to this trend, there is a new form of senior housing in India. This is resort retirement housing for India's new, postindustrial elites. These retirement resorts are often gated communities featuring Western amenities and menus. Rental retirement and assisted living are not options in India. However, continuum-of-care homes are now on the drawing board.

In the future, India will have a two-tiered system of senior housing. There will continue to be old-age homes for the poor and there will be a greater variety of senior housing for the rich. Architecturally, the future will be more diverse than ever before. Socially, there will be a growing gap between the housing options for India's poor and India's new elites.

TRADITIONAL VERSUS MODERN HOUSEHOLDS

Mrs. Duta has moved in with her son, Sagar, his wife, and their two children. Now that she lives with them, she is not getting along with her daughter-in-law,

Shyamoli. Shyamoli complains that Mrs. Duta's traditional ways are beginning to disrupt her modern household. The daughter-in-law does not want Mrs. Duta to cook so much traditional food ("It's too greasy," she says. "There's too much cholesterol."). Mrs. Duta does not know how to operate the washer/dryer in her new and modern home. Actually, she is happier washing her clothes by hand. She refuses to place leftovers back in the refrigerator because they are "contaminated *jutha* things"[1] that, in the Hindu religion, would make other food in the refrigerator unclean. Mrs. Duta soon feels unwelcome and unloved.

This story is fictitious. An aging woman from Calcutta has come to live with her oldest son, Sagar, and his family. In this story, Sagar and his family live somewhere in Southern California. But gerontologically speaking, the story could have been set in Calcutta or almost anyplace in India. Divakaruni's story captures the strains and tensions that surface in Indian families when older people are widowed or sick. Even under the best of circumstances, housing a man's mother and his wife under the same roof can cause problems for Indian families. The changing demographics and booming economy of India today are making this arrangement even more volatile.

Where will an older person live when he or she is widowed or sick? The answer to this question is more complicated than ever before because of economic and demographic changes on the Indian subcontinent. India's rapidly growing economy has been not only a fiscal blessing but also a gerontological nightmare.

Many Indian families—the traditional support system for elderly people—have been dispersed nationally and globally. Two decades of rapid growth (Linton, 2005: 1) have created job opportunities in other parts of the nation and the world.

In addition to the miracle of economic growth, there has been a demographic miracle as well. Advances in public health and medicine are prolonging life in India and have created India's age wave of people over the age of 60. "India's single most stunning achievement... is longevity. While it took France 120 years for the population of the elderly to double, it took India just 25 years" (Das, 2005: 1). India now has one of the world's most rapidly aging populations. As a result, older people are turning to their families for care and support, but they are doing so at a moment when Indian family life is in transition. Like the fictional Mrs. Duta, many older people are finding that their families cannot or will not care for them. Even when families are willing to be caregivers, they may have relocated to Bangalore or Southern California. Home design in India is beginning to respond to these strains. New forms of senior housing, such as resort retirement or assisted living, are now available, and there are still the traditional old-age homes for older people who have been abandoned by their families, or cannot afford better housing.

A RAPIDLY AGING INDIA

The number of people aged 60 or older grew from 12 million in 1901 to more than 71 million a century later—a six-fold increase in this segment of the Indian population (Das, 2005: 1; Liebig and Ramamurti, 2006: 237). And while the youngest age group (people aged 0 to 14) only increased 6.7 percent between 1991 and 2001, the oldest group (people aged 60 or older) increased 38.4 percent during that same period of time (Ponnuswami, 2000: 124). The result has been a population experiencing two demographic changes. The first is that the sheer number of elderly people is increasing, as it is throughout much of the world. But India is unique because the percentage of people aged 60 or older, relative to the rest of the population, is also rising rapidly.

In year 2000, there were 71 million people aged 60 or older, and that number is expected to triple by the year 2050 (Linton, 2005: 1). And according to Liebig and Rajan (2003: 12), in 2050, the two most populous nations in the world, China and India, "will share the major proportion of the world's elderly." The gerontological difference is that China will need to house very old people who will not have much longer to live. India, however, will have to provide housing for people who are relatively young and will have many more years ahead of them.

China will gray into old age (see Chapter 5, "China: The New Revolution Is Gray, Not Red"), while India will gray into middle age. By 1995, life expectancy in India had increased 15 years for men and 16 years for women (Government of India, 1999). This means that India now has a greater percentage of people aged 60 or older than ever before, but many of them are aged 60 to 75 (Iyengar, 2005:1). Actually, speaking, they are still relatively young: They will have many years ahead of them, and they will need years of housing and health care. Rural and urban India will face different challenges because the aging population is not distributed evenly across India. Most of this age wave is occurring in the rural countryside—often in substandard housing.

Almost 70 percent of India's elderly people now live in the rural countryside, where housing is in short supply. Older people in rural areas tend to be older than their counterparts in India's cities and are apt to require more social services and health care. Many are also candidates for India's rural old-age homes, which tend to be overcrowded and underfunded (*Global Action on Aging*, 2003: 1; Shah, 2004: 3).

The creation of senior housing in India is also complicated by poverty and illiteracy, which often "travel together" in aging populations. In addition to being disproportionately rural, 80 percent of elderly people in India who need better housing are illiterate, and 40 percent of them currently live below the poverty level (*Global Action on Aging*, 2003: 2). This combination of poverty, illiteracy, and rural residence makes it difficult for many of India's elderly

TABLE 9.1 INDIA'S AGING POPULATION, 1991

PERCENTAGE OF PEOPLE AGED 66 + IN INDIA'S STATES

STATES	1991 POPULATION (000'S)		PERCENT OF TOTAL POPULATION	
	(60+)	(70+)	(60+)	(70+)
Andhra Pradesh	4,306	1,425	6.47	2.14
Arunachal Pradesh	37	12	4.23	1.42
Assam	1,186	448	5.29	2.00
Bihar	5,227	1,803	6.05	2.09
Goa	74	27	6.34	2.27
Gujarat	2,540	966	6.15	2.34
Haryana	1,230	528	7.47	3.21
Himachel Pradesh	402	164	7.79	3.18
Kashmir	432	163	5.78	2.18
Kamataka	3,041	1,149	6.76	2.56
Kerala	2,529	1,006	8.77	3.46
Madhya Pradesh	4,254	1,583	6.43	2.39
Maharashtra	5,453	1,934	6.91	2.45
Manipur	109	40	5.94	2.19
Meghalaya	82	29	4.62	1.64
Mizoram	34	12	4.93	1.77
Nagaland	65	28	5.40	2.31
Orissa	2,217	794	6.98	2.51
Punjab	1,532	625	7.56	3.08
Rajasthan	2,666	917	6.06	2.08
Sikkim	19	6	4.59	1.51
Tamil Nadu	4,073	1,408	7.29	2.52
Tripura	192	87	6.96	3.17
Uttar Pradesh	9,250	3,403	6.65	2.45
West Bengal	9,250	3,403	6.65	2.45
Andaman Islands	10	3	3.55	1.18
Chandigarh	29	11	4.52	1.73
Dadra Nagar	6	2	4.40	1.24
Daman & Diu	6	2	6.32	2.43
Delhi	444	154	4.71	1.63
Lakshadweep	3	1	5.22	1.68
Pondicherry	56	21	6.90	2.55
All India	**60,754**	**22,154**	**6.58**	**2.40**

(Source: Irudaya Rajan S., Mishra,U.S. and Sarma, P.S. *India's Elderly: Burden or Challenge?* New Delhi: Sage Publications, 1999. Data in Table 9.1 comes from India's 1991 census.)

TABLE 9.2 INDIA'S POPULATION: BROAD AGE GROUPS, 2001

AGE GROUPS	POPULATION	MALES	FEMALES
6 years and below	150,421,175	77,322,151	73,099,024
	17.94%	17.77%	18.12%
7–14 years	161,943,487	84,405,295	77.538,192
	19.31%	19.39%	19.22%
15–59 years	464,826,476	241,411,392	223,415,084
	55.43%	55.47%	55.39%
60 years and above	56,681,640	29,363,725	27,317,915
	6.76%	6.75%	6.77%

(Data Source: 1991 Census of India.)

people to get the care they need. One observer estimates that 50.78 percent of the rural elderly and 57.35 percent of the urban elderly are "totally dependent" on others for economic support, and it is not clear that they can afford to buy the care that they need (Ponnuswami, 2000: 124). Like Mrs. Duta in Divakaruni's short story, these elderly people often have no choice but to turn to family members for care and support.

SENIOR HOUSING IN A RAPIDLY AGING INDIA

In India, it has long been assumed that the family will provide care and shelter for its aging members. Years ago, Ross offered this wonderful image of care and obligation in the traditional Hindu community: "The joint family, the caste, and the village . . . circled each individual Hindu, radiating out like rings around a thrown stone" (1961: 3). These circles were not only a form of control but also a source of care and security. Of the three (family, caste, and village), the Indian family is still the most important source of care and control. In the traditional joint family, the ideal was for "all the married sons to live together in a single household with their parents" (Ross, 1961: 97). Studies of traditional Indian villages showed that it was indeed customary for at least one married son (and his wife) to continue living with his parents in their home (Shah, 1974: 50). Technically, this is called "patrilocal residence" because one or more sons (and their wives) will reside in the father's home.

The traditional joint family is losing its dominance in Indian life, but a recent survey of 1,000 Indian adults (HSBC, 2004) finds that most respondents still assume they can rely on their family to care for them in their old age. Interestingly, the same survey found that most respondents would agree to be caregivers to an elderly person, but they assumed that most other people of the same age would refuse to do so (HSBC, 2004).[2] The results of this survey are worth a closer look because they have implications for senior-home design in India.

Of all 10 nations and territories included in the HSBC bank survey, India was the most traditional in terms of housing arrangements for elderly people.[3] It was the nation where the norm of filial piety was perhaps most deeply engrained. Respondents from India were the ones who most often assumed they would someday be "caring for elderly relatives." In traditional Indian families, this means moving into the home with an aging, widowed parent, though it is now more acceptable for an aging parent—usually the widowed mother—to move in with a married son or daughter.

Compared to similar samples of adults from the nine other aging nations involved in the survey, the Indian sample was the least worried about "being a burden to my family" when they eventually grow old (HSBC, 2004: 13). The HSBC survey confirms that in India it is still widely believed that older people should be invited to live with other members of their family when they can no longer take care of themselves.

Actual housing patterns in India reflect this social norm. An estimated 66 percent of older men and 68 percent of older women in India "reside with one or more adult children, usually with a male child. The pattern is even more pronounced in rural areas of India, where 90 percent of the elderly have at least one grown child living in the house with them. Almost 72 percent of India's elderly people now live in households with four or more members, which reflects the fact that there are children and grandchildren living with them (Liebig and Ramamurti, 2006: 246).

Yet there are class- and caste-based differences in how the norm of filial piety actually plays out. The following excerpt comes from the diary of a married Indian woman who comes from a wealthy family. She explains that in wealthier families, a son and his wife would typically have their own room when they moved in with his parents. Arrangements would be more haphazard among lower-caste and lower-income families:

> Usually the mother-in-law does not move. It is her home, and the son brings his bride into it, traditionally. If the family is well-to-do, she remains in her room and the new couple get another. If not, they get the bedroom with maximum privacy—I know of mothers-in-law who sleep in the drawing room, or even on the floor in the kitchen to allow the youngsters marital privacy. . . . I know Indian mothers here (i.e., in the United States) who sleep in the living room because they have only one bedroom in the apartment (Diary of Vibhuti Patel, March, 2006).

The following describes social-class differences in sleeping arrangements for a widowed woman: "Living conditions vary in India. Wealthy urban families enjoy modern homes, servants, and cars. In a larger house, or *kothi*, a widowed mother or aunt would almost always have a bedroom or suite of rooms of her own and, perhaps, a servant to help care for her. The middle classes usually live in apartments or smaller homes, and middle-class families often convert or subdivide a bedroom to provide a place for her to sleep. In the more humble *johnpris*, or cottages of the poor, a widow would have to sleep where she could" (cd-pc.ca/English/India/family.html, 2001).

The traditional patrilocal pattern brought one or more sons (and their wives) to the father's home or cottage where there might be two or three bedrooms. India's clasic stone and wooden cottages, or *jhonpris*, have changed little over the centuries. The heart of every dwelling is the *brahmasthalam*, or courtyard. The courtyard is then surrounded by blocks or modules, each oriented toward a cardinal direction (Cooper and Dawson, 1998: 149). The house could be expanded to accommodate children, relatives, and aging family members by adding to each of these four modules. Historically, there were eight variations on this housing form, each one suitable for a particular caste (Cooper and Dawson, 1998: 149), though these caste-based distinctions in home design are no longer enforced. Figure 9.1 illustrates the bedroom of a typical home of a higher-caste family.

Figure 9.1. An older family member may have a bedroom much like the one in this Jaipur home.

The bedroom in this home could be curtained or partitioned into smaller, more intimate spaces. There are storage niches and wooden pegs on the walls for clothing. The room looks out on the home's central courtyard, allowing both privacy and access to the rest of the house.

The vernacular architecture sometimes substitutes a veranda for the courtyard. In such cases, the veranda would encircle the house, and bedrooms would all look out onto the verandah instead of looking into an internal courtyard (Cooper and Dawson, 1998: 146–47). Whether looking out onto a courtyard or veranda, there is always an effort to locate bedrooms so that they receive maximum shade and breezes.

Yet, the patrilocal pattern is already breaking down among educated and affluent families. Older people with more education are less likely to have children living with them and are more likely to be living either with their spouse or alone (Bongaarts and Zimmer, 2002). Especially in India's larger cities, the presence of studio flats and other rental units has given older people the option to live alone or apart from their family if they can afford to do so (Figure 9.2). There are also retirement resorts and ALFs for those who can afford them.

Figure 9.2. The growing number of studio apartments and ALFs in India now make it easier for older people to live alone or apart from the patrilocal family.

Retirement resorts and ALFs are both examples of senior housing that side-step the family. They now appeal to older couples and widowed people who want to live independently and can afford to do so.

Unlike Sweden (see Chapter 6), where older people have traditionally lived apart from their families, this *neolocal* pattern of residence is just beginning to emerge in India. One reason for this is that younger family members are more dispersed than ever before; another reason is that there are now more housing options available for India's older people.

CULTURE SHAPES THE DESIGN AND OPERATION OF INDIA'S OLD-AGE HOMES

The Rajaji Elders' Home near the city of Chennai is named after Rajaji, a guru who lived "as an ideal elder citizen well worthy of emulation." The brochure for Rajaji Elders' Home describes it as *"a peaceful home for elders of children who live away in a foreign land"* (Rajaji Elders' Home, 2005: 1, italics added). A trustee of an old-age home in Gujarat echoes this image of old-age homes coming to the rescue when parents have been abandoned by their ambitious children. The trustee says, "There are people whose children are settled abroad. Such couples do not have a shortage of money. They just want a good, comfortable home. And with more youngsters migrating abroad, there are more parents in this predicament" (Adhuanu, 2005: 1). These are reminders that old-age homes in India are still seen by many as a last resort—a place to go when family members cannot or will not be involved.

Old-age homes in India actually date back to the eighteenth century (Nair, 1989) but have not been perceived as mainstream housing for most of India's elderly people, only for those elderly people who were destitute or had been abandoned by their families.[4]

A survey by HelpAge India, one of India's most age-friendly social agencies, confirms that this belief is still well entrenched in India's culture. HelpAge India surveyed the living arrangements of India's elderly population in 1998 and found that less than 1 percent of India's aging population—an estimated 16,000 people out of India's 566,581,640 people aged 60 or older—was living in old-age homes (HelpAge India, 1998: 132).

Until recently, it was the norm for the joint family, with its tradition of filial piety and patrilocal residence, to provide care and shelter for most of India's aging population. Rajaji Elders' Home is typical in this regard: It positions itself as a place for older people who do not have a patrilocal option because, to para-phrase the brochure, the children have moved away to a foreign land (Figure 9.3). In its form and function, this home is typical in many other ways as well. The

Figure 9.3. Rajaji Elders' Home houses older people whose children have moved abroad.

design and operation of Rajaji Elders' Home, like so many others in India, has been shaped by Hindu norms and the ever-present caste system.

Throughout Part II of this book, there are examples of how culture has shaped the design and operation of senior housing. Chapter 8, for example, looks at the phenomenon of NORCs in Israel, and Chapter 6 explains that Sweden's commitment to help older people to age in place has created a society where almost 90 percent of older people do not relocate to nursing homes or ALFs but instead live independently in their own homes or apartments.[5]

Culture also shapes the form and function of senior housing in India. Centuries of history and tradition have left their mark on the architecture and interior design of housing for older people. But there are now new influences as well. The high-tech lifestyle of India's new financial and social elites is shaping the architecture and interior design of new senior housing in India.

Traditional architecture and new design are happening side by side in India today. One observer puts it like this:

> Colossal changes have taken place in India over the last two decades. . . . When one sees e-mails being sent through mobile telephones from impoverished villages, one is apt to believe that the old order has changed, yielding to the new. But in the next breath, one notices that water is still being drawn from a well . . . that villagers still plough their fields with their own hands. . . . And only a few miles away . . . we can see workmen using pickaxes to dig up ridges to lay fiber-optic cables (Das, 2006: 1).

The architecture and design of housing for older people in India today reflects both of these influences. Housing being built for the poor and homeless looks the same as it has for years, if not decades, while gated communities and new-age villages now attract the elite of India.

THE OLD-AGE HOME: CHARITY, WORK, AND MEDITATION

More than half of India's old-age homes are places where the destitute or indigent elderly live free of charge, and the design of these homes reflects the religious values and social norms of India. Old-age homes in India have typically been charitable organizations that are operated by Hindu or Christian orders such as Little Sisters of the Poor. A handful of old-age homes are operated by organizations such as the Rotary Club. The free old-age homes provide food, shelter, and companionship to people who would otherwise be destitute. Such homes are open to all, "without any restriction of caste, creed, and sex" (Prasnathi Old Age Welfare Home, 2005: 1), though it is doubtful if any members of the elite Brahmin caste live there. The people who do live there enjoy a level of comfort that they would not otherwise have.

The remainder of old-age homes charge fees. Based on monthly charges, there are three categories of for-pay homes:

1. Homes where rent is based on the income of the elderly resident
2. Homes that charge less than $1,000 rupees/month
3. Homes charging more than $1,000 rupees/month (Karmayog, 2005: 1)

Old-age homes, whether "free" or "for pay," are places for older people to live, not retire. The architecture and design of such places puts the emphasis on dormitory living, making privacy all but impossible. The designs of sleeping quarters, bathing and toileting facilities, and meditation areas underscore this gerontological point.

GUIDELINES FOR DESIGNING OLD-AGE HOMES IN INDIA

Senior Indian magazine provides the following guidelines for designing old-age homes:

- Old-age homes can be dormitory type, independent rooms, or cottages.
- The rooms should be well ventilated. Facilities should be at ground level. If upper floors have to be built, then a sloping ramp has to be provided.
- Toilets and bathrooms should have rough flooring so that elders do not slip.
- Suitable railings should be provided for support.
- A room should be set apart where sick people needing short-term care can be housed.
- There should be at least one recreation room (*Senior Indian*, 2005: 1).

Advertising for 25 old-age homes in India, both in print and online, indicates that the actual design comes close to these recommendations in most cases.

DORMITORY LIVING

Privacy is almost nonexistent in most of India's free old-age homes. In fact, the most striking aspect of the design is the public nature of sleeping space. Residents usually sleep in dormitories, which typically house between 3 to 10 people in a single, open bedroom. Many of the residents in these free old-age homes sleep in dormitories without curtains or partitions between their beds.

Sada Sukhi Ashram, a rural old-age home near the city of Chennai, is a good example of public sleeping spaces. Sada Sukhi Ashram consists of 10 rural hut blocks. Each of these hut blocks has five rooms that are "interconnected to each other and are . . . semi-open in between the walls." Residents are assigned cots or beds where they sleep, but they are free to wander within the hut block (Project Sada Sukhi Ashram, 2005).

Many old-age homes in rural India simply have a single sleeping space for anywhere from 3 to 10 people (all of the same sex). Such dormitories are unheard of in U.S. nursing homes or ALFs; the same is true for Sweden, Japan, and Israel. However, dormitory living is common in India's old-age homes, especially in the free homes for poor or abandoned elderly people (Liebig, 2003: 172). These dormitories, or sleeping rooms, rarely have curtains or partitions between the beds. Storage consists of "perhaps a table or a locker to hold one's possessions" (Liebig, 2003: 173) (Figure 9.4).

It may come as a surprise to Western readers, but most Indian residents do not resent this lack of privacy. The presence of other people is often taken for

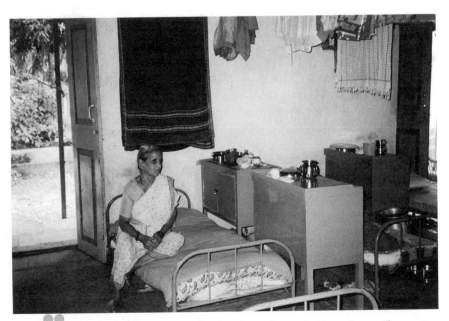

Figure 9.4. The women's dormitory of a rural old-age home: There are no curtains or partitions between the beds. Some of the occupant's clothing hangs from ropes above her bed.

granted and reflects the Hindu norm that the house is an "unprivate place" (Riley, 2003: 4), and that it is karma, or fate, for people to be living in such close proximity (Lighig in Liehig and Rajan, 2003: 160).

Figure 9.5 shows the residents of a women's dormitory having an afternoon chat. The dormitory space also doubles as their living room.

India's poor or indigent people's acceptance of this lack of privacy is an example of how belief in karma affects perceptions of crowding. India's Hindu culture encourages people to accept "the unprivate house" without complaint, and most residents of old-age homes, especially the free old-age homes, do exactly that.

Many of India's old-age homes are located in the rural countryside, where they do not look much different from the surrounding village huts and houses (Liebig, 2003: 165). There is little to distinguish them except for the occasional gate and fence that are designed to prevent senile residents from wandering away.

Rajaji Elders' Home, mentioned earlier, is a more upscale home where residents pay monthly rental fees. Dormitory living is an option at Rajaji Elders' Home, but it is just one of three possible sleeping arrangements.

Figure 9.5. This dormitory space doubles as the living room for the women in this rural old-age home.

Depending on their budgets, residents can live in Rajaji's dormitories, or they can rent single or double rooms at higher rates. The gerontological point is that there will still be people who opt to live in the dormitory and will not be shunned for doing so.

BATHING AND TOILETING FACILITIES IN OLD-AGE HOMES

In addition to the sleeping arrangements, there is not much privacy for residents during bathing and toileting in India's traditional old-age homes. Western toilets are still rare in most old-age homes, especially in rural old-age homes, where almost a third of the residents still rely on squat-toilets, and most still provide buckets for bathing (Liebig, 2003: 172). Even squat toilets are an improvement. "Hundreds of millions of homes across India lack running water and, therefore, toilets" (Nunan, 2005: 1). Groups such as Sulabh International have brought squat toilets and showers to many of the free old-age homes. The squat toilet is a "simple canvas-and-wood shed around a simple Asian squat-toilet that empties into a compost pit" (Baldauf, 2004: 2).

Squat toilets and showers with cold water (which are common in India) are now available to many residents in free old-age homes. If and when residents have hot water for bathing, it is most likely at a for-pay facility. At Rajaji Elders' Home, for example, every resident who rents a single or double room has a bath with hot water, but those who live in the dormitories do not.

ROOMS FOR MEDITATION AND YOGA

Many of India's old-age homes will have prayer or meditation rooms, which reflect the importance of spirituality for Hindus and Muslims. Hindu religion, in particular, emphasizes *vanaprastha* as the ideal for older people. This is the belief that an older person should give up active life and devote himself to meditation and self-realization. *Vanaprastha*, at least in theory, involves giving up worldly pursuits and leaving home for the forest and a life of meditation (Das, 2005: 1). It is for this reason that so many of India's old-age homes provide space for meditation and yoga. In the rural Sada Sukhi Ashram, the meditation room has a "junglelike atmosphere" (Sada Sukhi Ashram, 2005: 1). At the more upscale Dignity Lifestyle Village in Mumbai, there is a state-of-the-art meditation center that not only offers "daily bhajans and spiritual discourses for a soul-stirring experience" but also in-house psychologists who conduct group-therapy sessions in that very same space (Dignity Lifestyle Village, 2005: 4).

CONNECTION TO GROVES AND GARDENS

Many of India's old-age homes advertise their landscaping as an inducement for residents to meditate and stroll outdoors. This is another expression of *vanaprastha*, which includes the image of older people retreating to groves or forests to meditate (Das, 2005: 1). It may not be realistic to relocate permanently to groves or forests, but India's old-age homes often try to provide access to groves and gardens as a gesture to *vanaprastha*. Many of the brochures and websites that advertise India's old-age homes will mention that there are shade trees, groves, or shaded paths where residents are welcome to stroll. In this sense, the landscape design of these old-age homes grows out of the relationship between home and garden in vernacular Indian architecture, where access to gardens and groves is important (Cooper and Dawson, 1998: 57).

A PLACE TO WORK, NOT TO RETIRE

Indian culture also affects the activities and operation of most old-age homes. Most important is the focus on work rather than retirement. It is rare for older people in India to retire. "Retirement for many older Indians has not been, and is not, the norm today" (Kumar, 2002: 15). *Vanaprastha* was supposed to coincide with retirement, but the social and economic fact is that most elderly people cannot afford to retire (Kumar, 2003: 47). Older people today are likely to work well into their sixties or seventies because they have no other means of support. Residents in India's old-age homes, especially those that are for the destitute or indigent, are often expected to work in the garden or in local crafts shops.

Nava Nir, in Calcutta, is perhaps an extreme example of this work ethic. It is an old-age home where the residents themselves run the day-to-day affairs of the facility because "there is no one else to do it" (Cohen, 1998:116). The welfare organization that sponsors this old-age home cannot afford to staff it; the home will literally cease to exist if the residents do not oversee daily operations (Cohen, 1998: 116–117). Nava Nir has become a home for homeless widows who have created a family and community of their own and who have become self-supporting because they had to.

VEGETARIAN MENU

Hindu and Muslim sensibilities shape the menu in old-age homes, especially those where poor people are housed. Residents in these places are discouraged from having "intoxicating drinks, liquor or drugs, non-vegetarian food, snuff, or tobacco . . . in their rooms" because this violates religious norms (Project Sala Sukhi Ashram).

GATED COMMUNITIES: NEW HOMES
FOR INDIA'S AGING ELITES

Across the way from Bangalore Old-Age Home is a new resort retirement community complete with gates, security guards, villas, and a state-of-the-art fitness center. In terms of form and function, they might as well be worlds away from each other.

An estimated 38 percent of all old-age homes in India have been created in the past 10 years (Liebig, 2003: 167); much of this new construction is closer to being Western-style retirement resort communities than traditional Indian old-age homes. Actually, it may be more appropriate to call them resorts for seniors than old-age homes. Many of the communities sprouting up near New Delhi or Bangalore are clusters of cottages or villas with access to upscale shopping, fitness facilities, spas, and—in deference to Hindu tradition—yoga and meditation centers.

A recent article in *The Times of India* referred to India's new senior communities as "new-age housing" (Sharma, 2005: 1) or "customized retirement *resorts*" (Nayar, 2004: 1, italics added). One of the newest—the Ashiana Village—is billed as a gated residential community that may be the first retirement village in India to have gates, electronic alarms, and security guards (Figure 9.6).

GATED BUT BARRIER-FREE

Villas and cottages in India's retirement resorts are typically barrier-free environments (Nayar, 2004: 2), featuring homes built on one level and bathrooms with railings in the showers and faucets with levers. Residents take comfort in knowing that they live in a community of care with easy access to shopping, dining, social activities, and medical assistance. Ashiana, on the outskirts of New Delhi, will be the prototype for similar retirement resorts in Bangalore, Mumbai, Hyderabad, and other large Indian cities (Nayar, 2004: 3).

The market for India's new senior housing reflects the massive social and economic changes that have been transforming India over the past two decades. Instead of appealing just to Brahmin families—India's traditional elite class— the market for these new, gated communities consists of "people from the middle and upper classes" who have made their fortunes more recently (Nayar, 2004:2). Prodeepta Das, for example, observed that one retirement community in Calcutta rents almost exclusively to "people from professional backgrounds" (Das, 2005: 3).

HOUSING FOR INDIA'S NEW ELITES

Advertising for one of these retirement resorts, Clasic Kudumbam Village, even included testimonials by physicians, attorneys, and members of Chennai's technological elite. Doctor Venkat Memi, for example, says this is a "great facility," and Mr. Srinivasachar, Advocate, says the resort is "exceptionally good" (www.Kudumbam.com, 2006). These testimonials (there were easily 50 of them on the website at the time this chapter was being written) call attention to the fact that India's new retirement communities are appealing more to men, married couples, and upscale professionals who come from India's new, technological and financial elites. This is a dramatic departure from traditional old-age homes whose residents are widowed women with little or no income.

Advertising for India's new senior housing almost always mentions that wealthy residents who live there are still on good terms with their families. MK Dixit, for example, is a retired school principal who tells *The Times of*

Figure 9.6. Ashiana Village is one of India's first gated retirement communities.

India that "mine is a very happy family. It's just that I want to live on my terms and conditions" (Sharma, 2005: 1). On a similar note, a retired corporate executive and his wife have moved to a retirement resort near New Delhi where they will enjoy "comfort, care, security, and even entertainment" (Nayar, 2004: 1). This is a far cry from accounts of the elder abuse, abandonment, or poverty that sometimes push elderly people into India's traditional old-age homes. In one typical account, a 74-year-old woman explains that "my son threw me out," which is the reason she now sleeps in the dormitory of a free old-age home in Calcutta (*The International Development Magazine*, 2005:1).

INDIA'S RETIREMENT RESORTS: AMENITIES FOR BODY AND SOUL

The amenities available in India's retirement resorts are designed to satisfy the exquisite tastes of the wealthy residents (Figure 9.7). Dignity Lifestyle Village, on the outskirts of Mumbai, for example, offers residents a choice of villas, twin-bed cottages, or single-bed cottages; there is no option for dormitory living. Cottages are luxuriously furnished, with twin beds and "wardrobes, [a] writing table, [a] television, [a] refrigerator, [a] safe deposit locker, and [a] decorative *puja* [meditation] alcove" (Dignity Lifestyle: Senior Citizens' Retreat for Active Living, 2005: 2). Bathrooms in these new retirement resorts are not much different from the luxury toilets available to elites in India's largest cities (Beni, 2005: 1), but worlds away from the squat-toilets in free old-age homes. Bathroom suites in Ashiana Village or Dignity Lifestyle Village offer everything from bidets to jacuzzi tubs.

Bedrooms also appeal to the Westernized tastes. Residents can always expect air-conditioning and interior decoration. At Clasic Kudumbam there are villas with one or two bedrooms and studio cottages. The bedrooms typically include "modern wooden beds, [a] pooja shelf, [a] coat/umbrella stand, and broadband Internet access" (www.Kudumbam.com, 2006). This calls attention to the architectural norms and standards that are emerging in India's senior resort communities.

Most important, there is the norm of privacy. The new resort villages build homes that provide Western-style privacy. The "unprivate house" (Riley, 2003:6), which is a familiar part of Hindu culture, is nowhere to be seen. Dormitory living is out of the question in Ashiana Village and other enclaves for India's elites. Instead, there are spacious villas, cottages, or studios.

The architecture is modern, but with a nod toward traditional Hindu and/or Muslim detail. It is not uncommon to find a Hindu temple on the premises or nearby (Figure 9.8). For example, Clasic Kudumbam Village maintains a "beautiful temple with daily *pujas*" (www.Kudumbam.com, 2006). But all of the new resort communities also have in-ground swimming pools, gyms, and/or spas. In short, there is a deliberate mix of traditional and Western amenities.

Daily activities in these new retirement communities focus on leisure and self-development rather than work. At Ashiana Village, for example, there is "computer surfing and e-mailing, a well-stocked library, a health club and fitness center, a meditation center, and a 500-seat auditorium" (ashianahousing.com) (Figures 9.9 and 9.10).

These new, upscale communities are successfully reaching out to India's new elites—individuals and families who have reaped the benefits of India's entry into the global economy. They cater to an affluent, healthier, and more independent clientele. And they offer amenities that appeal to more secular tastes. For example, Dignity Lifestyle Village has two segregated kitchens that serve up traditional (i.e., vegetarian) and Western (i.e., meat meals). The same is true at Ashiana Village, which has a cafeteria-style dining room with vegetarian and non-vegetarian meals and a multicuisine restaurant called Ashiana Gymkhana for formal dining. Clasic Kudumbam offers only hygienic vegetarian food, but advertises that other food is just a short walk away.

Figure 9.7. This two-bedroom villa is now available for wealthy retirees.

Figure 9.8. There is a Hindu temple on the grounds of this new retirement community.

ASSISTED LIVING: ANOTHER OPTION FOR INDIA'S ELITES

Care Homes Limited is nestled in the suburbs of Bangalore. It was one of the last buildings to be built in those suburbs, but among the first ALFs in India. Assisted living is a new concept in India, but is "gaining ground these days" because it offers a level of care unavailable in retirement resorts (*The Hindu*, 2006: 1). The resorts are, by and large, for the able-bodied and physically active. At present, there is no place for people who need ongoing assistance with feeding, dressing, toileting, or wound care.

Care Homes Limited consists of 98 cottages where residents can and do age in place. The cottages are designed to promote safety and convenience. Every cottage—whether it has two bedrooms, one bedroom, or just studio space—has skid-free flooring, glare-free surfaces, an instant alarm system, a telephone, a television, Internet connections, and an entertainment center (*The Hindu*, 2006: 3). There are also home-health aides, a nurse on the premises, and a

Figure 9.9. Women at this retirement resort can enjoy a mix of traditional and Western activities.

Figure 9.10. Residents enjoy Web surfing and other leisure activities at this new retirement community.

hospital within easy reach of the community. Cottages are available to people aged 50 and over who are able to afford the monthly rent.

An advocacy group called Senior Citizens in India explains that assisted living is the ideal solution for those senior citizens who "cannot take full responsibility but still want to be independent." The solution for such people is "specially designed homes for the elderly who have resources to afford not only homes but also nursing care. . . . [They are] equipped with 24-hour medical services, dining and recreational facilities, and ramps for wheelchairs" (Swami, 2005: 1).

The message has begun to catch on. Care Homes Limited built a prototype in the suburbs of Bangalore and is now constructing similar projects near Kochi and Calcutta (Swami, 2005: 2). A competitor known as Elders' Village is also branching beyond Bangalore and is building ALFs in Mumbai and Calcutta (*The Hindu*, 2006: 1).

THE FUTURE

The demand for new housing in India will continue to increase; it will not be long before assisted living and resort retirement become as commonplace as old-age homes. India is also making breakthroughs in product design that will enhance the lives of older people and places where they live. For example, India's *Harmony Magazine* has an ongoing section called "Products and Services," which showcases devices "that promise to make the lives of silvers (i. e., seniors) easier" (Mukherjee, 2005: 38). Not only do some of these devices make life easier for India's seniors, but they also make senior housing safer and more attractive.

ISOLATION AND ABANDONMENT OF THE POOR IN OLD AGE WILL BECOME AN EVEN GREATER PROBLEM

The continued growth of India's economy is one reason why older people will become isolated and abandoned. During the past two decades, India has been the beneficiary of economic growth that has resulted in job opportunities for men and—increasingly—for women. This will result in more families that cannot adequately care for their elderly relatives. A recent expose by India's Dignity Foundation offers the following real-life cases in which older people had been abandoned or abused:

- "I have a home but am not allowed to live there" laments a 67-year-old woman whose two daughters have evicted her.

- "I live alone but have a daughter problem," which has turned out to be the fact that the daughter is mentally ill and the mother is suffering from caregiver overload.
- "Married daughter's interference," which amounts to harassment by a daughter-in-law
- "I have four children and want to go to an old-age home." "No!" said the children. An 87-year-old man can no longer negotiate the stairs in his home, but his children will not let him move (Dignity Foundation, 2005: 1–4).

These four real-life cases call attention to the fact that old-age homes continue to have a place in Indian society: They are a place where older people can go when there is strife or isolation at home.

ATTITUDES TOWARD INDIA'S OLD-AGE HOMES WILL CONTINUE TO CHANGE

The Times of India reported growing interest in passing legislation to require families to take care of their aging family members, apparently in response to the growing number of real-life cases involving intergenerational strife or isolation (*Khaleej Times*, 2005: 1). One government official actually complains that "the younger generation is increasingly unwilling to look after parents and provide them with food, shelter, and emotional needs" and goes on to say that the advent of retirement homes across India is "diluting Indian family structure" (*Khaleej Times*, 2005: 1–2). Or as one commentator puts it, "changes in values, work styles, and in the social order have weakened traditional family- and community-based support systems for the aged and led to the growth of homes for the aged" (Sandesh India, 2005: 1). Although they may be perceived as diluting Indian family structure, India's old-age homes are often an important option for some older people and their families.

SENIOR HOUSING FOR INDIA'S ELITES WILL BECOME EVEN MORE OF A STATUS SYMBOL

The new senior housing satisfies a very different need in India. It is becoming a status symbol—a sign of wealth and power—for India's new elites. The new senior housing appeals to families that are both affluent and, increasingly, Western in their outlook. This means that they do not rely on the patrilocal family for care, as they once might have. Instead, they see assisted living and resort retirement as an extension of their elite lifestyle.

NOW THAT YOU'VE READ CHAPTER 9

KEY TERMS AND CONCEPTS

bagh
jhonpris
kothi
neolocal residence
old-age home
patrilocal residence
resort retirement community
saas
unprivate home
vanaprastha

QUESTIONS FOR STUDY AND DISCUSSION

1. By custom, where do most older people in India live?
2. Who typically ends up in India's old-age homes and why?
3. There is now a surge in construction of senior housing in India. What is the market for this new senior housing?
4. More Indian families are becoming nuclear instead of being extended, or joint, families. How will this impact the housing options of older people in India?
5. How does the design of old-age homes in India reflect cultural norms and values?
6. How are India's new retirement communities different from the traditional old-age homes?
7. Why has it taken so long for ALFs to be available in India?

HELPFUL WEBSITES

apnabangalore.com/html. (Old-age homes in Bangalore)
calcuttayellowpages.com/oldage.html (Old-age homes in Calcutta)
cp-pc.ca/english/india/family.html (Family Life in India—2001)
dignitylifestyle.org   (Dignity Lifestyle: Senior Citizens' Retreat for Active Living—2005)
dignityfoundation.com/reallifecases.php (Senior housing: real-life cases)
janakalyansevashram.com (Senior-citizen homes across India)
Kudumbam.com (Clasic Kudumbam Gated Retirement Community, 2006)

prasanthioldagehome.com (Prasanthi Old Age Welfare Home, 2005)
seniorindian.com/grandparenting.htm (Grandparenting)
seniorindian.com/old_age_homes.htm (Guidelines for establishing old-
    age homes)
seniorindian.com/seniorsandchildren.htm (Senior-children relationship)
siis-india.com/projectsadasukhi.html (Project Sada Sukhi Ashram)

NOTES

1. Chitra Banerjee Divakaruni, "Mrs. Duta Writes a Letter," *The Unknown
   Errors of Our Lives*. New York: Anchor Books, 8.
2. HSBC Bank, 2004: The Future of Retirement in a World of Rising Life
   Expectancies. HSBC surveyed 1000 people in each of the following nations
   and territories: Canada, USA, Japan, UK, France, Hong Kong, China,
   Brazil, Mexico, and India.
4. Liebig and Ramamurti estimate that prior to 1900 there were no more
   than 29 old-age homes in all of India. That number had increased to 300
   by 1990 but it is still an aberration for older people to live in India's old-
   age homes (Liebig and Ramamurti, 2006: 246–47; Liebig, 2003: 160).
5. For other examples of how culture impacts architecture and interior
   design, see Day and Cohen, 2000; Hadjiyanni, 2004; Gustafson, 2001; and
   Stafford, 2001.)

PART III
POLICY AND PROSPECTS

"*A power shift is under way, and a tough new business rule is emerging: Harness the new collaboration or perish. Those who fail to grasp this will find themselves ever more isolated—cut off from the networks that are sharing, adapting, and updating knowledge to create value.*"

—D. Tapscott and A. D. Williams, *Wikinomics*

10

Are We Ready for Aging?

OVERVIEW

The age wave was first identified in the United States in the 1970s, but it has since become a global phenomenon. People in nations as diverse as China, Brazil, Sweden, India, Japan, Israel, and the United States are living longer than ever before. And the world's gerontocracies are now addressing the issue of senior housing.

The form and function of the family is changing in all of the world's rapidly aging nations. Along with changes in the family, there are new patterns of migration that are breaking even close-knit families apart. It is no wonder that senior housing has become a major issue worldwide.

International comparisons show that the age wave has generated different architectural responses and experiments. Some of these have been well received, such as the *residencial* in Brazil. Others, like Japan's *nisetai jukatu*, have been social and architectural failures that paved the way for more successful forms of senior housing.

There was a time when most geriatric product design was being done in England or the United States. But in recent years, nations as diverse as Israel, Japan, and Sweden have also become geriatric-design centers.

Senior housing in the twenty-first century appears to be divided into housing for the upper class and housing for the masses. The housing available for the affluent aging is now converging. India's elite resort communities, for example, have more in common with the *residencial* in Brazil or premier senior housing in the United States than it does with housing for the masses in India. Nations such as Japan, Sweden, and China are building elite senior housing that offers Internet access, health spas, fitness centers, gourmet cuisine, and more. The world's elite senior housing is also starting to converge because developers in one nation are bringing successful formulas to senior housing in other nations. This has been the case in China, where elite senior housing has been built by developers from Hong Kong or Taiwan.

Senior housing for the masses continues to be vernacular. It is shaped by local architectural styles and norms. While there are waiting lists for openings in elite-senior housing, the senior housing for the masses in places like India, Japan, and Israel is a last resort.

The future will be more collaborative, as architects, designers, and gerontologists from all around the world share information online. The second generation of the Internet, known as Web 2.0, allows for mass collaboration through blogging, open-source software, and global outsourcing. Senior-home design in the United States already depends on collaboration among architects, designers, and gerontologists. Web 2.0 will make the collaboration even more dynamic and allow older people and their families to give input on senior-home design.

Senior housing will be to the twenty-first century what the age wave was to the twentieth (Dychtwald, 1990: 16). Starting around 1970, there was a growing awareness that millions of people were living longer. The age wave started as demographic shorthand for the rapid aging of the U.S. population. But by the end of the twentieth century, it was clear that *many* of the world's populations were aging rapidly (Bengston et al., 2003). Statistically speaking, a number of nations have become gerontocracies because the percentage of older people has grown so rapidly in a very short time. Seven of those gerontocracies—the United States, China, Japan, India, Sweden, Israel, and Brazil—have had to develop more senior-housing options to meet the needs of these aging populations.

HOUSING THE WORLD'S GERONTOCRACIES

The Japanese, for example, now call Japan *Choujukoku*, or "the Land of Longevity." Average life expectancy for Japanese women in 2002 was 85.23, the longest life expectancy in the world, and the average life expectancy for Japanese men in the same year was 78.32; more than 20,000 Japanese people are already aged 100-plus (*Trends in Japan*, 2003: 1).

Brazil is also a rapidly aging nation. The phrase for this in Portuguese is *Onda de Pessoas*, but *Onda de Pessoas* does not capture the impact of the age wave on this youth-obsessed culture. More to the point, Brazilian newspapers now cover the geroculture (Garcez-Leme et al., 2005: 2022) and promote the joys of life after 50. In response to the needs of the geroculture, Brazil has developed a form of senior housing known as the *residencial*. The *residencial* is more like a luxury hotel than a nursing home, and for the first time, a form of senior housing in Brazil offers older people a range of activities and cultural events. Brazil, like many of the world's rapidly aging nations, now has senior housing for actively aging people, along with the more traditional arrangements.

The Brazilian *residencial* would have been unthinkable even 20 years ago, when older people either lived with their families or lived in nursing homes called *clinicas geriatricas*. But the age wave has had implications for senior housing in Brazil and everywhere that the percentage of older people is increasing. This is because more people than ever before are living into their eighties or nineties, but they do not have the support or communities to care for them. Home design becomes even more of an issue when family systems weaken or disperse and when housing solutions that work in one aging culture are not well received in another.

There are two major ways in which the age wave has had an impact on senior housing around the world. First, it has weakened family structures worldwide, which means that older people must turn elsewhere for care. Secondly, it has prompted a variety of architectural responses and forms. Nations as diverse as Brazil, China, and India are developing their own forms of senior housing.

FAMILY CAREGIVING DECLINING

Family support for the elderly is weakening in the most rapidly aging nations, and many of the world's aging nations are experiencing changes or breakdowns in family structure. These breakdowns include a decline in fertility, higher divorce rates, an increase in the number of living grandparents, and the expectation that the state should assume more responsibility for the care of older people (Bengston et al., 2003: 2).

India's Changing Family Structure

The great irony of the twenty-first century is that families are becoming more nuclear and more dispersed at the very moment when family members are living longer (Bengston et al., 2003: 11). Senior housing worldwide has begun responding to these changes in family structure, sometimes with standardized forms of housing and sometimes with senior housing that is unique. For example, India has been experiencing a "brain drain," as younger people migrate in search of well-paying jobs. The Indian family structure has traditionally been based on norms of filial piety, which means that the oldest son, or one of the sons, looks after an aging parent. And until recently, it would have been unthinkable for "respectable" people in India to live in old-age homes; residents of old-age homes were pariahs and people without family. But because well-educated men are migrating—often abroad—parents are being left behind in India. Nursing homes and ALFs are becoming more common in India as a result of the migration. Rajaji is one of a small but growing number of senior residences for "respectable" people whose children have moved abroad (india9.com/RajajiEldersHome).

Sweden's Changing Family Structure

It is possible that the experience of older people in Sweden will become the prototype for aging worldwide. Sweden has a long history of independent aging. An estimated 40 percent of seniors in Sweden live independently and do so by choice. In fact, 70 percent of Swedish women over the age of 70 live on their own, and the remainder live mostly in adult communities around Sweden. Adult communities are cohousing that is reserved for people aged 40 and older (Wikipedia, 2005: 1). In Sweden, there is no expectation that the oldest son or daughter will care for an aging parent. Home design in Sweden reflects the norm that older people will either age in place or live with other adults. This is very different from Japan, where senior-home design is being shaped by the decline in filial piety.

Japan's Changing Family Structure

It was once the norm for older people in Japan to live with or near their children. Yet more Japanese people than ever before now live on their own in collaborative homes. The emerging model for senior housing in Japan is aging in place, with help from a combination of live caregivers, robotic helpers, and information technologies (Almekinders, 2005: 23). Japan is also exploring other forms of senior housing that are evidence of the massive changes in Japanese life. One of the most intriguing developments is based on the fact that Japan is a nation where people often work a lifetime for the same corporation. Some of Japan's largest corporations are now developing corporate retirement barracks as the final phase of lifetime employment (Wiejers-Hasegawa, 2003:1).

Israel's Aging Immigrants

Migration patterns are also shaping home design in an aging world. Israel, like India, for example, has had to develop new forms of senior housing because traditional caregiving has been disrupted by migration. Israel has developed new forms of senior housing, but for the opposite reason that India had to: vast numbers of older people have immigrated to the Holy Land. Israel attracts older people who sometimes migrate to the Holy Land but leave their families behind. This is especially true of older Jewish people from the former Soviet Union. In response to this migration, Israel has established sheltered-housing settlements where aging immigrants, often from the same country now live together in Israel. There are currently 46 sheltered-housing settlements, containing 4,750 apartments, for elderly immigrants, and other "supportive communities" for elderly immigrants in most Israeli cities (Brodsky and Morginstin, 1999: 78–79).

The decline of filial piety, along with global migration, makes traditional housing arrangements difficult, if not impossible. Architects and designers are responding with diverse and divergent housing forms. There is no "one size fits all" in a world where family support is changing so rapidly.

GREATER VARIETY OF HOUSING SOLUTIONS IN AN AGING WORLD

The world's most rapidly aging nations are beginning to develop new forms of senior housing in response to the need caused by the breakdown of family structure and the change in migration patterns. Some of these housing developments are very Western in form and function, but others are not.

China's Senior Housing Boom

China has turned to the West for ideas, but it has built senior housing in ways that incorporate Chinese norms and values. There has been an impressive surge in the construction of Western-style nursing homes and ALFs. In fact, an estimated 18 percent of older people in China now live in senior housing. Chinese economists estimate that the senior housing industry is experiencing a growth rate of 15 percent per year (Daniels, 2004: 1), and a recent national survey finds that 20 percent of elderly Chinese people would prefer to live in senior housing if they could afford to (*Liaoning Daily*, 31 August 2004: 1). The newest development in China's senior-housing market is the coming of nursing-home chains within and across China's largest cities (Lai-kwok, 2004: 1; *Shanghai Daily*, 18 October 2004).

But senior housing in China also pivots on Chinese form and function (Xu, 2005: 1). Chinese nursing homes and ALFs are often sited and designed to have good *feng shui*. For some senior-housing developments in China, the design may be Western, but the lighting, the colors, and the floor plan are Chinese.

Japanese Robotics and Collaborative Housing

Japan is experimenting with information technology and robotics to build collaborative homes with a mix of human, robotic, and electronic care. For example, there will be visits from not only home-health workers but also robotic caregivers and electronic sensors that relay information (such as data on blood pressure, body temperature, and medication regimens) to a nurses' station or physician's office. The Japanese have been architecturally experimental. For example, the *nisetai jukatu*, a Japanese version of the mother-daughter house, was a breakthrough in senior housing. But it was a relatively brief experiment: The *nisetai jukatu* was only marketed in Japan for about 10 years, and it was then superseded by other, more relevant forms of senior housing. But the *nisetai jukatu* gave the Japanese a new architectural model, or paradigm (Brown, 2003: 63). It was a transitional form of housing that liberated sons or daughters from housing elders in their homes. For the first time, there were alternatives. In response to the *nisetai jukatu*, more elderly people in Japan began to voice their preferences; it became clear that they preferred to age independently. As a result, the Japanese began constructing collaborative homes where older people could age in place with the help of home-health aides, networked appliances, and robotic helpers.

Israel's Sheltered Settlements and NORCs

Israel's sheltered-housing settlements are the response to migration patterns. Apart from building for elderly immigrants, Israel has had to deal with the increased longevity of its original settlers. Israel has perhaps the largest number of NORCs of any postindustrial society. Seventy-five of Israel's 267 kibbutzim have become NORCs (Miles, 2005: 3) because the original settlers and their families have all aged in place. Architecturally, this has meant that these kibbutzim have had to retrofit homes and have had to construct nursing homes and, in some cases, dementia units for aging settlers.

Places to Age "Youthfully" in Brazil

Senior housing in Japan and Israel reflect social and demographic trends that are reshaping the postindustrial world: the breakdown of extended-family systems and migration in search of white-collar careers. In contrast, senior housing in Brazil only became an issue when Brazilian cities began to modernize—and not because Brazilian family structure has changed so very much. Architect and urbanist Sandra Perito (2005: 2) traces the development of senior housing to *verticalizacao*—the rise of high-rise apartments—in Brazil's largest cities. During the 1970s, Brazil began an ambitious program of high-rise construction. The high-rise apartments that came to dominate Rio de Janeiro, São Paulo, and Curitiba had fewer bedrooms. The new apartments encouraged conjugal families and created a demand for more senior housing. The original nursing homes were almost indistinguishable from their counterparts in the United States, Israel, or Japan. But Brazil has also responded to the *Onda de Pessoas*, or age wave, with *residencials*, which are more like hotels than senior-housing complexes, but they are far more expensive.

The expense of aging gracefully and youthfully in a Brazilian *residencial* calls attention to perhaps the most troubling aspect of home design in an aging world. Home design for people who are aging but poor is basic and very traditional at best. And there is great divergence in senior housing for the world's poor aging populations. For example, elderly people in India who are lower-caste can

Figure 10.1. Top of the line in China: Cheerful Court offers the same amenities as upscale retirement communities in the United States.

only expect dormitory-type housing and outdoor plumbing (Liebig: 2003: 172). Senior housing for lower-caste people and other pariahs in India has changed very little over the years. Medical capacity in most Chinese nursing homes is basic at best (Xinhua General News Service, 2004: 1). And in Brazil, the elderly in the most poverty-stricken towns and villages must still make due with a hammock strung between two trees (Camargo, 2004: 6).

In contrast, senior housing for the wealthy all over the world is becoming standardized (Rosenfeld, Chapman, and McCulough, 2007: 3). For example, Cheerful Court, in Beijing, will feature "an indoor swimming pool, [a] Jacuzzi, [a] gymnasium, [a] library, [a] grooming room, [a] hair salon and more" (Lee, 2003: 1) (Figure 10.1). And India's aging elites are moving to gated communities and luxury retirement resorts complete with luxury spas and Internet access (Sharma, 2005: 1). These have more in common with Brazilian *residencials*, Swedish adult communities, or top-of-the-line housing in the United States than they do with India's local old-age homes.

SENIOR-HOME DESIGN: THE FUTURE IS GLOBAL

Along with the aging of nations around the world, there has been a change in how senior housing is created and delivered. Perhaps the most significant change of all is how innovative the designs are. Senior housing is no longer a clone of what has developed in the Western world. Other rapidly aging nations are developing their own designs and architectural forms. There are lessons to be learned from how these nations are housing their aging populations. A look at Israel, Sweden, India, China, Brazil, and Japan reveals that they are experimenting with a variety of architectural forms and product designs. In addition to architectural differences, there are new products being designed in other nations, and innovative ways of keeping older people in their homes are being developed. All three of these factors—architectural innovation, creative product design, and new systems of delivery services to the elderly—are creating diversity and vitality in senior-home design.

INNOVATIONS IN ARCHITECTURE AND INTERIOR DESIGN

Sweden, for example, has bypassed the nursing home in favor of the *servicehus*, where residents live in apartments furnished with their own possessions. The

Figure 10.2. IT makes it possible for people to age in place in this apartment building in Sweden instead of moving to a nursing home.

servicehus deliberately avoids the standardization and institutional feel of nursing homes. Instead, residents of the *servicehus* are encouraged to live as independently as they are able to. They may have moved to a *servicehus* when they are no longer able to live independently, but this does not mean they give up their independence. There is a common dining room where residents eat lunch together, but they prepare breakfast and dinner in their own flats, often with the help of family members. The Swedish government is also developing new forms of housing for people with Alzheimer's disease and is now experimenting with smart homes where people with Alzheimer's can live independently, with the help of IT that enables a continuum of care within apartment buildings (Lundberg, et al, 2005: 1) (Figure 10.2). Residents move into less-wired apartments when they are independent, but relocate to more-wired apartments as they lose their ability to live independently (Sandstrom, 2006: 20).

Brazil and Japan have also developed indigenous forms of senior housing. The *residencial* offers a cross between a hotel and a high-rise apartment and is different from senior housing in the West. Brazil is also in the forefront of universal design and is building prototypes in Rio de Janeiro, São Paulo, and Curitiba (Brasileira, 2006:1-7). And Japan is exploring intergenerational and multigenerational housing, which are departures from Western models.

PRODUCT DESIGN

Even if they are not innovative architecturally, many of the world's rapidly aging nations are developing unique products that enhance the senior-housing experience. No single nation has a monopoly on product design. Nations as diverse as Israel, India, and Japan are marketing products designed for older people and their caregivers.

Sweden's Assistive Products

For example, Sweden has developed assistive products that are beginning to receive attention worldwide. Photo Messenger, for example, is a telephone that displays photographs of a user's significant others when their phone numbers are dialed. Photo Messenger allows cognitively impaired people to make phone calls without having to remember or dial telephone numbers. They merely touch the photo image on the directory, and the number is automatically dialed. When phoning a person on the directory, his or her photo lights up, and it blinks when that person makes an incoming phone call. Photo Messenger allows people with Alzheimer's disease to continue doing something familiar (i.e., talking on the telephone) even though they may have forgotten the relevant phone numbers or other details about the person they are phoning.

Israel's Assistive Technologies

Israel is also developing assistive technologies and products that are being marketed worldwide. GeronTech, an Israeli company, is at the forefront of assistive-technology development. GeronTech's mission is to develop products that help older people to live independently and age in place. This includes body-weight support systems that help with gait rehabilitation. In addition to developing assistive technologies for physical well-being, GeronTech has also pioneered the CogniFit series of software programs that are designed to help elderly people maintain their cognitive abilities (Figure 10.3). Of more interest to architects and design professionals is the Israeli-made Homecare Bed (yad-sarah.org, 2006: 8—Homecare Bed). The Homecare Bed operates like hospital furniture, but it has the appearance of bedroom furniture.

Japanese Robotics and Networked Appliances

The assistive technologies coming out of Israel help today's seniors to age in place, but the robotics coming out of Japan will be the assistive technologies of the future (Figure 10.4). Japan has turned to robotics in an effort to care for an increasingly aging population. Japanese citizens now enjoy the longest life expectancy in the world (*Trends in Japan*, 2003: 1). But there is a shortage of caregivers, and the Japanese have turned increasingly to robots and robotics to meet the need for caregivers. In fact, Mitsubishi Heavy Industries has developed a robot called "Wakamaru, whose purpose is to let me help the senior citizen" (Pacific Research Consulting, Inc., 2003:1). Wakamaru's caregiving abilities include reminders to take medications, online reports to family members, and sharing of digital photos taken inside the home using a camera that is built into this robotic caregiver (MSNBC, 2005: 1).

Figure 10.3. CogniFit is at the forefront of assistive technology to help older people age in place.

Japan is also linking networked appliances and home-based telecommunications systems to create interactive environments. The goal is to help people regulate their home environments and to allow appliances in the home to regulate one another (Toshiba, 2006: 1; *Japan Information Network*, 2002: 1). Voice-activated systems, for example, are especially helpful to older people whose mobility may be limited. A person can say, "I'm going to the kitchen," and lights in the hall leading to the kitchen "will be switched on" (*Japan Information Network*, 2002: 1). And there are now telecommunications systems coming out of Japan that make appliances self-regulating, as when the refrigerator can send an e-mail to the grocery store and order more milk or orange juice when the supply of these runs low (*Japan Information Network*, 2002: 1). Toshiba is trying to make self-regulating appliances a feature in senior housing. If this comes to pass, it will be possible for older people to live in homes where appliances automatically notify the repair company if they break down and can wirelessly monitor one another. If Japan is developing interactive appliances, India is nurturing the interactive capabilities of older people.

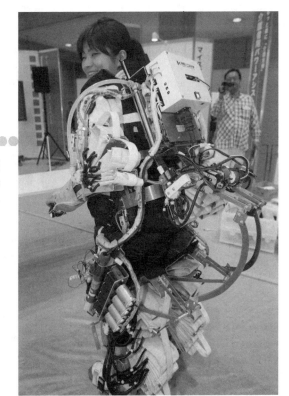

Figure 10.4. Japan has turned to robotics to help care for its aging population.

India: Blogging About Gadgets

India's *Harmony Magazine* is very similar to the AARP's MODERN MATURITY and encourages older people to develop online caring communities. *Harmony Magazine* is of interest here because it has a column that regularly focuses on product design and encourages readers to acquaint themselves with new gadgets that can make life easier for older people. A recent issue of *Harmony Magazine* featured new gadgets and offered readers facts on how the gadgets worked, how much they cost, and where to get additional information (Sharma, 2006: 70–71). Although directed at older audiences, *Harmony Magazine*'s review of new gadgets also refers readers to blogs and home pages where there is additional information. GadgetGuru .com is an increasingly popular link for older people who want to keep abreast of gadgets and other support systems coming out of India. In addition to promoting new gadgets and support systems, websites like Gadget-Guru.com become collaborative by giving older people opportunities to input on the development and distribution of especially useful gadgets (Tapscott et al, 2006: 11).

SERVICE DELIVERY

One of the great insights from looking at senior housing worldwide is that nations have developed other ways of maintaining older people in their homes. After all, older people eventually need social support to live independently, even in the best-designed homes.

Home-Health Workers

Sweden, more than any other nation, has made home-health workers available to older people. Many of Sweden's home-health workers are municipal employees who are paid by the city or state to make home visits. An estimated 20 percent of Sweden's elderly people received more than 50 hours of intensive home-health care per month from municipal caregivers (Socialstyrelsen, 2005: 3). In addition to the municipal workers (who visit at no charge), there is a growing number of for-profit providers and producers of care. In Sweden today, an older person can create a community of care that includes municipal caregivers, private companies, cooperative associations, and even some of Sweden's largest insurance companies. Older people are able to age in place more easily because they can create the home-care systems that they need. The Swedish approach has been to weave together a variety of caregivers. In Japan, the mix is more likely to include people, robots, and technologies.

Support Services: Taxis, Mobile Vans, and Other Transport

Japan recently revised its nursing-care insurance law to emphasize support and maintenance of older people in their homes (Web-Japan, 15 July 2005: 2). In addition to home-health aides, Japan now reimburses taxi companies for driving older people to hospitals and doctors' offices (Web-Japan, 18 August 1997: 2) and is turning to robotic helpers and telemedicine to link older people with health-care providers.

Emergency Home Repair

Israel has devised yet a third way to help older people age in place. Israel sponsors a number of organizations that send volunteers to the homes of elderly people in need of assistance. When elderly people need emergency home repairs—including electrical and plumbing repairs—they can phone volunteer organizations and receive assistance. They can also phone for help if they need to repair or replace the locks on their doors. Yad Sarah, the largest of Israel's volunteer organizations, actually has a fleet of mobile vans that transport volunteer electricians, locksmiths, plumbers, and tradesmen to the apartments of homebound elderly people. They do so either free of charge or for a nominal fee.

There is a similar development in Japan, where a mobile bathing service now literally brings a bath unit to the homes of disabled people. The van includes a system that features a specially made wheelchair and bath unit into which "the wheelchair can be slipped." The van was developed in response to complaints that caregivers hurt themselves while assisting disabled people in or out of the bath. The van is especially welcome in a nation where bathing has social and ritual significance (E-Medica Corporation, 2006: 1). And in this case, it is another way of including older and disabled people in socially significant activities. As the world's population ages, it will become increasingly important to think about home design in more gerontological ways.

LESSONS TO BE LEARNED FROM THE WORLD'S GERONTOCRACIES

The lesson to be learned from Sweden, Israel, and Japan is that the best-designed homes are not only livable but also they are *accessible*. Aging in place often requires the help, advice, support, and encouragement of others. Global comparisons show how different these supports can be. Visiting nurses and home-health workers are the most familiar providers. But other nations are making home more livable by calling in locksmiths, plumbers, cabdrivers, and even robotic helpers when they are needed. Israel's volunteer program in particular shows the value of listening to older people and giving them what they need. Architects and interior designers are also beginning to listen. Humanistic design is an approach to senior housing that builds on "the input of older adults and family members" (Marsden, 2005: 29).

HUMANISTIC DESIGN: ACTIVE LISTENING GOES GLOBAL

Humanistic design encourages architects and designers to incorporate the realities of aging, as articulated by older people. This requires a process of active listening in which architects and designers hear and then process comments by older people. When asked about home design, older people explain what they expect or need from senior housing. Professionals only begin the design process after considering what older people and their families have to say.

Making things nice, as Ralph Caplan notes, is not the same as making them right (2005: 123). The goal of humanistic design is to strike the ideal balance between nice and right by revealing the needs and wants of older people. This has also been called "user-centered design" (Fisk et al., 2004: 34–37) because it brings geriatrics and family dynamics into the creative process.

USER-CENTERED DESIGN IN THE UNITED STATES

The goal of user-centered design is to bring the user (along with the user's tasks and goals) into the center of the design effort (Quesenbery, 2004: 6). Active listening reminds architects and designers, for example, that arthritic people may not be able to turn doorknobs or handles and that aging couples may want to sleep in separate bedrooms. Input from older people is vitally important background information that gets factored into the architecture and interior design of a building (Shulman, 2001:2).

Active listening can be done on a project-by-project basis, but it is also a technique with national and global implications. John Marsden has developed a "collaborative" model that integrates the viewpoints of researchers, designers, and consumers (Masden, 2005:31). Marsden's approach includes active listening as older people and their families react to pictures of assisted-living facilities. He asked more than 500 respondents to look at images of the interiors and exteriors of ALFs and compiled their responses. Marsden's research shows that other people and their families do not necessarily perceive environments the same way that architects, designers, or gerontologists do. Marsden's humanistic approach to design would have architects and designers be more mindful of how older people and their families perceived assisted-living facilities. Using this approach would create better housing cues and caring cues. It brings what Marsden (1005: 103) calls "human scale" to the construction and design of assisted-living facilities.

USER-CENTERED DESIGN GOES GLOBAL

User-centered design is also finding a place in the design and construction of senior housing outside the United States, in some of the world's most rapidly aging nations. Active listening may still be in its infancy in places like Brazil and Japan, but it is already making an impact on senior housing in those nations.

Brazil

Humanistic design has come to São Paulo, where elderly people now have a voice in the creation of senior housing. The Permanent Commission on Accessibility (CPA) has actively solicited input from disabled and elderly people in lower-income neighborhoods of this Brazilian city. CPA is responsible for constructing senior housing in lower-income neighborhoods and is committed to humanistic design, so the organization gets input from the poor and powerless before authorizing the construction of senior housing in their neighborhoods (Medieros, 2004: 1).

Japan

The Japanese housing industry launched an unsuccessful form of housing called *nisetai jukatu*. The experiment was declared a failure in less than 10 years (Brown, 2003: 60) and was abandoned in favor of senior housing. The failure of *nisetai jukatu* speaks to the need for humanistic design. *Nisetai jukatu* was created without listening to older people or their families. It was created by Japanese developers who were nostalgic for a social structure and living arrangement that had already become obsolete in Japan: the multigenerational household. Japanese real-estate developers had assumed that there would be widespread demand for mother-daughter houses where elders could live with their children or grandchildren. *Nisetai jukatu* was developed and marketed without enough input from older people or their families. As senior housing, it proved to be a failure. Developers had not counted on the fact that most of Japan's elders now wanted to live near but not with their children. *Nisetai jukatu* never had robust sales, and the few that did sell created family discord. A new and different form of senior housing emerged when Japanese developers finally sat down with older people and actively listened to their housing needs.

Instead of wanting multigenerational homes, Japanese elders said they wanted retirement communities and senior housing (Brown, 2003: 68). The *nisetai jukatu* was abandoned in favor of housing that allowed older people to age in place near their friends and neighbors. This is what the seniors had wanted all along.

Sweden

Sweden has a tradition of humanistic design. Humanistic design is consistent with the tolerant social attitudes of Sweden. Sweden, more than any other nation, is inclusive and responsive to the needs of older people because older people are valued members of society in Sweden. Older people often want to live independently, and they are generally content with their housing situation. Only 1 percent of Sweden's elders complained of having unmet housing needs, as compared with 30 percent of older people in the United States (Peck, 2006: 1). In 1998, Sweden instituted a policy of care at home whereby older people would be entitled "to help of high quality" (Ministry of Health and Social Affairs, 2005: 1). Part of the policy includes having architects and designers listen to what older people say they want and need. Humanistic design was written into Swedish social policy.

As a result, senior housing in Sweden has begun to reflect the changing needs of older people in this nation. For example, focus groups revealed that many older people are working or volunteering outside the home. In response, designers have added home and away programs to monitor the use of water, electricity, and water. The away programs allow for remote control of gas, water, and electricity inside the home. This is a realistic response to new roles and relationships that take older people away from home for long periods of time (Sandstrom, 2005: 19), but it would have gone undetected if not for focus groups with older people.

GLOBAL PATTERNS: SENIOR HOUSING FOR THE RICH AND FOR THE POOR

Senior housing is now a global issue. As the twenty-first century unfolds, there is every reason to believe that there will be two global patterns: one for the world's affluent aging populations and another for those older people living in poverty. Senior housing for the wealthy is becoming a status symbol. This is especially striking in Brazil, Japan, and India, where wealthy families put their names on waiting lists for openings in elite homes such as Green Tokyo in Japan or Santa Catarina in São Paulo, Brazil.

HOME DESIGN FOR ELITES

There is already evidence of convergence in the architecture and design of senior housing for affluent older people (Rosenfeld, Chapman, and McCulough, 2007: 13). Housing for elites around the world is becoming remarkably similar. India's luxury retirement resorts—places like Ashiana Village and Classic

Figure 10.5. Clasic Kudumbam provides a variety of amenities for affluent older people.

Kudumbam—provide amenities that are very similar to those available in premier communities throughout the United States. These include spa facilities, Internet access, gourmet meals, and adult education (Figure 10.5).

Of course there are cultural differences. The cuisine at an elite Indian establishment will reflect Hindu dietary norms, which will be different from a kosher kitchen at an elite community in Israel or the dining room at a Sunrise or Del Webb community in the United States. Still, the similarities across cultures are striking. Elite communities in Japan, for example, have vans available for transporting residents to doctors' appointments, which is not very different from transport arrangements at elite communities in Brazil, India, and the United States.

Convergence is also a result of corporate growth, as companies that build upscale senior housing in one nation begin expanding into other nations. This has been especially true in China, where most of the upscale senior housing is being built by foreign investors, often from Taiwan and Hong Kong, but increasingly from European nations (Wu, 2004: 1; www.building.com.hk, 1999). Senior housing for the world's wealthy may be converging, but the architecture and design of senior housing for lower-income people continues to be vernacular.

HOME DESIGN FOR THE MASSES

Housing for the poor in nations like India or China has barely changed, even as housing for the wealthy becomes more sophisticated. In India, for example, the poor continue to live in old-age homes where they sleep in dormitories and often use outdoor privies (Liebig, 2003: 160) (Figure 10.6). Even today there are accounts of poor people in rural areas of Brazil who still sleep in hammocks in the *barraca* (Camargo, 2004: 12). Also, accounts of senior housing in Japan, while still preliminary, suggest that group homes in rural areas are indistinguishable from local, vernacular buildings, while group homes in Japanese cities are more international in their design and construction (Yokohama, 2005: 11).

The exceptions are Sweden and Israel, where housing is state-subsidized and the standard of living for older people is perhaps the highest in the world. Home design for older people in China, Japan, Brazil, India, and the United States continues to reflect the differences between the poor and the wealthy.

THE UNITED STATES: COMMUNITY BUILDING AND EDENIZING

It is no exaggeration to say that senior housing worldwide is shaped by home design in the United States. American designers are finding global markets for products designed for older people and their homes; some of the largest

Figure 10.6. These lower-income women sleep in a dormitory in this Indian old-age home.

real-estate developers in the United States, including groups such as Sunrise and Del Webb, are even beginning to develop senior housing abroad.

THE DESIRE TO AGE IN PLACE

A recent AARP survey finds that 83 percent of people over the age of 60 want to stay in their homes (NAIPC.org/guide to aging in place). Preliminary data from other cultures indicate that this is universal. The chapters in Part II of this book indicate that older people in nations as diverse as Japan, Sweden, Israel, Brazil, and China want to live independently for as long as they can. The one exception is India, where there is still popular support for the traditional pattern of moving into the home of a married son or daughter.

Given the universal desire to age in place, it is worth mentioning that the United States has become a worldwide source of information on home modification. The AARP now makes such information available online and in print, and there is no shortage of material on do-it-yourself repair.

Older people wishing for more professional input can also turn to the United States. There are currently two professional approaches to home modification that are thriving in the United States. One of them is gerontologic design, which is grounded in a medical model of aging and provides medical intervention: modification for kitchens or bathrooms in response to health problems. The other approach is more gerontological and aims for universal design. Universal design is a more inclusive design paradigm that works for people of all ages. Brazilian architects have already picked up on the universal design paradigm, and the very same approach is making headway in Israel and Japan.

Perhaps the most interesting development in the United States is the beginnings of home design for the baby-boom generation, who are now approaching their retirement years. Other nations, especially Sweden, China, and Japan, are also dealing with the aging of their own baby-boom contemporaries. American designers are already anticipating the housing needs of Boomers in retirement: smaller "castles" with spaces for entertainment, home offices, and physical fitness. These innovations will impact the design and development of real estate for aging boomers in these other cultures.

QUESTING FOR COMMUNITY

Perhaps the most significant change in senior home design to come out of the United States is the cohousing movement. It is already common for older people to move to retirement communities. Ever since the 1960s, communities like Sun City have been magnets for older retirees. But in recent years, there has been a movement toward senior cohousing that is different from retirement communities both in form and function. Senior cohousing refers to intentional communities that older people plan and sometimes develop on their own. Senior cohousing is inclusive; it gives older people the opportunity to select their friends and neighbors and build a community where they can enact a common vision (Figure 10.7). This vision can be spiritual, environmental, political, or social—as in the case of senior cohousing communities that create welcoming places for friends who have known one another for a lifetime.

The United States is also leading the way in the creation of service delivery to NORCs. Many U.S. suburbs and, increasingly, urban neighborhoods are now aging in place. Residents in NORCs now need services—medical, social, and psychological—that they did not need when they first moved to the community. NORCs are developing strategies for home repair and renovation that will also become more relevant worldwide in years to come.

LONG-TERM CARE: MORE HOMELIKE

There has been a paradigm shift in the design of nursing homes and long-term-care facilities in the United States that is also having an impact worldwide

Figure 10.7. The Elder Co-housing Network helps place older people in elder cohousing communities throughout the United States.

(Schwarz, 1996: 36). The medical model is losing influence. Architects and designers are now working in a new and different paradigm. The new paradigm emphasizes homelike environments rather than hospital-like ones. There is also a movement within senior housing to make long-term-care facilities part of the neighborhoods or communities in which they are situated. Traditionally, nursing homes and ALFs have been "in" but not "of" the community. The new social movement promises to make long-term care a more integral part of the local community. Inspired by the design of long-term care in Holland, this movement is finding greater acceptance in other rapidly aging nations as well. Win Bakker, for example, describes how the Dutch have incorporated assisted-living facilities into local communities: "[The facility] looks like a normal contemporary apartment building, not an institution . . . tenants do their own housekeeping independently . . . common areas are located on the ground floor . . . they [have] a grand café [and] Internet café. . . . The services in this building are also expressly used by the neighborhood inhabitants" (Bakker, 2006:2). Following Bakker, it is possible to do more than make an institution more "homelike." It is also possible to make it part of the surrounding community.

WEB 2.0: A COLLABORATIVE WORLD

Don Tapscott and Anthony D. Williams insist that the Internet has already created a more collaborative world, where people will work together to create "information-based" products and services. They locate this new, collaborative world in "Web 2.0, known also as 'the hypernet'" (Tapscott and Williams, 2006: 19) because it allows for more "peering" and "peer-production communities" (Tapscott and Williams, 2006: 23).

THE COMING OF A COLLABORATIVE CULTURE

The twentieth century, says Jeremy Rifkin, was the Age of Access when people first became aware of the Internet and how it could broaden their social networks (2000: 30-45). The twenty-first century will be the Age of Participation, in which new Internet platforms, known as Web 2.0, will allow for mass collaboration. This will be possible because collaborative infrastructures—the Internet, open-source software, and global outsourcing platforms—will give people opportunities to create and expand their knowledge in new and dynamic ways (Tapscott and Williams, 2006: 17).

The prototype, and most familiar example of mass collaboration, is *Wikipedia*, the peer-produced online encyclopedia. *Wikipedia*, which expands daily, is proof of what can come from peer production, when "masses of people or firms collaborate openly to drive innovation and growth" (Tapscott and Williams, 2006: 11). *Wikinomics*, the influential book by Tapscott and Williams, introduces readers to the coming of collaboration in a variety of fields—everything from banking and electronics to chemical engineering. Conspicuously absent from *Wikinomics* is any discussion of mass collaboration in the design disciplines. But Whitney Quesenbery indicates that mass collaboration is also impacting architecture and interior design.

Quesenbery, writing two years earlier than Tapscott and Williams, noted the beginnings of a "convergence effect" because the Internet is impacting the design process and how the design disciplines interface with one another (Quesenbery, 2004: 8). Disciplines that once worked separately, with little or no overlap, are now able to use the Web as a platform to create better, more collaborative products. Following Quesenbery, the new Web is about participating in the design process and not about passively receiving a design after it has been created. Web 2.0 allows for mass collaboration for user-centered design; designers from a variety of disciplines can react to what older people say they need or want.

The design of senior housing is already a collaborative culture in the sense that it builds on architecture, interior design, and gerontology (Masden, 2005:

29-47; Tapscott and Williams, 2006: 45). The growing influence of humanistic design includes older people and their families in the collaborative culture. Web 2.0, with its blog sites and open-source software, is providing new cyber-formats for collaboration. Professionals and laypeople can add value and watch designs become more senior-friendly. There are already signs that some older people are now using the Web to share information and caregiving advice. They "look in" on one another virtually, using e-mail and chat rooms (Belkin, 2006: 91).

THE COLLABORATIVE CULTURE GOES GLOBAL

The collaborative culture will eventually go global. Ideas for senior housing in countries as diverse as Japan, Brazil, India, and the United States will come from professionals and older people around the world. Web 2.0 already provides global outsourcing platforms. In the not-too-distant future, the design and construction of housing in one part of the world will be the result of collaborative efforts worldwide.

THE FUTURE

The nations of the world are experiencing an age wave, which is prompting the design and construction of senior housing worldwide. At this point in time, the design of senior housing for wealthy people is converging: From India to Brazil, luxury housing is becoming strikingly similar. In the meantime, senior housing for the masses—older people who are poor, powerless, and isolated—continues to be vernacular. In other words, it is dramatically different, albeit substandard, around the world.

HUMANISTIC DESIGN

One of the great changes in senior housing is the growing popularity of humanistic design. This involves getting input from older people and their families and modifying architecture and interior designs accordingly. Nations as disparate as Israel, Brazil, and the United States are seeking input from older people and their families at preliminary stages of the design process.

GLOBALIZATION

Globalization means that nations all across the world are developing products and new systems for delivering services, home care, and information to the elderly. The result is collaborative design in which ideas about products, technologies, and delivery systems are shared across national boundaries.

THE IMPACT OF WEB 2.0

The future will see even more such collaboration as Web 2.0 empowers design professionals, older people, and service providers to share ideas and build on mutual interests to create more relevant and workable senior housing.

NOW THAT YOU'VE READ CHAPTER 10

KEY TERMS AND CONCEPTS

accessible
adaptable
adult communities
age wave
collaborative homes
corporate retirement barracks
Edenizing
filial piety
geroculture
gerontocracy
humanistic design
residencial (Portuguese for "luxury retirement hotel")
servicehus (Swedish for "nursing home")
sheltered-housing settlements
verticalizacao (Portuguese for "verticalization" or high-rise apartment life)

QUESTIONS FOR STUDY AND DISCUSSION

1. Why is luxury housing for seniors becoming so similar worldwide, and why is housing for poor people still so vernacular and local?
2. What are some non-Western architectural responses to the age wave, and how are these different from the nursing homes and ALFs being built in the United States?
3. Why would it be difficult to introduce Sweden's *servicehus* in the United States?
4. What is the Eden Alternative, and how has it revolutionized nursing-home design in the United States?

5. How is Web 2.0 creating mass collaboration among designers, gerontologists, and older people?
6. How do blogging, open-source software, and global outsourcing platforms create new approaches to senior-home design?

HELPFUL WEBSITES

building.com.hk
NAIPC.org (National Aging in Place Council)

Appendix
Learning from Architects and Designers

OVERVIEW: FROM ACCESSIBLE HOMES
TO MORE LIVABLE COMMUNITIES

The next step for elder housing will be the merger of universal design and urban planning. We will see more accessible homes in more livable communities. In fact, architect and social visionary Witold Rybczynski makes precisely this point in *The Last Harvest: How a Cornfield Became New Daleville* (2007: 279). New Daleville, Pennsylvania, was still being developed at the time Rybczynski wrote about it. Yet even in its infancy, the community provided spaces where people could connect with one another. In addition to universally designed homes, they had opportunities to interact on front porches, at local parks, and in swimming pools. Says Rybczynski:

> Invisible bonds of community are already beginning to form. . . . People are on their porches, and [they] start talking. How much of this activity is encouraged by the proximity of the houses and the presence of front porches is difficult to say, but it's hard not to believe that people are affected by their environment. Put them in a village, and they begin to behave like villagers (Rubczyaski, 2007: 279).

The stories in this appendix represent the diversity and synergy of home design for the elderly. The contributors are architects (and one gerontologist) whose work embodies this diverse field. As in other areas of architecture and design, they bring the diversity of age, gender, and culture to the design of senior housing.

The contributors range in age from an 82-year-old man to a woman in her early twenties. They are an international group who hail from Sweden, Japan, Brazil, and the United States, among other places. One of the contributors is now semi-retired; a few of them are young people who are just entering the design field.

The respect for older people and their social worlds is palpable in all of their work. Douglas and Ellen Gallow—an architect and a gerontologist—describe aging-friendly improvements to a vacation home. They redesigned the home with the hope that family members would not have to "surrender certain experiences or opportunities" as they get older.

The same is true for Hanson's work in Sweden, the work of Studio 16 in Japan, and Marianne Cusato's flexible design for the award-winning Katrina Cottages. These are designs for homes and communities that maximize experiences and opportunities for occupants as they get older.

The material in this appendix reflects new and important shifts in the design of senior housing. There is a growing emphasis on maintaining connection to community and to the outdoors. There is also much interest in homes that are both affordable and accessible.

MAINTAINING CONNECTION TO THE OUTDOORS

Douglas and Ellen Gallow renovated a vacation house that now enables occupants of all ages to enjoy the outdoors. Studio 16 in Japan revitalized neglected city parks in Hiroshima and transformed the park space at the same time as offering seniors a living area in the city. Windows have been designed so that the outdoors can be viewed, even when it is no longer possible to go for walks in the woods. Hanson has created a similar relationship to the outdoors, but in a nursing-home setting. Hanson's design for a senior apartment complex has indoor glassy spaces that function in much the same way as the windows in the single-family home designed by Gallow and Gallow. The goal is the same in both designs: to give elderly people more access to the outdoors—even if the access is only visual.

AFFORDABLE HOUSING

Marianne Cusato has designed attractive and affordable alternatives to HUD trailers. Her award-winning Katrina Cottages are designed to be affordable. They have become part of the landscape along the Gulf Coast that was ravaged by Hurricane Katrina.

Cusato also sees them as an increasingly popular option for older people and their caregivers because they are so affordable. Hanson has also designed housing with older people and their fixed incomes in mind.

ACCESSIBLE HOUSING

All of the designs featured in this appendix are accessible. However, Brazilian architect Sandra Perito has designed a universal home that is especially attractive as well as safe and accessible for people of all ages. Perito's houses have kitchens, bathrooms, and bedrooms that accommodate people of all ages and those with disabilities. Building on the principle of universal design, three senior projects are included here from students in the interior design department at Parsons The New School for Design, and their plans for a universally designed dream home.

THE QUEST FOR COMMUNITY

Perhaps the most significant new trend in senior housing is the quest for community. More senior housing is being designed to help people remain connected to friends and neighbors. The Katrina Cottages, for example, can be built in clusters that create close-knit neighborhoods. The cottages are raised and have porches, which allow people to look out on their neighborhoods and socialize with friends and passersby.

In addition to Cusato's cottages, Allan Chapman has designed single-level clusters of four-unit houses, a low-density approach to independent living for older people. Chapman's design assumes that people are still mobile and are able to drive. It is a vision of community in which people are active and live independently.

Hanson's futuristic design for high-density housing creates community for people who are too frail to be living on their own and who need assistance. The apartments are clustered in ways that create "communities of care" in at least two ways. Older people live close enough to become friends who "look in" on each other. The proximity also allows home-health workers to move more effectively from one apartment to the next.

The progression from Perito to Cusato and from Chapman to Hanson and Studio 16 reflects the continuum of care as people get older. They move from independence to congregate housing, from being self-sufficient to depending on friends, neighbors, and caregivers.

The work of Perito is of singular significance because it allows people to live independently for most of their lives. The designs by Cusato, Chapman, and Hanson ease the journey from independence to the nursing home, or *servicehus*.

CASE STUDY 1: DIGNIFIED HOUSING FOR THE ELDERLY IN SWEDEN
Designed by Hanson

BACKGROUND

Most housing for the elderly in Sweden has been criticized for its lack of functionality and quality. This has created a need for new suitable buildings that will give the elderly the chance to live a dignified life.

Accommodations for the elderly in the final leap of life means is housing for individuals who may not be fully aware of their whereabouts, and perhaps have no perception of their surrounding.

Relatives search for worthy alternatives for their family members. Mistreatment is a sensitive subject that has been extensively discussed in the Swedish media.

TYPOLOGY

Partly depending on a stressed budget, the basis for these projects is an industrial building method consisting of volume elements, where the individual housing units are delivered as a finished product. Facades, roofs, and all other elements are built on site.

The typology is organized as follows. Common spaces for social activity have a central emplacement, surrounded by a number of housing units. Two departments, or wards, are organized around one nursing staff. This organization is repeated on each floor, thus creating effective wards.

The green atriums bring nature into the buildings and create intimate spaces for socializing outside the individual housing unit.

THE METHODS

The process has been based on diagrams that can be linked to an ideogram, and the specific case has been studied based on the site and its urban complexity, giving each project individual character.

A unique plan and design should be treated with focus on the outstanding character concerning both the interior and the exterior. The materiality and tactility of the buildings adds emphasis to each project's certain concept.

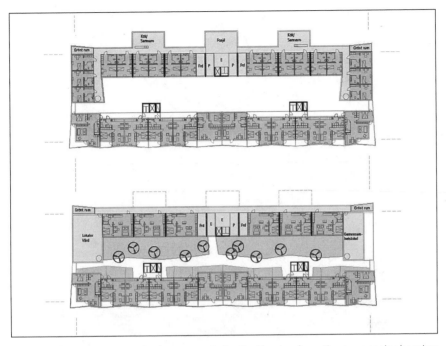

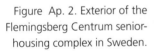

Figure Ap. 1. Design concepts for the Flemingsberg Centrum senior-housing complex in Sweden.

Figure Ap. 2. Exterior of the Flemingsberg Centrum senior-housing complex in Sweden.

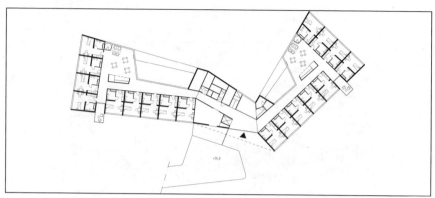

Figure Ap. 3. Floor plan for the Norrtalje senior-housing project in Sweden.

Figure Ap. 4a. Exterior rendering for the Norrtalje housing project.

Figure Ap. 4b. Interior rendering for the Norrtalje housing project.

CASE STUDY 2: A PARK FOR ELDERLY PEOPLE IN HIROSHIMA, JAPAN
Designed and developed by Studio 16

This project involved a housing development for the elderly centered around two existing parks in Hiroshima, Japan. In planning this project, the developer discovered that many elderly people were living by themselves. In many cases, housing developments for the elderly are outside of the city, and people have to leave their familiar environment if they need to live in an ALF or nursing home.

Therefore, one of the main purposes of the developers and designers for this project was to improve the lifestyle of the senior inhabitants in the city by developing something new. In combination with the development for the senior housing, the developers were interested in preserving city parks. Parks in the city of Hiroshima have been deteriorating since 2000. There is much less maintenance now, and parks are used by fewer and fewer people. However, their locations are perfect places for people to meet.

For this project, the designers used two existing parks in Hiroshima and converted them into a small community area where older people can meet and spend time with others. New functions include a day-care service, cafeteria, clinic, and short-term residence, and a new landscape for the park will create a cover for these functions. The designers tried to create strong visual connections between these new functions and the street level and make the park more present.

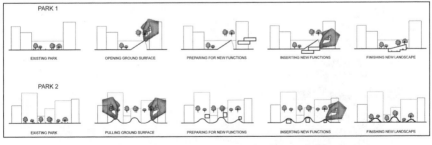

Figure Ap. 5. Design concepts for the development of urban parks for the elderly living in Hiroshima, Japan.

Figure Ap. 6. Site plans and floor plans for the development of urban parks for the elderly living in Hiroshima, Japan.

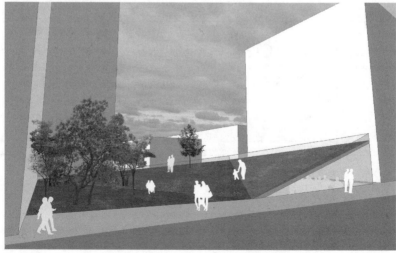

Figure Ap. 7. Exterior perspectives for the development of urban parks.

CASE STUDY 3: PLANNED COMMUNITY FOR OLDER PEOPLE IN AN AMERICAN SUBURB

Designed by Allan Chapman

SCHEME A: LOWER DENSITY FOR FAIRLY INDEPENDENT LIVING

Scheme A is planned for the relatively independent elderly and has 1,000 square feet of enclosed space. The unit provides a parking space with covered access for an automobile. The mechanical systems are accessed through the garage, allowing residents to control appliances without entering the house.

The house entrance is only a few steps from the car, and the kitchen is close to the entrance. At the entry, there is a large closet that includes the clothes washer and dryer, plus space for outside garments, boots, and so on. There is also room here for a wheelchair or walker, and there is additional storage in the garage.

There are two bedrooms and two baths located at each end of the single-level layout. One bath has access from the living area. The kitchen is open to the living/dining area and features a small bar counter. It is assumed that this unit is for people who will prepare their own meals, and so the design includes all of the appliances of a complete kitchen.

Each unit will also have an enclosed garden fenced with a gate, enabling access to a path system that will possibly lead to a common facility. This house is designed to be built with two or four units attached.

SCHEME B: HIGHER DENSITY WITH MORE DEPENDENCY FOR DAILY ROUTINES

Scheme B is planned as an apartment in a larger building, probably on several levels with elevator access. It is expected that there will be very few occupants with their own automobiles. Parking under the building is a possibility and will be accessed by the elevator. Each unit is reached by a passage from the elevator. This could open to a shared space, possibly a pool. This passage could be screened or glazed, depending on climate. While each unit has a small balcony, the corridor could be widened in some areas to provide an alternate place to sit and observe the activities at the ground level.

One bedroom is shown here; a second bedroom and even a second bath are optional add-ons. As in Scheme A, the bedrooms in Scheme B are at each end of the living area for added privacy. The one bath shown is accessible from the living area.

We assumed that these occupants will need considerable assistance, including transportation, with some meals served in a common area or brought to the unit. Varying levels of health care may be required.

If arranged around a courtyard as shown in the sketch, the units to the north may be three or four stories high, with those to the south limited to one or two stories, assuming that the courtyard would be fairly sunny.

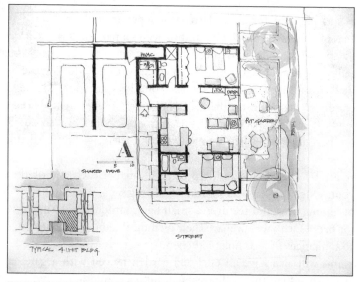

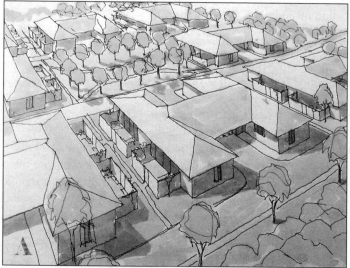

Figure Ap. 8. Design layouts for planned communities for older people.

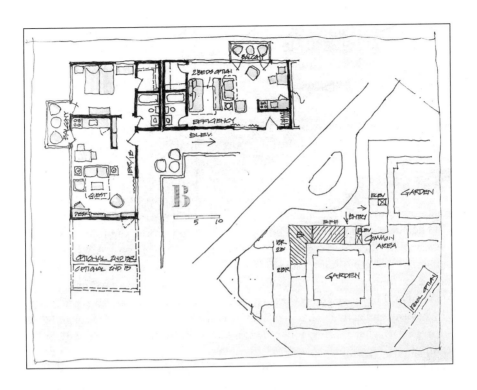

BALCONY

2 BEDS OPTION

EFFICIENCY

BR/B

ELEV.

BALCONY

GUEST

DESK

B

5   10

OPTIONAL 2ND BR
OPTIONAL 2ND B

GARDEN

ELEV.

ELEV.

BFE   ENTRY

COMMON
AREA

1BR
2B

2BR

GARDEN

POOL OPTION

B

CASE STUDY 4: AGING-FRIENDLY MAKEOVER FOR A LAKESIDE RETREAT

Designed by Ellen Gallow (gerontologist) and Douglas J. Gallow Jr., AIA; NCARB; Lifespan Design Studio, LLC, Lebanon, Ohio

Like most remodeling projects, the renovation of a lakeside vacation home for a fifty-something couple in upstate New York didn't start out as an exercise in design for aging. The couple had recently acquired the camp, a family heirloom spanning multiple generations, from the wife's parents, who are now in their eighties. The expressed goal was to re-create the spaces that in recent years had started falling down around them, thus preserving treasured memories and enabling future generations to enjoy similar experiences.

The client's elderly parents plan to continue to visit the camp for as long as possible, and her four siblings will gather for annual retreats. A writer and a self-employed consultant, she and her husband plan to live and work at the lake house for four or five months each year. She is a former dancer and he is an avid sportsman. They joke about their trick knees and bum hips, but they are generally healthy and active. They recently welcomed their first grandchild and look forward to having another generation of kids to swim, fish, and boat with at the camp.

The architect's walk-through with the owners was eye-opening on numerous levels. The charmingly rustic structure was a patchwork of disjointed rooms and spaces, pieced together over decades, as dictated by inspiration and necessity. Its layout expressed the core values that draw the extended family there every summer: togetherness, and the lake. The living and sleeping spaces on the lake side of the house were large and open with sweeping views, while the rest of the house was segmented by function—cooking, bathing, changing clothes, laundry—its arrangement inconsequential in the minds of the owners. There was little that they could imagine changing other than the stairs to the second floor: Three bottom steps that blocked passage to the kitchen were literally pushed in and out of position as needed.

PROJECT VALUES

What appeared on the surface to be a fairly simple request to draw up floor plans so that the camp could be replicated soon became a more complex challenge to merge tradition with aging-friendly improvements. Although the clients were open to the architect's suggestions, they had never given thought to the ways that the existing layout defined and might eventually compromise the experience of being there—especially for their elderly parents. Like most people, they regarded the constructed environment as "a given," embedded with the power to dictate when it was time to surrender certain experiences and opportunities, trusting it would never happen to them or their loved ones. Changing it seemed somehow disloyal and, since expense was a significant concern, potentially frivolous.

THE NEW LAYOUT

Like the original, the new camp is a two-story structure for a variety of reasons. Although air-conditioning is essentially unnecessary in the breezy, heavily treed setting, midsummer sleeping is most comfortably achieved on the large screened second-floor sleeping porch that the family shares dormitory-style. The existing sleeping porch and dining porch below it—both of which had been renovated in the last five years—were incorporated into the new structure: The rest of the old camp was razed. Also included on the new second floor are a private bedroom, communal changing room, full bathroom, and large laundry room. A new switch-back staircase with a large landing in the middle limits the number of steps that must be traveled at one time. The landing, which will double as a writer's nook, is naturally lit from a window above. Handrails have been added to both sides of the stairs.

The new main floor was designed to provide everything that someone unable to go upstairs would need. The zero-step entrance and core living spaces (living room, kitchen, porch, and dining room) are contiguous and open to one another—each positioned and studded with windows to frame the best views. A master bedroom and full bath with roll-in shower are discretely tucked beyond the new stairwell. The bathroom is accessible from both the living area and the bedroom. The bathroom door swings outward, making it impossible for someone who has fallen to become trapped in the space. Although the owners opted not to install the washer and dryer on the main floor, a linen closet was sized and located where it could be easily adapted for a stackable unit in the future. Thus, in combining a universally accessible ground floor with a strategically planned second floor with amenities for guest use, the new camp will function effectively in its dual roles as home away from home for the clients and their parents and a vacation spot for their young children and grandchildren.

DESIGN DETAILS

A variety of features were designed to support and enhance the user-friendliness of the new layout. Because the camp is not air-conditioned, the placement and ease of use of windows is essential to maintaining a comfortable temperature. Additional consideration was given to the location and size of those windows to provide the best views (from a standing or seated position) of the lake, dock, and beach areas where guests frequently gather. Should a family member become unable to move comfortably outside of the camp, they can sit and watch from one of several strategically located settings in the house and on the porch.

The living room fireplace around which the family gathers on cooler evenings has an elevated hearth, making it easier to maintain the fire and providing appealing supplemental seating. The old mantel was reused as a sentimental and cost-saving measure. Although the family most often gathers around large tables on the porch for meals, a bar-height peninsula dividing the kitchen from the living room will double as a lunch counter. This element could be modified to regular (and thus handicapped-accessible) seating height in the future.

The repositioned entrance is off of a covered porch, with the approach graded for zero-step access. Thirty-six-inch-wide doors were used at the entrance and throughout the first floor, and a minimum five-foot (in diameter) clear turning space was provided in all first-floor rooms. Wood floors were utilized in the living, dining, and sleeping spaces, and vinyl was used in the kitchen and bathrooms, for easy navigation as well as ease of maintenance and durability in the setting without heated and air-conditioned setting. Vinyl siding that simulates cedar-shake shingles and a standing-seam metal roof were selected for their long-term cost-effectiveness and minimal maintenance requirements.

Figure Ap. 9. This summer retreat was renovated so that people of all ages could enjoy the outdoors for years to come.

EXISTING PORCHES

Figure Ap. 10. Exterior sketch of redesigned house with existing porches.

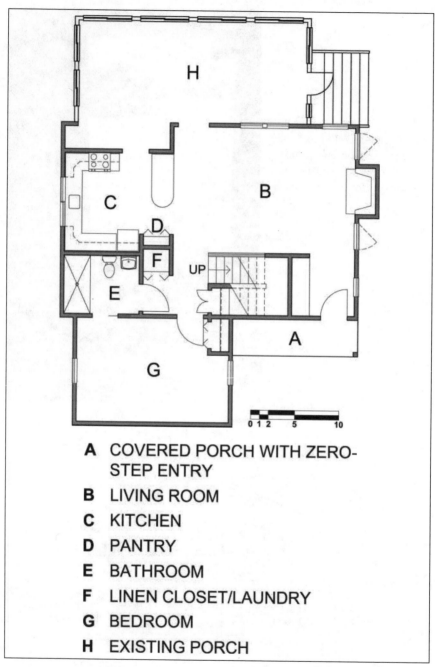

A COVERED PORCH WITH ZERO-
STEP ENTRY

B LIVING ROOM

C KITCHEN

D PANTRY

E BATHROOM

F LINEN CLOSET/LAUNDRY

G BEDROOM

H EXISTING PORCH

Figure Ap. 11. Interior floor plan layout of the house.

CASE STUDY 5: KATRINA COTTAGES FOR THE GULF COAST
Designed by Marianne Cusato

A Katrina Cottage is a dignified alternative to the FEMA trailer. It is a small permanent house that is safe and affordable and can be assembled quickly. Architect and planner Andres Duany developed the concept for the Katrina Cottage just after Hurricane Katrina in response to the overwhelming need for emergency housing along the Gulf Coast.

Since its debut at the 2006 International Builders Show, Katrina Cottage 1, the 308-square-foot cottage designed by Marianne Cusato, has attracted nationwide attention. This idea, born out of the tragedy of our nation's worst natural disaster, has brought hope to thousands and has reached well beyond the emergency-housing market. From affordable and elderly housing to in-law units and guest houses, and even vacation homes, the cottages have struck a chord in the hearts of Americans.

KATRINA COTTAGE FOR THE ELDERLY OCCUPANT
The idea of this plan is that the first piece of the plan can be built as a stand-alone building, which is 576 square feet for a single elderly person. But there is also an option for a second bedroom for a caretaker or for use as a study. When

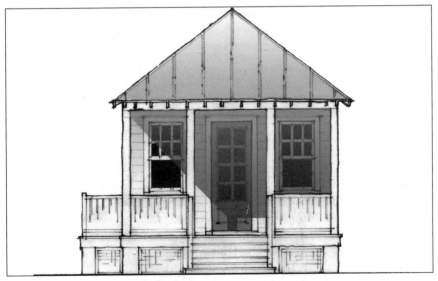

Figure Ap. 12. Exterior rendering of a Katrina Cottage.

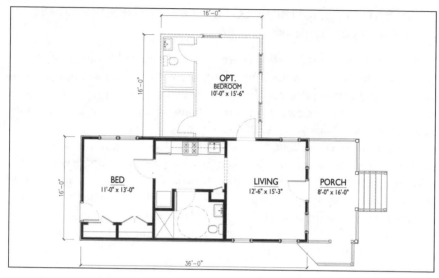

Figure Ap. 13. Typical Katrina Cottage floor. The plan layout optional bedroom can be for a caregiver or home-health aide.

the entire house is built, it is 772 square feet. The second bedroom can be built with the first phase of the house or added at a later date.

The elevations show alternatives that can be ordered for the front and sides. The cottage is raised, so when people are sitting on the front porch, they are up at eye level with people on the street. This makes the porch element a more usable space. A ramp goes off to the side of the house and wraps around to get down to grade.

The house has been designed in the same building style to fit into New Orleans, as well as a more generic American vernacular. The same plan could be adapted in any number of styles or variations.

CASE STUDY 6: UNIVERSALLY DESIGNED HOME IN BRAZIL

Designed by Sandra Perito, architect and PhD in inclusive architecture by the Faculdade de Arquitetura e Urbanismo of the Universidade de São Paulo, President-Director of the Instituto Brasil Acessível, Associate-Director of Marcondes Perito Construções, Engenharia E Arquitetura (São Paulo, Brazil), member of the commission for the definition of the Universal and Visitable Housing Label. The aging of the population, a worldwide phenomenon, is also evident in

Brazil. Therefore, the permanence and use of the home environment becomes even more important. This environment, if not adequate for the limitations deriving from age, may hinder the full use of the space and put at risk the safety of the elderly residents. Adaptable housing that can absorb the changes imposed by age advancement may assure the safety, independence, individuality, and privacy of the elderly users.

In the Brazilian socioeconomic context, the ultimate desire of any individual is the acquisition or construction of his or her own house. Brazilian elderly want to continue to live in their own houses, within the community with which they are familiar, as observed through research conducted by the designer.

PROJECT CONCEPT

This project was based on the concept of universal design, whose main premise is to design spaces and products that can be used by all, with comfort and safety, independent of physical capacity or age. Its principles should be fused in the infrastructure of the building and promote the investment in the capacity of space and products, based on the adequacy of use, practicality, and safety.

Also, some of the characteristics of energy conservation were considered, such as solar heating for the water; outside brightness–adjustable, presence-sensor switches; and toilet flushes with controlled flux. The construction of the building and the orientation of the openings had the objective of facilitating the air flow and natural lighting. Also, the foliage in the landscaping was chosen so that the mechanical systems were simplified, reducing the costs of use and conservation of the construction.

The house was built on a lot with 510 square yards in a residential condo in the city of Taubaté, 80 miles from São Paulo, in the Parafba Valley. The Taubaté Village is a medium-high standard condo, located well inside the urban area and in a quite plain area.

The option for this location was a consequence of the difficulties in finding financially accessible lots in residential areas of large cities, especially in highly regarded and safe neighborhoods. Normally the lots available are in degraded downtown areas that have a fair price and reasonable proximity to urban services, or in suburban areas that are not well served by transportation and infrastructure.

The implementation took into account that the potential users of the residence would be anonymous. For this reason, its universal characteristics should function properly for the greatest number of people or families that could live there. The project is a two-story house with 320 square yards of total built area, including the garage, terrace, and annex.

Figure Ap. 14. Exterior of a two-story house.

The option for a two-story house was selected because it is a very common type of housing in the market and, at first, the most difficult solution to be considered in terms of accessibility. Also, the two-story house allows a larger garden area, which can be used for leisure activities.

The ground level is totally accessible with a moderate slope ramp, a consequence of the landfill built to better prepare the lot for the construction of the house and improve sunlight exposure, which takes people from the street up to the front door. A leisure area was created to allow social interactions in the front part of the lot, allowing for an interesting visual contact with the neighbors and the surrounding activities. Although people avoid direct exposure to sunlight when they are not in specific areas such as swimming pools, clubs, or the beach, everyone can benefit physiologically and psychologically from the sunlight, especially those with advanced age. When aging, people become less mobile and their world seems to "shrink." This tendency of introspection can be countered by project strategies that prioritize not only the privacy and safety but also social interactions.

The rooms were planned with enough room to maneuver wheelchairs. The living room, for instance, allows layout flexibility and, because it has an open

Figure Ap. 15. Bedrooms and living rooms were planned with open-area designs for maximum flexibility of use by people of all ages.

design, allows for comfortable use with well-defined spaces, but without visual or mobility restrictions.

Given the characteristics of adaptability that were attempted to be applied to the project, besides the installed infrastructure for an elevator placement, one of the rooms on the ground floor, next to an accessible bathroom, enables a diversified use: complement for the living room or television area, an office, an extra bedroom for an assistant, or even an accessible suite, in the case of temporary or permanent mobility limitation of one of the residents. In that case, there is a provision for the installation of a wheelchair under the staircase. The accessible bathroom on the ground floor also allows for the accommodation of visitors who might have mobility limitations.

The proposed program was of a house that can accommodate an average family with five people, and the rooms were distributed as shown in the figure below:

ACCESS AND CIRCULATION

The access from the street to the main door is a ramp with a 6-percent slope and a lowered curb wide enough for two people and with slight inclines to the sides to avoid water accumulation.

The main entrance is protected by a covered portal that creates a protected transition between the outside and the inside, with room for a supporting bench.

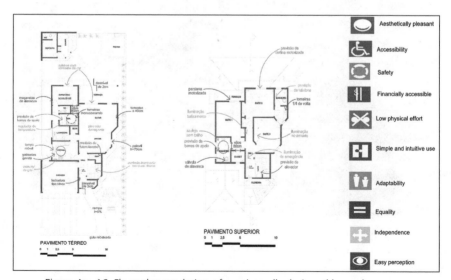

Figure Ap. 16. Floor-plan rendering of a universally designed home by renowned designer Sandra Perito.

Figure Ap. 17. Main entrance hall of the Universal Home.

The entrance hall has room for wheelchair maneuvering and it is the distribution center of the house. The corridors are three feet wide, enabling the installation of handrails without interfering with the circulation. The staircase was designed to allow space for handrails, which were installed in two levels, with lighting to serve safely both children and adults.

The steps of the stairs were designed to assist the passage for elder users or people with mobility restrictions, with contrasting colors on the edges. Dry tubing and a shaft necessary for the installation of a residential elevator were also built.

DETAILING

The detailing took into consideration the use of the residence under several circumstances: limited flexibility, reduced strength, reduced mobility and coordination, and visual and hearing limitations. The following details of the project take these considerations into account:

- Kitchen and laundry: The kitchen, of all rooms in the house, can be the most important, and at the same time, it is where a great

Figure Ap. 18. Universally designed kitchen.

number of barriers can be found. Many accessories and equipment that facilitate the use of this space are currently available in the market, but careful planning is fundamental. It is hard to have an independent life if you cannot prepare your own meals. For that reason the project has considered triangular distribution of the activities, a free area for wheelchairs, top boards with varying heights and an adjustable-height sink-board top, allowing people of different heights or who are sitting down to use it comfortably; a removable cabinet under the cooktop allows the attachment of a chair to be seated while working; the space for an oven and a micro-wave to be placed at a comfortable height, with a shelf with retractable support between them; lateral space for fridge and freezer, for access to both appliances; granite tops with rounded corners and contrasting borders for easy touch and visual identification, to avoid hits and injuries, to those who are visually impaired; lever sink faucets with a quarter rotation, which can be used even when one's hands are wet; drawers in the lower cabinets facilitate visualization and access by people with limited flexibility or motion impairment. The pantry and laundry room are also part of the main body of the kitchen, avoiding the need to leave the house to access them. The ironing board is foldable, drawer style, allowing the user to iron while sitting or standing; the crank-operated clothesline reduces the effort to use it up to 10 times; the laundry-tub-lever faucet that can be operated at any position; clothes baskets placed inside the cabinets don't obstruct circulation.

Bathrooms: Safety and independence are important objectives for the design of the bathrooms; therefore, all the space was considered as a wet area, not only the shower. For many people, the bathroom may be an obstacle to inde-pendent life and, because of that, special attention was given to these rooms. Five critical elements were incorporated into the bathrooms, in addition to the whole building having at least one accessible bathroom on each floor: Empty space under the sink, provision for the installation of support bars, antiskid flooring, an accessible and safe shower area, and simplified-to-use hardware. Faucets and pressure valves with a quarter turn or mono-command require minimal effort to operate; shower box doors with outward opening two and a half feet wide are better in the case of an accident and help is needed; a level difference of one inch between the bathroom floor and the shower box and color differentiation assist with identification; the bathroom mirrors are lower and larger than usual.

Figure Ap. 19. Bathroom design with safety in mind.

- Landscaping: The benefits of a garden area are many, from the simple stimuli, such as senses of smell, sight, and sound, to daily activities that keep the residents occupied and provide them with a goal to reach. The spaces must not only be accessible but also safe. The following elements were considered: The plants selected change their shape and colors throughout the year, helping to keep track of the seasons, plants, flowers, and varied fruit were placed to attract birds, stimulate the resident's sense of smell, and allow variations of scenarios; flower beds were installed and are accessible for activities such as cultivating flowers, aromatic herbs, and spices; the project was built with good drainage of the external floors; the identification number of the house was made in a large size that can be easily read from the street; the mailbox was installed in the front garden to offer visual contact with the neighbors; and a bench was placed under a midsize tree in the front yard for leisure and reading outside.

Figure Ap. 20. Attention to detail was given to the landscape of the home. These flower beds can be cultivated without kneeling on the ground.

CASE STUDY 7: STUDENT WORK FOR UNIVERSALLY DESIGNED DREAM HOME FOR ANYWHERE IN THE WORLD

These three projects were completed by seniors in the interior design department at Parsons The New School for Design in the fall of 2006. This was for a professional practice class taught by Kimberly Sheppard and Michael Gabellini. In this two-week exercise, students studied ADA (Americans with Disabilities Act) guidelines and then made floor plans of their universally designed dream home. The seniors showcased here are Kyungsung So (Korea), Ling-Zhi Hew (Singapore), and Marlene Mendez (United States).

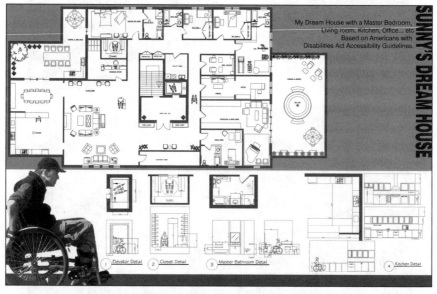

Figure Ap. 21. [Sunny's] dream house.

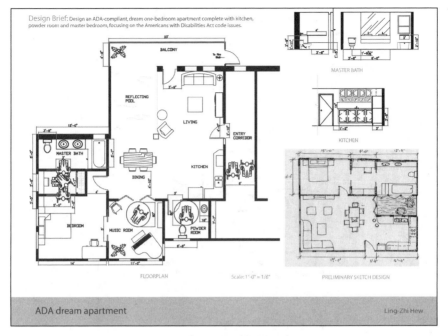

Figure Ap. 22. ADA dream apartment.

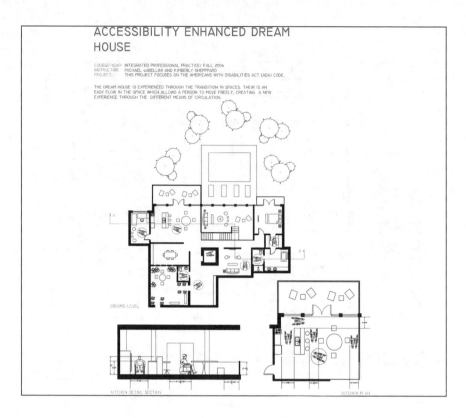

Figure Ap. 23. Accessibility-enhanced dream house.

References

Introduction

AARP. (2000). Fixin To Stay: Understanding Senior Housing. Washington, DC.

AARP. (1998). *Aging Everywhere: Global Aging Report*. Washington, DC.

Bakker, W. (2005). Evolution of living. *AARP Global Report on Aging*. Washington, DC: AARP Research International, p. 1.

Baldwin, D. (10 January 2006). Main street as memory lane: Familiar landmarks guide Alzheimer's patients. *The New York Times*, p. F1.

Belkin, L. (5 March 2006). A virtual retirement home. *The New York Times*, p. 9.

Brown, N. Under one roof: The evolving story of three-generation housing in Japan in Traphagan, J. and J. Knight (eds). (2003). *Demographic Change and the Family in Japan's Aging Society*. State University of New York Press, p. 53–71.

Brown, P.L. (10 September 2006). Growing old alone together in a new kind of commune. *The New York Times*, p. 1.

Cotsalas, V. (23 October 2005). Designing homes for easier living. *The New York Times*, p. 3.

DelWebb.com/lifestyle/Adult_Lifestyle.

Eckholm, E. (26 May 1998). Homes for the elderly are replacing family care as China grays. *The New York Times*, p. A1.

ElderCo-housingNetwork.com (also see Directory.co-housing.org/us).

———. Floating hotels. (7 April 2004). *Trends in Japan, Web Japan*, p. 1.

French, H. (24 November, 2005). China's online revolution. *The New York Times*, p. 1.

Gawnde, A. (24 May 2007). Rethinking old age. *The New York Times*, p. 27.

GenerationsOfHope.com.

Gwynn, A. (23 April 2006). A place to age in grace. *San Francisco Chronicle*, p. 9.

Hamilton, W. (23 April 2005). The new nursing home. Emphasis on "home." *The New York Times*, p. A1.

Hoevel, A. (23 May 2007). Don't let disabilities or age rob you of a stylish home. www.CNN.com.

HSBC. (2004). *The Future of Retirement*. London: HSBC Group Head Office.

Jackson, R. and N. Howe. (2004). *The Graying of the Middle Kingdom*. Prudential Foundation: Center for Strategic and International Studies.

———. (11 November 2002). Japanese attitudes on aging: Online survey. web-japan.org/trends.

Hui, P. (30 August 2004). Old folks want to be more independent. *South China Morning Post*, p. 1.

Kerkstra, P. (Summer 2006). Back on campus: Some seniors return to alma mater for retirement. *Mature Adult*, p. 18.

Knox, N. (24 March 2006). Home, senior-friendly home. *USA Today*, p. 5B.

Lai, C. (9 June 2004). More flats to cater for needs of elderly. *South China Morning Post*, p. 1.

Levine, E. (Fall 2006). The gay 60's, 70's and 80's. *Key*, p. 76.

Liaoning, T. (21 June 2004). Investors wanted for elderly care in Liaoning. *Business Daily Update*, p. 1.

Lifetime Homes: http://www.lifetimehomes.org.uk. Accessed November 2007.

Nakamura, A. (19 January 2006). Elderly of tomorrow can count on technology, researchers say. *The Japan Times*, pp. 1–4.

Nayar, L. (31 August 2004). Retirement homes becoming middle-class lifestyle statement. *Yahoo! India News*, pp. 1–3.

———. (1 January 2006). *Networked Home Appliances*.

The Center for Sustainable Design: http://cfsd.org.uk. Accessed November 2007.

———. (18 October 2004). Nursing homes opening up across the city. *Shanghai Daily*, p. 1.

Otis.com/products/detail/residential elevators.

Parker, R. (25 October 2004). Will cruise ships become old age nursing homes? *Future Pundit*, p. 1.

Ramanathan, S.K. (27 May 2003). Old age homes come of age. www.rediff.com.

Tapscott, D. and A. Williams. (2006). *Wikinomics: How Mass Collaboration Changes Everything.*

———. (3 July 2006). *The Design Hub: A Design and Architecture Company*, pp. 13–64. www.indiamart.com/thedesignhub.

———. (3 December 2005). Japan leads the world in developing new products for the elderly. *The Economist*, p. 59.

———. (28 September 2006). The Elder Co-housing Network. www.directory.co-housing.org/us.

Weijers-Hasegawa, Y. (2 April 2003). Homes for seniors not all created equal. *The Japan Times*, p. 1.

Weil, E. (5 March 2006). A condo on a permanent luxury cruise. *The New York Times Magazine*, p. 81.

Williams, J. (June 2005). Designing neighborhoods for social interaction: The case of co-housing. *Journal of Urban Design* (vol. 10, no. 2), pp. 195–227.

Yan, Y. (June 2005). Private Life Under Socialism: Love, Intimacy and Family in a Chinese Village, 1949–1999. Ca: Stanford University Press, p. 122.

Chapter 1

2002 National Older Adult Housing Survey, Secondary Analysis of Findings National Association of Home Builders. (2005). Upper Marlboro, MD.

Achenbaum, A. (2005). *Older Americans, Vital Communities*. Johns Hopkins University Press.

http://adaptiveenvironments.org. Accessed July 2007.

Adler, J. (20 June 2004). Ranch house a prototype for senior living. *The Chicago Tribune*, p.4.

Armour, L. (2006). Spying on Mom. FSB, p. 29.

Bakker, W. (2005). Evolution of Living. AARP (2005) Global Report on Aging. *Special Issue: The Promise of Livable Communities*, pp. 1–9.

Bakker, R. (1999). Elderdesign: Home Modifications for Enhanced Safety and Self-Care. *The Care Management Journals* (vol. 1, no. 1, winter), pp. 47–54.

Bauhaus-dessauide. Gerantopolis 2030. Accessed July 2007.

Basler, B. (December 2005). Declaration of independence: Home is where you want to live forever. *AARP Bulletin*, p. 14.

Berry, B. (7 August 2006). Architect suggests methods to make houses safer. *Ventura County Star*, pp. 1–2.

Binstock, R.H. (2003). Making a house a home. *The Gerontologist*, 43(6), pp. 931–934.

Butrica, B. & Schaner, S.G. (2005). Satisfaction and engagement in retirement. Perspectives on productive aging. *The Urban Institute's Retirement Project*.

Campbell, G. (2005). The promise of livable communities. *AARP: Global report on aging* (special issue), pp. 1–8.

Chamberlain, L. (7 January 2007). Design for everyone, Disabled or not. *The New York Times*, p. 10.

Clark, C. Jr., (1988). Ranch House Suburbia: Ideals and Realities, in Larry May (ed.), *Recasting America: Culture and Politics in the Age of the Cold War*. Chicago: University of Chicago Press, pp. 172–91.

Cotsalas, V. (23 October 2005). Designing homes for easier living. *The New York Times*, p.3.

Della Cava, M.R. (15 May 2006). When mom or dad moves in. *USA Today*, p.1.

Dyck, I. et al. (June 2005). The home as a site for long-term care: Meanings and management of bodies and spaces. *Health & Place* (vol 11, issue 2), pp. 173–185.

Dychtwald, Ken. (1999). *Age Power: How The 21st Century Will be Ruled by the New Old*. New York: Tarcher/Putnam.

Elderhouse: (2004). Planning Your Best Home Ever. *National Association of Home Builders*. Upper Marlboro: MD.

Esterbrooks, J. (26 October 2006). Baby boomers change senior housng trends. *The Daily Transcript* (San Diego), p. 1.

Fessenden, F. (16 July 2006). When it feels right at home. *The New York Times*, p.1.

———. (2000). Fixing to Stay: Understanding Senior Housing. Washington, DC: AARP.

Gold, M.R. (28 June 2005). Aging in Place and Multi-Generational Households. *Realty Times*, pp. 1–2.

Gross, J. (9 February 2006). Aging at home: For a lucky few, a wish come true. *The New York Times*, p. F1.

Gross, J. (14 August 2007). Grass roots effort to grow old at home. *The New York Times*, p.1.

Gumpert, G. and Drucker, S.J. (1998). The mediated home in the global village. *Communication Research* (vol 25, no. 4), pp. 422–438.

Haberman, C. (20 May 2005). Aging in the city easily beats other options. *The New York Times*, p.3.

Hansen, EB and Gottschalk, G. (2006). What makes older people consider moving, and what makes them stay where they are? *Housing, Theory and Society* (vol 23, no. 1), pp. 34–54.

Hayden, D. (1999). *The Power of Place: Urban Landscapes as Social History*. Cambridge: MIT University Press.

Hayden, D. (2004). *Redesigning the American Dream* (Revised edition). NY: W.W. Norton & Co.

Hevesi, D. (14 May 2000). The elderly face complicated housing choices, *The New York Times*, (Real Estate Desk), p.1.

———. (2004). Hidden in plain sight: Capturing the demand for housing near transit. *Reconnecting: America's Center for Transit-Oriented Development*.

Higdon, N. (14 July 2006). CAPS Certification prepares contractors for expertise in aging-in-place remodeling. *Home Builders Journal*, p. 1.

Holstein, A. (April 2006). Rethinking Senior Housing. *Dwell*, pp. 173–175.

———. (2006). Home Modification: Your Key To Comfort, Safety and Independent Living. *AARP*. Washington, DC.

———. (2 August 2002). Homes of the future: smart home watches out for you. *Infinitech.Org*, p. 1.

———. (Summer 2005). How and where to live: determining your specific needs. *AARP Mature Adult*, pp. 18–22.

Interiors 07. (15 March 2007). *From Dream to Reality: Case Studies in Universal Design*, p. 1.

intel.com/research. Digital technologies for aging in place. Accessed July 2007.

Kamerick, M. (30 November 2005). Boomers push interest in universal design homes, *Bank Rate*, pp. 1–2.

Kelly, J. (2004). Universal design: transparent, inclusive, attractive. ASID ICON (summer), p.2.

Knox, N. (24 March 2006). Home, senior-friendly home. *USA Today*, p. 5A-B.

Kovach, S. (17 July 2005). High-tech home: best new smart homes can 'take care' of elderly owners. *Palm Beach Post*, p.1.

Lanks, B. (October 2006). Solid state: new flair for the accessible home. *Metropolis*, p. 90.

Larson, K, Intille, S. et al. (October 2004). Open source building—reinventing places of living. *BT Technology Journal* (vol 22, no. 4), pp. 187–200.

Lasch, C. (1991). *Haven In a Heartless World: The Family Besieged*. WW Norton & Co.

Luscombe, B. (September/October 2003) This bold house. *AARP Magazine*, pp. 23–31.

Mathew, A. House wired for health. *Architecture Week*. 15 February 2006, 1–6.

McKeough, T. (August 2006) Future Perfect. *Metropolis*, p. 69.

Miller, A. (3 August 2004). Behind the aging curve. *Times Union*, pp., 1–4.

National Association of Home Builders. (2005). National Older Adult Housing Survey, secondary analysis of findings.

National Association of Home Builders. (July 31, 2006). 1,000 NAHB members trained for specialized aging-in-place remodeling, p. 1, www.NAHBrc.org.

Nisbet, R. (1969). *The Quest For Community*. N Y: Oxford University Press.

Novelli, W. (2005). Nurturing Communities. *AARP Global Report on Aging: Special Issue 2005, The Promise Of Livable Communities*, pp.2–5.

Nyren, C. (6 May 2006). Selling universal design to baby boomers. *The Mature Market*, pp. 1–4.

Paquette, C. (26 September 2004). Affordable housing for the elderly. *The New York Times* (Real Estate Desk), p. 22.

Parmelee, P. and Lawton, M. (1990). The design of special environments for the aged. In J. Birren and K. Schaie, eds. *Handbook of the Psychology of Aging*, 3rd ed. New York: Academic Press.

Percival, J. (2002). Domestic spaces: Uses and meanings in the daily lives of older people. *Aging & Society* (vol 22, no. 6), pp. 729–749.

Pine, V. (2002). The face of New York: the people.

Project 2015: The future of aging in New York. *NYS Office for the Aging*.

Preventing slips, trips and falls. *Business & Legal Reports* (2006 edition).

Pristin, Terry. (15 February 2006) Hot niche in the rental market: Housing for the elderly. *The New York Times*, p. C6.

Rhode Island School of Design. (1999). The Universal Kitchen (design exhibition).

Robinson, J.T. and Moen, P. (2000). Future housing expectations in late-midlife: The role of retirement, gender, and social integration. *Social Integration in the Second Half of Life*, pp. 158–189.

Rosenfeld, J.P., Chapman, W. and McCulough, E. (Fall 2006). Going global: Senior housing in three aging nations, *Live Wire*, pp. 12–14.

———. (2006). Saving lives, saving resources. *Floor Safety USA*.

Schafer, Robert. (2000). *Housing America's Seniors*. Cambridge, MA: Joint Center for Housing Studies of Harvard University.

Schwarz, B. and Brent, R. (1999). *Aging, Autonomy, and Architecture*. Baltimore, MD: Johns Hopkins University Press.

Schwennsen, K. (2006). Best practices: Lessons from the latest "design for aging review." *AIA Design for Aging Review.*

Sisson, M. (21 August 2006). Keeping the elderly at home. *The Health Care Report*, p.1.

Sluis, W. (Summer 2006). Making a move: Downsizing to a home that matches your needs. *Mature Adult*, p. 19.

Smart Homes and Beyond International Conference on Smart Homes and Health Telematics (May 2006).

Taylor, J. (June 2004). A second coming of age. *American Demographics*, pp. 36–38.

Tedeschi, B. (3 December 2006). The graying of the housing market. *The New York Times.*

Trager, C. (13 May 2006). What's hot in senior housing. *Newsday—Long Island, NY*, p. B-4.

Weisman, G. (1987). Improving wayfinding and architectural legibility in housing for the aging in Regnier, V. and J. Pynoos, Eds., *Housing for the Elderly: Design Directives & Policy Considerations.* NY: Elsevier.

Wilkinson, D. (10 September 2006). Taking the dangers out of hanging around the house. *The New York Times*, p. 18.

Wylde, M. (2001). *Boomers on the horizon: Housing Preferences of the 55+ market.* NY: Builder Books.

Chapter 2

1. Of General Interest: Quests For Communities

AARP. (1991, revised 2000). *The Doable Renewable Home.* Washington, DC: AARP.

Achenbaum, A. (2005) *Older Americans, Vital Communities.* Johns Hopkins University Press.

adaptiveenvironments.org. Accessed July 2007.

ap.buffalo.edu/idea/projects. Accessed July 2007.

Basler, B. (December 2005). Declaration of Independents: Home is where you want to live forever. Here's how. *AARP Bulletin*, pp. 14–17.

Binstock, R.H. (2003). Making a house a home. *The Gerontologist*, 43(6), 931–934.

Bradspries, R. (2007). Personal correspondence.

Butrica, B. & Schaner, S.G. (2005). Satisfaction and engagement in retirement. Perspectives on productive aging. *The Urban Institute's Retirement Project.*

Campbell, G. (2005). The promise of livable communities, *AARP: Global report on aging.* Special issue, 2005: 1–8.

Clark, C. Jr., (1988) "Ranch House Suburbia: Ideals and Realities," in Larry May (ed.), *Recasting America: Culture and Politics in the Age of the Cold War.* University of Chicago press, pp. 172–91.

Dychtwald, Ken. 1999. *Age Power: How The 21st Century Will be Ruled by the New Old.* Tarcher/Putnam.

Hayden, D. *The Power Of Place: Urban Landscapes As Social History.* Cambridge: MIT University Press.

Hayden, D. (2004). *Redesigning the American Dream.* Revised edition. NY: W.W. Norton & Co., 2002.

Hevesi, D. (13 May 2000) The elderly face complicated housing choices, *The New York Times, (Real Estate Desk)*, p.1.

Larson, C. (27 November 2006). Taking care of mom and dad: a boomer's guide. *U.S. News*, pp. 61–73.

Massis, J. (2006). Chelsea senior facility an urban model for eldercare, *The Jewish Advocate*, 29 September, pp. 1–2.

Nisbet, R. (1969). *The Quest For Community.* NY: Oxford University Press.

Novelli, W. (2005). Nurturing Communities. pp. 2–5 in *AARP Global Report On Aging: Special Issue 2005, The Promise Of Livable Communities.*

Paquette, C. (2004). Affordable housing for the elderly, *The New York Times (Real Estate Desk)*, September 26, p. 22.

Parmelee, P. and Lawton, M. (1990). The design of special environments for the aged. In J. Birren and K. Schaie, eds. *Handbook of the Psychology of Aging*, 3rd ed. New York: Academic Press.

Pristin, Terry. (2006) Hot niche in the rental market: Housing for the elderly, *The New York Times*, 15 February, p. C6.

pwc.gov.org/ud. Accessed July 2007.

Regnier, V. (2002). *Design for Assisted Living: Guidelines for Housing the Physically and Mentally Frail.* NY: Van Nostrand Reinhold.

Rosenfeld, J.P., Chapman, W. and McCulough, E. (2006). Going global: Senior housing in three aging nations, *Live Wire*, pp. 12–14.

Rybczynski, W. (1997). *Home: A Brief History of an Idea.* New York: Penguin Books.

Schafer, Robert. *Housing America's Seniors.* (2000). Cambridge, MA: Joint Center for Housing Studies of Harvard University.

Schwarz, B. and Brent, R. (1999). *Aging, Autonomy, and Architecture.* Baltimore, MD: Johns Hopkins University Press.

Suttles, Gerald. (1972). *The Social Construction Of Communities.* Chicago: The University of Chicago Press.

Trager, Cara (13 May 2006) What's hot in senior housing. *Newsday,* p. B-4.

Weisman, G. (1987). Improving wayfinding and architectural legibility in housing for the aging. In Regnier, V. and J. Pynoos, Eds., *Housing for the Elderly: Design Directives & Policy Considerations.* NY: Elsevier.

2. NORC's (Naturally Occurring Retirement Communities)

AARP (2006), Aging in place and naturally occurring retirement communities (NORC's), *Statement before the Senate community on health, education, labor, and pensions.*

Ahrentzen, S. (2004) On their turf: facilitating health-promotive activities in a naturally occurring retirement community. *University of Wisconsin, Milwaukee, Center on Age & Community.*

Binstock, R.H. (2003). Making a house a home. *The Gerontologist,* 43(6), 931–934.

Bleyer, J. (2006). In the land of gray hair, anxiety, then accord. *The New York Times,* 13 March, p.3.

Gozonsky, M. (1991). A look at naturally occurring retirement communities (norcs). *Perspectives on Aging,* 20, 33–34

Manheim, A. and Friedman, E.B. (2005). Plainview/Oyster Bay cares: Seniors helping seniors, *JCC Circle,* 2005, p.1.

Marek, K.D. & Rantz, M.J. (2000). Aging in place: A new model for long-term care. *Nursing Administration Quarterly,* 24(3), 1–11.

Ormond, B.A., Black, K.J., Tilly, J. et al. (2004). Supportive services programs in NORC's. *U.S. Department of health and human services.*

Peck, R.L. Universal design for aging in place. *Nursing Homes Long-Term Care Management,* 51(6), 16–20.

Pine, P.P. & Pine, V.R. (2002). Naturally occurring retirement community- supportive service program: An example of devolution. *Journal of Aging & Social Policy,* 14(3/4), 181–193.

Piturro, M. (2002). Neighborhoods age together. *Caring for the Ages,* 3(10).

Poliakoff, R. (2004). Aging in Place: Naturally Occurring Retirement Communities and Condominium Living. Florida and the World, pp. 1–11.

Stuart, M. and Weinrich, M. (2001). Home is where the help is: Community-based care in Denmark. *Journal of Aging & Social Policy,* 12(4), 81–101.

Sykes, J.T. (1997). NORCS: What can we learn from them? *Perspectives on Aging,* 26(1), 16–19.

Toy, V.S. (2006). Helping the elderly stay in their own homes, *The New York Times,* 12 February, p.1.

Vladeck, F. (2004). A good place to grow old: New York's model for NORC supportive service programs, New York: *United Hospital Fund.*

3. The Baby Boomer's Quest for Community

Boomers Are Driving The Housing Market. NewRetirementCommunities.Com 2006.

Esterbrooks, J. (2006). baby boomers change senior housing trends. *The (San Diego) Daily Transcript.* 26 October, pp. 1–3.

Gardiner, Virginia (2006). Easing Into Retirement Housing: Rock 'n' Roll Apartments for baby boomers," *Metropolis,* October, pp. 33–34.

Kamerick, M. (2005). Boomers push interest in universal design homes, *Bank Rate,* 30 November, pp. 1–2.

Miller, A. (3 August 2004). Behind the aging curve, *Times Union,* p. 1–4.

Neville, T. (6 April 2007). Birds of a feather. *The New York Times.*

Nyren, C. (2006). Selling universal design to baby boomers, *The Mature Market,* 6 May, pp. 1–4.

Pine, V. (2002). The face of New York: the people. Project 2015: The future of aging in New York. *NYS Office for the Aging.*

Robinson, J.T. and Moen, P. (2000). Future housing expectations in late-midlife: The role of retirement, gender, and social integration. *Social Integration in the Second Half of Life,* 158–189.

Taylor, J. (2004). A second coming of age, *American Demographics,* June 2004, 36–38.

Wylde, M. (2001). *Boomers on the horizon: Housing Preferences of the 55+ market.* NY: Builder Books.

4. Cohousing and Alternative Housing for Seniors.

Brown, P.L. (2006). Growing Old Alone Together in the New Kind of Commune, *The New York Times,* September 10, p.1.

Durrett, C. (2005). *Senior Cohousing: A Community Approach to Independent Living: The Handbook.* Habitat Press.

Eheart, B., Hopping, D. et al. (2005) *Intergenerational Community as Intervention,* April, unpublished paper.

Eheart, B., Power, M.B., et al. (2006) Aging well in an intentional intergenerational community: Meaningful relationships and purposeful engagement, unpublished paper.

Fornoff, S. (31 August 2005). "Fill Your Empty Nest With Friends," *The San Francisco Chronicle,* pp. 1–6.

Gross, J. (2004). Older women team up to face their retirement years together. *The New York Times*, p. 22.

Hopping, D.(2006). *Parameters of Site Design for Replication of the Hope Meadows Neighborhood Model*. Unpublished paper. Generations of Hope.

Kerkstra, P. (2006). Back on campus: Some seniors return to alma mater for retirement. *Mature Adult*, Summer, p. 34.

Levine, E. (2006). The gay 60's, 70's, 80's and 90's. *Key*, Fall, p. 76.

Martin, B. (2006). Author discusses alternative housing for seniors. *Kodiak Daily Mirror.* 2 October, pp. 1–3.

Rajewski, G. (2006) Developer Takes Novel Approach To Seniors' Housing. *Affordable Housing Finance*. July, pp. 1–3.

Ritter, J. (2006) Gay Seniors Settle Into A Niche. *USA Today*, July 5, pp.1–2.

Scott-Hanson, C. and Scott-Hanson K. (2005). *The Cohousing Handbook: Building a Place for Community*. 2nd edition. New Society Publishers.

Thomas, W. (1999) *The Eden Alternative Handbook: The Art Of Building Human Habitats*.

Williams, J. 2005. Designing Neighborhoods for Social Interaction: The Case of Cohousing. *Journal of Urban Design*, Vol. 10, No. 2, 195–227.

Wilson, C. (2005). Gay retirement communities are growing in popularity. *The New York Times* (real estate section), p. 16.

Yeoman, B. (2006). Rethinking the Commune. *AARP Magazine*. March & April, pp. 1–4.

Chapter 3

1. Assisted Living and Continuum of Care

The American Institute of Architects. (2006). *Design for Aging Review*. Images Publishing.

The American Institute of Architects. (2004). *Design for Aging Review*. Images Publishing.

Bakker, W. (2005). Evolution of living. *AARP Global Report on Aging, 2005*. AARP Research International: 1.

Bane, E. (2006). Color and wayfinding: Helping residents and patients get from point A to point B. *ASID Annual Meetings*, unpublished paper.

Belluck, P. Creating a village to foster a child. *The New York Times*. 16 August 2007: F1.

Bunker-Hellmich, L. (2003). Aging and the designed environment. *Implications: A Newsletter by InformeDesign*. Vol. 1, Issue 1: 1.

Carr, R. (2005). Nursing Home. *National Institute of Building Sciences*, pp. 105.

dychtwald.com/highlights. Accessed July 2007.

Glynn, A. (2006). A place to age in grace. *San Francisco Chronicle*, p. 1–6.

Green, J. (2005). Older, and living in Manhattan. *The New York Times*, p. A1.

Gross, J. Aging at home: For a lucky few, a wish come true. The New York Times. 9 February 2006, p. F1.

Gross, J. (30 January 2005). Under one roof: Aging together yet alone. *The New York Times*, p. A1.

Guerin, D. (2002). Color meaning across cultures. *Implications: A Newsletter by InformeDesign*, pp. 1–4.

Gwynn, A. (2006). *A place to age in grace*. San Francisco Chronicle. April 23, p. 9.

Hadjiyanni, T. (2004). Culturally sensitive housing. *Implications* (vol 3, no. 1), pp. 1–6.

Hoover, R. (1995). Healing Gardens and Alzheimer's disease. *Journal of Alzheimer's Disease and Other Dementias*. vol. 10, no. 2:1–9.

Kershaw, S. (2003). Many immigrants decide to embrace homes for the elderly. *The New York Times*. October 20: A1.

Knez, I. and Kers, C. (2000) Gender and age affect response to indoor lighting. *Environment & Behavior*, Vol. 32, No. 6: 817–831.

Leib, C. (2000). *Design Details for Health: Making the Most of Design's Healing Potential*.

Marsden, J. (2006) *Humanistic Design of Assisted Living*. Johns Hopkins University Press.

National Association of Home Builders. *National Older Adult Housing Survey* (2002)

newretirementcommunities.com/homeguide/active_adult.nhg. New communities for a new lifestyle. Accessed July 2007.

newretirementcommunities.com/homeguide/active_adult.nhg. Roomers are driving the housing market. Accessed July 2007.

Paquette, C. (2003). Residences for the elderly stress hotel-like touches. *The New York Times*, p. A1.

Pearce, B.W. (2006). *Senior Living Communities*. Johns Hopkins University Press.

Petersen, A. (2004). Social engineering hits the senior set. *The Wall Street Journal*. October 20: D10.

Proffitt, M. and Briller, S. (2005). *The Unit's Edge: Exploring the Boundary between Public and private Domains in Residential Settings for Older Persons*. Milwaukee, WI: University of Wisconsin Press.

Pristin, T. Hot niche in the rental market: Housing for the elderly. *The New York Times*. February 16:A1.

Regnier, V. (2002). *Design for Assisted Living: Guidelines for Housing the Physically and Mentally Frail*. NY: John Wiley & Sons.

Regnier, V. (1993). *Assisted-Living Housing for the Elderly: Design Innovations from the United States and Europe*. John Wiley & Sons.

Schwarz, B. and Brent, R.(eds.) (1999) *Aging, Autonomy and Architecture: Advances in Assisted Living*. Johns Hopkins University Press.

Tanner, F. (2005). Red light, green light: Keys to successful assisted-living development. *Assisted Living*: October 1: 1.

Zimmerman, S., Sloane P. and Eckert, K. (eds) (2004). *Assisted Living: Needs, Practices and Policies in Residential Care for the Elderly*.

2. Nursing Homes and Dementia Units

Anderson, L. (2006). With one site, much input, Village Care set to build. *The Villager*. September 27-October 3, p. 1.

Andershon, J. (2006). Designs for Alzheimer's care. *Assisted Living* Success. October 1: 2.

Babwin. D. (2004). Ethnic nursing homes on the rise. (2004). *The Associated Press*. October 12: 1.

Baldwin, D. (2002). Main street as memory lane: Familiar landmarks guide Alzheimer's patients. *The New York Times*, January 10: F1.

Barisas, M., Calkins, M., Chaudhury, H. et al. (2005). *Environments for People with Dementia*. Milwaukee, WI: University of Wisconsin Press.

Belkin, L. (2006). A virtual retirement home. *The New York Times*, March 5: 91.

Brawley, E. (1997). *Designing for Alzheimer's Disease. Strategies for Creating Better Care Environments*. John Wiley & Sons.

Brush, J. (2004) *Improving Dining for People with Dementia*. Milwaukee, WI: University of Wisconsin Press.

Caron, W. Living with Alzheimer's. *Implications: A Newsletter by InformeDesign*, Vol. 3, Issue 1: 1–4.

Clemetson, L. (2006). U.S. Muslims confront taboo on nursing homes. *The New York Times*. June 13: 1.

Davis, E. (1922). *Illinois Federation of Colored Women's Clubs (1922)*. New York Public Library, Images, Africana and Black History.

Day, K. and Cohen, U. (1993). *Contemporary Environments for People With Dementia*. Baltimore, MD: John Hopkins University Press.

Day, K. and Cohen, U. (2000). Culturally-specific design supports dementia patients. *Environment & Behavior* (vol 32, no. 3), pp. 361–399.

Day, K. and Cohen, U. (2000). The role of culture in designing environments for people with dementia. *Environment & Behavior*. (vol 23, no. 3), pp. 361–399.

Gladwell, M. (1997). The Alzheimer's strain. *The New Yorker*. October 26, 97–112.

Hamilton, W. (2005). The new nursing home: Emphasis on Home. *The New York Times*, p. A1.

Hensler, K. Sun Health Residence for Alzheimer's care. *Interiors*, September: 77–83.

Hoglund, J. and Ledewitz, S. (1999). Designing to meet the needs of people with Alzheimer's Disease. in Schwarz. B. and Brent, R. (eds). (1999) *Aging, Autonomy and Architecture*. Baltimore: Johns Hopkins University Press: 229–61.

Hutchings, J. (2000) Color in folklore and tradition: The principles. *Color Research & Applications*. (vol 29, no. 1) pp. 57–66.

Hutchings, J. (2004). Culture informs color. *Implications. Color Research & Application*. 29, 1: 57–66.

Israel, C. (2005). Green homes project brings new approach to nursing homes. *CBN Newswatch*, August 23:2.

Kepley, D. (2005). The case against aging in place: design criteria for more aging-resident-friendly care. *Nursing Homes*. October 1: 1–5.

Knez, I. and Kers, C. Gender and age affect response to indoor lighting. *Environment and Behavior*. Vol. 32, No. 6: 817–31.

Krejci, D. (Fall). The cluster: A design for the future. *Aging*, p. 1.

McDowell, E. (13 November 2004). Getting ready for aging baby boomers. *The New York Times*, p. A1.

Nursing home, wikepedia.org, 2005.

Ou, L. et al. (2004). A study of color emotion and color preference. *Color Research and Application* (vol 29), pp. 32–40.

Park, Y. and Guerin, D. (2002) Color, meaning, culture & design. *Journal of Interior Design* (vol. 28, no. 1), pp. 27–39.

Parker, R. (26 October 2004). Will cruise ships become old age nursing homes? *Future Pundit*, p.1. See also Belkin, L. (5 March 2006). A condo on a permanent luxury cruise. *The New York Times*, p. 81.

Passini, R. et al. (1998). Wayfinding for patients with dementia. *Journal of Architectural and Planning Research* (vol 15, no 2), pp. 133–151.

Peck, R. (March 2005). Getting closer to the goal. *Design for Senior* Environments, pp. 7–15.

Schwarz, B. (1996). *Nursing Home Design.* Garland Publishing, Inc.

Schwarz, B., Chaudhury, H. and Brent, R. (2005). *Impact of Design Interventions in Nursing Home on Residents with Dementia, Their Families, and Staff*. Milwaukee, WI: University of Wisconsin Press.

Thomas, W. (2006). *What are old people for?* Acton, MA: VanderWyk & Burnham.

Weinstein, D. (15 October 2006). New focus in nursing homes: Give residents some options. *The New York Times*, p. 2.

Weisman, G., Cohen, U. and Day, K. (2001). *Programming & Design for Dementia.* University of Wisconsin Press.

Wikipedia.org. Assistive technology, 2007.

Youngsoon, P. and Guerin, D. (2002). Meaning and preference of interior color palettes among four cultures. *Journal of Interior Design* (vol 28, no 1), pp. 27–39.

Chapter 4

Almekinders, M. (2005). *High tech-high touch*, AARP International Association of Homes and Services for the Aging. 6th International Conference. Unpublished paper.

———. (11 November 2002). Attitudes on aging: Online survey, web-Japan.org/trends, pp. 1–3.

———. (2000). Home helpers, 1986–1999. Annual report on health and welfare. *Ministry of Health and Welfare*, p. 1.

Brown, N. (2003). Under one roof: The evolving story of three-generation housing in Japan in John W. Traphagan and John Knight (eds). *Demographic Change and the Family in Japan's Aging Society.* Albany, NY: State University of New York Press, pp. 53–71.

Bunker-Hellmich, L. (2002). Aging and the designed environment. *Implications: A newsletter by InformeDesign*, p. 1.

Caring for a graying Japan, *web-Japan.org*, p.2. Accesssed 20 June 1997.

———. (23 March 2001). Changing roles in an aging society. *Mainchi Interactive*, p. 1.

Cohen, U. and Keith Diaz Moore. (1999). Integrating cultural heritage into assisted living environments in Benjamin Schwarz and Ruth Brent (eds). *Aging, Autonomy and Architecture.* Baltimore, MD: Johns Hopkins University, Press, pp. 90–110.

———. (7 April 2004). Floating hotel. *Trends in Japan, Web Japan*, p. 1.

Hadjiyanni, T. (2000). Culturally sensitive housing. *InformeDesign*, pp. 1–6.

Hall, K. (26 January 2005). Land of the falling birth rate. *The Herald*, p 6.

Hellner, B.M. (2005). Care at home, *AARP Global Report on Aging* (Special Issue), pp. 6–21.

Hewitt, P.S. (12 October 1999). Depopulation and aging in Europe and Japan: The hazardous transition to a labor shortage economy. *Global Action on Aging*, p. 1.

Hoover, Robert. (1995). Healing gardens and Alzheimer's Disease. *American Journal of Alzheimer's Disease* (vol 10), pp. 1–9.

———. (2003). Households by family type. *Ministry of Internal Affairs and Communications*, p. 123.

———. (2 April 2003). Homes for seniors not created equal. *The Japan Times*, pp. 1–2.

———. (21 December 2005). Housing in Japan. *Wikipedia*, p. 5.

———. (2004). Home networked appliances. *Human Factors Research and Design*, p. 1.

———. (26 October 2002). In Japan, happiness is a warm robot. *Asia Times*, p.1.

Ishii-Kuntz, M. (1999). Japan and its planning toward family caregiving in V.M. Lechner and M.B. Neal (eds). *Working and Caring for the Elderly: International Perspectives.* Philadelphia: Brunner/Mazel, p. 67.

Ishimoto, Tatsuo and Kikoyo Ishimoto. (1963). *The Japanese House: Its Interior and Exterior.* NY: Crown Publishers, Inc.

———. (3 December 2005). Japan leads the world in developing new products for the elderly. *The Economist*, p.59.

———. Ministry of public management, home affairs, ministry of internal affairs and communications, Table 9. "Households, by Family Type," p.123. *Japan Statistical Yearbook, 2003* (52nd edition).

———. (3 December 2005). Japan leads the world in developing new projects for the elderly. The Economist, p. 59.

Jones, W. (2004). Group home for the elderly in M' anazuru. *Architektur Wettbewerbe* (vol 197), pp. 8–11.

Kakuchi, S. (25 October 2002). In Japan, happiness is a warm robot. *SunWukong*, p. 1.

Leavitt, J. (1989). Two prototypical designs for single parents in Franck, Karen A. and Sherri Ahrentzen (eds). *New Households, New Housing*. New York: Van Nostrand Reinhold, pp. 211–24.

———. (21 November 2003). Living longer. *Trends in Japan*, p. 1.

Lytle, Mark J. (11 September 2003). A yen for the hi-tech life. *The Guardian*, pp. 1–3.

———. (21 February 2002). Robot care bears for the elderly. *BBC News*, pp. 1–3.

MacDonald, J. (2005). Making homes more accommodating for older or disabled residents. *Bankrate.com*. Bankrate, Inc., p. 1.

Morikawa, K. (28 January 2002). Digital old age home in Japan. *Global Action on Aging*, p. 1.

———. (18 August 1997). New ways to help the old: Elderly-care service industry enjoys boom, web-Japan, p. 1.

———. (1 January 2006). Networked home appliances. *Toshiba*, p. 1.

———. (21 June 2000). Nursing care boom. *Trends in Japan*, p. 2.

Ogawa, Naohiro. (7 March 1997). Demographic trends and their implications for Japan's future. *Japan Information Center*, p. 1.

———. (15 July 2005). Preventive care for the elderly. *The Japan Times*, pp. 1–2.

———. (21 July 2005). Robots to offer Japan's elderly a new lease on life. *MSNBC*, p. 1.

———. (21 July 2005). Robots to offer Japan's elderly a new lease on life. MSNBC, p. 1.

Sano, Chiye. (1958). *Changing Values of the Japanese Family*. Washington, DC: The Catholic University of America Press, Inc.

Schadler, Ted. (5 January 2005). Who will win the digital home? *Forrester Research, Inc.*, p. 1.

Schneider, Linda and Arnold Silverman. (2006). Japan: The importance of belonging, pp. 1–68 in *Global Sociology*, New York: McGraw-Hill.

Schreiner, Andrea S., Eiko Yamamoto and Hisako Shiotani. (2000). Designing for nursing home patients with dementia. *InformeDesign* (vol 3) pp. 1–6.

Schwarz, Benyamin. (1996). *Nursing Home Design*. NY: Garland Publishing.

———. (1997). Fukuoka welfare annuity home for the elderly. *Shin'ichi Okada* (vol 1), p. 167.

———. (2002). Sun City, Kashiwa. *Land Reform*, (vol 14), pp. 84–85.

Takahashi, Yumi. (2003). Pokkuri-dera: The meaning of longevity among Japanese elderly. Unpublished seminar paper.

Takeshi, Nakagawa. (2002). *The Japanese House In Space, Memory, and Language*. TOTO Shuppan, International House of Japan.

Tasukemasu, Otoshiyori. (25 May 2003). Mitsubishi Heavy Industry introduces Best Companion for Senior Citizen. Pacific Research Consulting, p. 1.

———. (12 August 2005). Teaching old houses new tricks: Traditional Kyoto townhouses enjoy a revival. *Trends in Japan*, pp. 1–2.

Thang, Leng Leng. (2003). Generational rearrangements: Changing demographic patterns and the revival of intergenerational contact in Japan, pp. 77–88 in John W. Traphagan and John Knight (eds). *Demographic Change and the Family in Japan's Aging Society*. Albany, NY: SUNY Press.

———. (11 April 2002). The house of the future: Networked appliances make life more convenient. *Japan Information Network*, p. 1.

———. (24 October 2005). The Silver Tsunami. *Belmont University*, p. 1.

———. (30 December 2004). The Silver Tsunami: A graphic depiction. *Rolling Rains Report*, p. 1.

———. (29 November 2004). The Yori-soi ifbot. *Akibalive*, p. 1.

Toto, Products, www.toto.co.jp/en/products/washlet, 2005: 1.

Traphagan, John W., "The Study of the Family in Japan," in John W. Traphagan and John Knight (eds). *Demographic Change and the Family in Japan's Aging* ___. (2003). *Society*. Albany, NY: State University of New York Press.

Webb, Michael. (2003). Care in Kyoto. *The Architectural Review* (vol 214), pp. 70–73.

Wijers-Hasegawa, Yumi. (2 April 2003). Homes for seniors not all created equal. *The Japan Times*, p.1.

Yokohama, Yuki. (2005). Group homes in Japan. AARP Conference on World Aging, pp. 1–16.

Chapter 5

Angus, Jean. (27 January 2003). Studio apartment scheme revised. *The Edge*, Shanghai, pp. 22–24.

Beal, Thom. (28 April 2000). Heard in Asia: At Hong Kong's quality healthcare, physicians' options include stock. *The Asian Wall Street Journal*, p.2.

Beslova, Antoaneta. (13 September 2004). Shanghai breaks China's second—child taboo. *Inter Press Service*, p. 1.

Chang, Leslie. (3 April 2000). Confucius said: Sons, care for your elders. Elders say: We sue." *The New York Times*, p.1.

Chang, Su-hsien. (23 April 2003). How many other children will avoid their obligations? *Shenyang Gazette*, p. 1.

China Statistical Yearbook, (2003). Compiled by National Bureau of Statistics of China. Beijing, China: China Statistics Press.

Daniels, Dwight. (5 January 2004). Respecting and protecting dignity of the elderly. *China Daily*, p. 1.

Eckholm, Eric. (20 May 1998). Homes for the elderly replacing family care as China grays. *The New York Times*, pp. A1, et. seq.

———. (25 September 2004). Empty nesters and community centers: How China copes with an aging population. *Xinhua General News Service*.

French, Howard W. (30 June 2006). As China ages, a shortage of cheap labor looms. *The New York Times*, p. 1 et seq.

French, Howard W. (24 November 2005). China's online revolution. *The New York Times*, p.1.

Hiatt, Lorraine G. (1991). *Nursing Home Renovation Designed for Reform*. Boston: Butterworth Architecture.

———. (11 June 2004). Home-care for elderly to expand across the city. *Shanghai Daily*, p.1.

Hui, Polly. (30 August 2004). Old folks want to be more independent. *South China Morning Post*, p. 2.

———. (21 June 2004). Investors wanted for elderly care in Liaoning. *Financial Times*. p.1.

Jackson, Richard and Neil Howe. (April 2004). *The Graying of the Middle Kingdom: The Demographics and Economics of Retirement Policy In China*. Center for Strategic & International Studies.

Knapp, Ronald G. (2000). *China's Old Dwellings*. Honolulu: University Of Hawaii Press.

Lai, Chloe. (9 June 2004). More flats to cater for needs of elderly. *South China Morning Post*, p.1.

Lai-kwok, Elaine Chung. (12 October 2004). *Housing For The Elderly: New Horizons, International Conference on Housing for the Elderly Today*, p.1.

Lee, Ella. (15 August 2003). HK gets its first retirement home for the middle-class. *South China Morning Post*, p. 1.

Lo, Felix. (4 September 2004). More land urged to house the elderly in retirement. *South China Morning Post*, p.1.

———. More flats to cater for the needs of elderly. *South China Morning Post*.

———. (23 October 2003). Nursing home funded by Hong Kong charity opens in shanghai. *Xinhua General News Service*.

———. (18 October 2004). Nursing homes opening up across the city. *Shanghai Daily*, p.1.

———. (23 June 1999). Old folks want to be more independent. *Liaoning Daily*, p.1.

———. (2 July 2004). Older generation gets special care in jing'an. *Shanghai Daily*, p.1.

Poston, Jr., Dudley and Peter A. Morrison. (14 September 2005). China: bachelor bomb. *Rand Commentary*, p.1.

Qin, Xu. (24 October 2005). Facing up to the graying of China. *Beijing Times*, p.1.

Riley, Nancy E. (June 2004). China's population: new trends and challenges. *Population Bulletin*, pp. 3–36.

———. (11 May 2004). Salesmen pressure elderly to renovate homes for better health. *Mainichi Daily News*, p. 1.

Saunders, Peter, Shang Xiaoyuan, Zhang Kaiti, and Sun Lujun. (May 2003). The structure and impact of formal and informal social support mechanisms for older people in China. A paper presented at the 4th International Research Conference on Social Security.

Schaff, Judy. (2001). *Jia*, Family and the Chinese house in Giskin, Howard and Bettye S. Walsh (eds). *Chinese Culture Through the Family*. Albany, NY: State University of New York Press, pp. 163–95.

———. (11 June 2004). Home-Care For Elderly To Expand Across City. *Shanghai Daily*.

Shen, Zaihong. *Feng Shui*. New York: Dorling Kindersley: 2001.

———. (5 April 2004). Tailoring healthcare policies for the elderly. *China View*.

———. Elderly daycare. http://english.www.gov.tw/e<->Gov/index.jsp.

Yan, Yunxiang. (2003). *Private Life Under Socialism: Love, Intimacy, and Family in a Chinese Village, 1949–1999*. Stanford, CA: Stanford University Press.

Yong, Wu. (21 June 2004). Investors wanted for elderly care in Shenyang. *China Daily*, p. 1.

Chapter 6

Andersson, Henrik O. and Fredric Bedoire. (2004). *Stockholm Architecture and Townscape*. Stockholm: Bokforlaget Prisma, pp. 282–91.

Bellevue Park, Malmo. (1992). *Arkitektur*, 6, 17–20.

Browall, C., Tollmar, K. and Petersson, F. Project Camelot. (2002). Roundtable talk and seminars around future living. (In Swedish) Vinnova-rapport VR, p. 13.

Brunnberg, Klas. (1992). Danish and typically un-Swedish. *Arkitektur*, pp. 71–72.

Caldenby, Claes, Joran Lindvall and Wilfried Wang (eds). (1998). *Sweden: 20th-Century Architecture.* New York: Prestel.

Caldwell, Christopher. (5 February 2006). Islam on the outskirts of the welfare state: Sweden is discovering that it has a Muslim-immigrant issue. *The New York Times Magazine,* pp. 54–59.

Dilani, Alan and Agneta Morelli. (6 November 2005). An environment that promotes health. *Aldreomsorg (Ward for the Elderly).*

Femia, Elia E., Steven H. Zarit and Boo Johansson. (1997). Predicting change in activities of daily living: A longitudinal study of the oldest old of Sweden. *Journal of Gerontology* 52B, pp. 294–302.

———. (2005). Gamlebyen. *Norsk Folkemuseum.* Accessed 2005, from www.folkemuseet.no.

———. Confusing terminology in the nursing jungle. Accessed January 2006, from http://gammel.viover60.no.

Gullbring, Leo. (July/August 2002). The "Swedish model": Rehabilitates community utopia. *L'Architecture D'Aujourd'hui,* pp. 61–66.

Hagford, Janet. (16 January 2006). Lyngblomsten care center. *Culture Change Now,* pp. 4–10.

Hayden, Dolores. (2002). Redesigning the American dream. New York: W.W. Norton & Co., p. 142.

Hellner, Britt Marie. (2005). Cure at home. *AARP Global Report on Aging,* p. 6.

Holst, G-M. *IT Sweden 2002: Information- and communication technology in a nutshell.* Accessed in 2003, from http://www.dfs.se/lankar/informtrl/teldok_kap13.asp.

———. (2005). How unique is Sweden. *Svenska Enskilda Banken Trigg Liv,* pp. 1–94.

———. (2005). Developments in care of the elderly in Sweden. *Socialstyrelsen,* p. 1.

Keijer, Ulf and Magnus Hunhammer. (March 1995). IT-supported dwellings in existent stock including augmented services for aging people and people with special needs: A Swedish development project. A paper presented at the second International Workshop on IT for Solving Housing Problems of Aged People.

Kephart, Gary. (1997). *Extraordinary Groups,* 1st edition. New York: Worth Publishers, p. 118.

Larsson, Hanna. (6 November 2005). The common good and at-home care. *Aldreomsorg (Ward for the Elderly),* p. 127.

Lennarth. (1 November 2004). A fork in the road for the Swedish model? *Aldre iCentrum (Older People in Focus).*

Liebig, Phoebe and S. Irudaya Rajan. (2003). *An Aging India: Perspectives, Prospects and Policies.* New York: The Haworth Press, Inc.

Lindvall, Joran and Max Plunger. (1992). *The Swedish Art of Building.* Stockholm: The Swedish Institute. Swedish Museum of Architecture.

Lundahl, Gunilla. (1983). Solbacka and blocks of communal service flats in *Gunilla Lundahl (ed), Recent Developments In Swedish Architecture: A Reappraisal.* Stockholm: The Swedish Institute and the Swedish Museum of Architecture, pp. 42–46; 101–114.

Lundberg, Stefan, Ulf Keijer and Greger Sandstrom. (2005). Design of an evaluation technology, organization and care for extended living at home by persons suffering from acquired brain injury or dementia. The Royal Institute of Technology.

Manteghi, Ladan. (2005). Affecting change globally. *AARP Global Report on Aging* (special issue), pp. 4–5.

———. (May 2005). *Ministry of Health & Social Affairs, Sweden.* (Fact Sheet #14), p. 1.

———. (2005). Nursing homes in Denmark Today and in the Future. IAHSA—Trondheim conference.

Peck, Richard. (14 January 2006). Sobering thoughts from Sweden. *Nursing Homes Magazine,* p. 1.

———. (30 December 2004). The silver tsunami. *Rolling Rains Report,* p. 1.

———. (2005). *Senior Citizen Sweden, 2005,* pp. 1–10.

Socialstyrelsen. (2005). *Current developments in care of the elderly in Sweden,* p. 11.

———. (25 January 2006). Nursing home resident surfs the net. *Sollentuna Journal,* p. 1.

———. Women and men in Sweden—Facts and Figures, 2004. Accessed 2004, from http://www.scb.se/default ____2154.asp.

———. Surftips-seniorer. Accessed January 2004, from www.surftips.blogspot.com.

———. (2005). *The World Factbook, 2005 (Sweden)* pp. 5–13.

Wikipedia. (2005). *Sweden,* p. 1.

Yamanoi, H. The Care of the Elderly in Sweden and Japan, #8 and #9. Accessed 2005, from www.wao.or.jp.

Yasujiro, Isayama. (2005). We can learn many things from Sweden in the coming years. *Osaka Group Study Exchange.* Accessed 2005, from www.gse2660.com, 2005.

Chapter 7

Andrade, Flavia and DeVos, Susan. (2002). *An Analysis Of Living Arrangements Among Elderly Women In Brazil,* unpublished paper presented at annual meetings, Brazilian Association of Population Studies.

Berquo, E. (1996). Some demographic considerations about the Brazilian population aging process in *Annais de I*

Seminario Internacional do Envelhecimento Populacional: Uma agenda para o final do seculo. Brasilia:MPAS,SAS, pp. 16–34.

————. (2002). Brazilian aging: Differences in well-being by rural-urban areas. *United Nations Research Institute for Social Development*, pp. 1–2.

————. (31 July 2006). Brazil's population forecast to increase by more than 40 percent by 2050. *Pravda*, p.1.

de Camargo, Erica Negreiros. (2004). *Today's Private Home Design and the Current Metropolitan Living Habits in Brazil*, unpublished paper presented at the ENHR Conference, Cambridge, UK.

deVos, Susan and Flavia Andrade. (2005). Race and independent living among elderly Brazilians since 1980. *Journal of Comparative Family Studies*, vol.36, no.4, pp. 569–581.

Fallender, Claire. "Age-old" solutions for senior citizens in Brazil. Accessed 2007, from www.globalenvision.org.

Garcez-Leme, Luiz et al. (November 2005). Geriatrics in Brazil: A big country with big opportunities. *Journal of the American Geriatics Society*, vol. 53, no. 11, pp. 2018–2023.

Gomes, Leticia Zioni. (8 April 2006). The universal home: A lifetime marriage. *Harmonia*, vol. 19, p. 50.

Hopgood, Mei-Ling. In surgery—happy Barzil, Fido gets a face-lift. Accessed 2003, from reflector.com/hp/contents/shared/news/brazil.

————. (2004). HSBC survey: *The Future of Retirement in a World of Rising Life Expectancies: Attitudes Towards Ageing and Retirement Across 10 Countries and Territories.*

Karsch, Ursula and Corina Karsch. (1999). Migration and urbanization in Brazil: Implications for work and elder care in Viola M. Lechner and Margaret B. Neal (eds). *Work and Caring for the Elderly: International Perspectives.* Philadelphia, PA: Brunner/Mazel, pp. 143–159.

Lloyd-Sherlock, Peter. (2005). Living arrangements of older persons and poverty. *Case Studies From Latin America.* University of East Anglia, UK, unpublished paper, pp. 1–12.

Mazenotti, Priscilla. Brazil approves plan to deal with the elderly. Accessed 26 June 2005, from www.brazzilmag.com, p.41.

McLaughlin, Daniel F. (31 July 2006). The old boys (and girls) from Brazil. *Brazil*, p. 1.

Medeiros, Marcelo. (August 2004). Architecture with a social conscience in Brazil. *Third Sector*, pp. 1–3.

————. First universal design project is launched in Brazil. Accessed 11 November 2005, from www.mercado.com.

Page, Joseph A. (1995). *The Brazilians.* New York: Da Capro Press.

Perito, Sandra. (14 January 2005). Life in minicities. *City Finance*, p. 2.

Social responsibility in Brazilian architecture. Accessed 5 April 2006, from primermao.com.br.

Ramos, L., Santos, C. et al. (1991). Profile of elder residents of Sao Paulo's urban community according to type of domicile: The role of multigenerational homes in *A populacao idosa e o apoio familiar. Informe demografio*, no. 24, pp. 11–86.

————. A house for a lifetime. Accessed 2005, from http://reumatologia.com.

Rebhun, L.A. (2005). Families in Brazil in Jaipaul L. Roopnarine and Uwe P. Gielen. *Families in Global Perspective.* New York: Pearson, pp. 330–344.

Rybczynski, Witold. (1986). *Home: A Brief History of an Idea.* New York: Penguin.

Schwarz, Benyamin and Ruth Brent. (1999). *Aging, Autonomy and Architecture.* Baltimore: Johns Hopkins University Press.

Schwarz, Benyamin. (1996). *Nursing Home Design.* New York: Garland Publishing.

————. (4 August 2004). Universal home: Appropriate for a lifetime. *Harmonia*, vol. 19, p. 36.

————. (2001). *The World Population Prospects: The 2000 Revision.* New York: The United Nations.

————. The renovation of a nursing home. Accessed 20 July 2004, from http://sentidos.uol.com.br.

Williams, Eugene. (2004). *Implementing Access Through Universal Design in Five Brazilian cities: Porto Alegre, Curitiba, Sao Paulo, Rio de Janeiro, and Belo Horizonte.* Design for The 21st Century, Plenary Session.

Chapter 8

Ames, Brianna. (26 March, 2006). Seniors' party hopes for youthful voters. *The Jerusalem Post*, pp. 1–3.

Ames, Brianna. (29 March 2006). Pensioners' party to define platform. *The Jerusalem Post*, pp. 1–3.

Amir, Eyal, Arza Churchman and Avraham Wachman. (2005). The Kibbutz dwelling: ideology and design. *Housing, Theory and Society*, vol.22, pp. 147–65.

————. (23 January 2002). An Israeli icon in decline: Changing times, values and economics spell trouble for Kibbutzim. *Today*, pp. 1–3.

Azaiza, Faisa. (1999). Services for the Arab elderly in Israel. *University of Haifa Focus*, pp. 1–3.

Be'er, S. (2001.) *Mashav—Planning for the Elderly.* A National DataBase, JCD-Brookdale Institute & ESHEL, Jerusalem, pp. 1–62.

Blumstein, Tzvia. (2004). The effect of a communal lifestyle on depressive symptoms in late life. *Journal of Aging and Health*, vol. 16, pp. 151–74.

Brodsky, Jenny. (2000). The challenges of a major success: The aging of Israeli society. *The Elderly in Israel—The 2000 Statistical Abstract*.

Brodsky, Jenny and Brenda Morginstin. (1999). Balance of Familial and state responsibility for the elderly and their caregivers in Israel, pp. 68–81, in Lechner, Viola M. and Margaret B. Neal (eds), *Work and Caring for the Elderly: International Perspectives*. Ann Arbor, MI: Brunner-Mazel.

Carmel, S. and A. Lazar. (1998). Health and well-being among elderly persons: the role of social class and immigration status. *Ethnicity and Health*, pp. 31–43.

———. (2000). *Central Bureau of Statistics*, annual reports, Jerusalem.

Ein-Mor, Nava. (2006). Connecting between the generations: philosophy and practice of "lifeline for the old." *Jerusalem*.

Fogiel-Bijaoui, Sylvie. (2005). Familism, post-modernity and the state: The case of Israel in Roopnarine, Jaipaul L. and Uwe P. Gielen, *Families in Global Perspective*. New York: Allyn and Bacon, pp. 184–207.

———. (2002). Israel: Aging population. Accessed 2006, from http://health.families.com.

———. (February 2003). "Israel's Elderly: Facts and Figures," *Mashav: Planning for the Elderly*—A National Database, JDC-Brookdale & ESHEL, Jerusalem.

Jacobzone, S., E. Cambois et al. (1999). The health of older persons in OECD countries: Is it improving fast enough to compensate for population aging? *Labor Market and Social Policy— Occasional Papers, no. 37. Organization for Economic Co-Operation and Development (OECD)*, Paris, pp. 112–143.

Kabilou, Jaacov. (2003). Quality assurance in homes for the aged in Israel. *Mashav: Planning For the Elderly*—A National Database, JDC-Brookdale & ESHEL, Jerusalem.

———. (2005). Kibbutz. *Wikipedia*.

Kroyanker, D. (7 April 2006). Fifty years of Israeli architecture as reflected in Jerusalem's buildings. *Israel Ministry of Foreign Affairs*, p. 3.

Leviatan, U. (1999). Contribution of social arrangements to the attainment of successful aging—the experience of the Israeli Kibbutz. *The Journals of Gerontology*, vol. 54 (Issue 4 P205-P213), pp. 55–61.

Litwin, Howard. (2004). Intergenerational exchange patterns and their correlates in an aging Israeli cohort. *Research on Aging*, vol. 26, no. 2, pp. 202–223.

Menirav, Limor. (February 2000). Nursing homes in Israel. Institute for Advanced Strategic and Political Studies, no. 45, pp. 1–2.

Meyers, Nechemia. (30 November 2001). The graying of Israel: Coping with aging population poses challenges. *The Jewish News Weekly*, pp. 1–2.

Miles, William F. (2003). Mid-life crisis, Kibbutz-style. *Shofar*, vol.21, no. 2, pp. 82–100.

Ran, Ami. (2000). A matter of fortune: mature building for the aged. *Architecture of Israel*, (Issue 41), pp. 22–41.

Rapoport, Amos. (2001). Understanding culture and housing design. *Housing, Theory and Society*, vol. 14, pp. 145–65.

———. (1 January 1998). Retirees—Making it in Israel. *HagShama: Department of the World Zionist Organization*, pp. 1–10.

Shenton, Shira. (1999–2000). House of the season: Integrated versus freestanding. *Architecture of Israel Quarterly*, vol. 4, pp. 16–23.

Shenton, Shira. (1999–2000). Simple yet not simplistic. *Architecture of Israel Quarterly*. vol. 4, pp. 25–29.

Sinai, Ruth. (6 September 2005). Research shows public nursing homes outshine private facilities. *Haaretz*, pp. 1–2.

Suleiman, K. and A. Walter-Ginzburg. (January 2005). A nursing home in Arab-Israeli society: Targeting utilization in a changing social and economic environment. *Journal of the American Geriatric Society*, vol. 53 (Issue 1),pp. 152–57.

Sykes, J.T. and Hunt, M. (1997). NORCs: What can we learn from them? *Perspectives on Aging*, vol. 26 (Issue 1), pp. 16–18.

———. Israeli home healthcare innovations, health and fitness. Accessed 2007, from http://yadsarah.org/index .asp?id=198.

Chapter 9

Adhvaru, Uday. (30 August 2005). *Old Age Homes in Gujaret, Where Elders Feel At Home*. Yahoo News, India, pp. 1–3.

Aggarwal, Yash. (17 September 2005). National convention of all India, Associations of Senior Citizens. *AARP Global Aging Program*, pp. 1–6.

———. (4 March 2006). Assisted living during sunset years. *The Hindu*, pp. 1–3.

Baldauf, Scott. (10 February 2004). India's new loos save lives. *The Christian Science Monitor*, pp. 1–3.

Beni, Joseph. (16 July 2005). Delhi's luxury toilets. *The Times Of India*, p. 1.

Bongaarts, J. and Zimmer, Z. (2002). Living arrangements of older adults in the developing world: An analysis of demographic and health surveys. *Journal of Gerontology: Social Sciences*, vol. 57B (Issue 3), pp. S145-S157.

Central Intelligence Agency. (2005). India. *The World Factbook*. Washington, DC: CIA Government Publications, pp. 1–16.

Cohen, Lawrence. (1998). *No Aging in India: Alzheimer's, the Bad Family, and Other Modern Things*. Berkeley, CA: University of California Press.

Cohen, Uriel and Kristen Day. (2000). The role of culture in designing environments for people with dementia. *Environment and Behavior*, vol. 32, no. 3, pp. 361–399.

Cooper, Ilay and Barry Dawson. (1998). *Traditional Buildings of India*. London: Thames and Hudson.

Das, Prodeepta. (15 March 2006) The old country. *The International Development Magazine*, p. 1.

Dignity Foundation. (7 October 2005). *Real Life Cases*, pp. 1–4.

Government of India. (1999). *National Policy on Older Persons*. New Delhi: Ministry of Social Justice and Empowerment.

Gustafson, Per. (2001). Understanding meanings of place. *Journal of Environmental Psychology*, vol. 21, pp. 5–16.

Hadjiyanni, Tasoulla. (2004). Culturally sensitive housing: considering the difference. *Informe Design*, vol. 3, (Issue 1), pp. 1–6.

HelpAge India. (1998). *Directory of Old Age Homes in India*. New Delhi.

Husain, Irfan. (31 October 2005). Karachi diary: Road to nowhere. *Daily Times: A New Voice for a New Pakistan*, pp. 1–2.

———. India. (21 December 2005). *Wikipedia*, pp. 1–13.

———. (2 July 2005). India plans law to force children to care for aging parents: Report. *Global Action on Aging*, pp. 1–2.

Iyengar, Jayanthi. (5 August 2004). Of aging societies, lost women, and lost consumers. *Asian Economy*, pp. 1–5.

———. (2 July 2005). India plans law to force children to care for aging parents. *Khaleej Times*, pp. 1–2.

Kumar, Vijaya. (2002). Social security for the elderly in India: Present status and future challenges. *Aging Indian Experience*, vol. 1, topic 10, pp. 1–21.

Kumar, Vijaya. (2003). Economic security for the elderly in India: An overview in Liebig and Rajan (eds), *An Aging India*. New York: The Haworth Press, pp. 45–66.

Liebig, Phoebe and P.V. Ramamurti. (2006). Living arrangements and social support for older adults in India in Hyunsook Yoon and Jon Hendricks (eds), *Handbook of Asian Aging*. Amityville, NY: Baywood Publishing Company, Inc., pp. 237–60.

Liebig, Phoebe. (2003). Old age homes and services: Old and new approaches to aged care, in Liebig, Phoebe and S.I. Rajan (Eds), *An Aging India*. New York: The Haworth Press, pp. 151–78.

Liebig, Phoebe. (2001). International perspectives on housing frail elders. *Journal of Architectural and Planning Research*, vol. 18 (Issue 3), pp. 208–222.

Linton, Leyla. (16 February 2005). UN: World's population is aging rapidly. *Political News*, pp. 1.

Mukherjee, Trina. (October 2005). Living easy: Simple devices that promise to make the lives of silvers easier. *Harmony*, pp. 38–40.

Nair, T.K. (ed). (1989). *Care of the elderly. Organizations caring for the elderly in India*. Madras: Madras Institute on Aging.

Nayar, Lola. (31 August 2004). Retirement homes becoming middle-class lifestyle statement, Yahoo News, India, pp. 1–3.

Nunan, Patricia. (21 March 2005). Indian group promotes development by bringing water, toilets to 700 million people. *VOA News*, pp. 1–4.

Ponnuswami, Ilango. (October–December 2000). Situation of the older persons in India. *Sarvekshna*. vol. xiv, no. 2, pp. 123–127.

Patel, Vibhuti. (2006). Personal correspondence.

Rajan, S.I., Mishra, U.S., and Sarma, P.S. (1995). Living arrangements among the Indian elderly. *Hong Kong Journal of Gerontology*, vol. 9 (Issue 2), pp. 20–28.

Ramanathan, S. Kalyana. Old age homes come of age. Accessed May 27, 2003, from www.rediff.com, pp. 1–3.

Riley, Terrence. (2003). *The Unprivate House*. NY: Harry Abrams, Inc., The Museum of Modern History Series, pp. 1–16.

Ross, Aileen D. (1961). *The Hindu Family in its Urban Setting*. Toronto: University of Toronto Press.

Sandesh India. (7 October 2005). *Old Age Homes*, p. 1.

———. Senior housing (In India): An overlooked opportunity. Accessed December 1, 1999, from www.rediff.com, pp. 1–4.

———. Senior Indian. (7 October 2005). *Guidelines for Establishing Old Age Homes*, pp. 1–3.

Shah, A. M. (1947). *The Household Dimension of the Family in India*. Berkeley, CA: University of California Press.

Shah, Bela. (9 September 2004). Tradition and the future in India. *Health News*, pp. 1–4.

Sharma, Radha. (7 August 2005). Old on the look-out for new-age homes. *The Times of India*, pp. 1–2.

Stafford, Phillip B. (2001). When community planning becomes community building, in Leonard F. Heumann, Mccall, Mary E. and Boldy, Duncan P. (eds). *Empowering Frail Elderly People*. Westport, CT: Praeger, pp. 137–152.

Swami, Mini. (19 February 2005). Senior housing India. *Indian Child*, pp. 1–3.

———. (2005). *The Future of Retirement in a World of Rising Life Expectancies: A Study Across 10 Countries and Territories*. HSBC (Together with Age Wave, Inc. and Harris Interactive).

———. (24 October 2004). The old country. *The International Development Magazine*, pp. 1–5.

———. (21 October 2003). What the elderly demand from us. *Global Action on Aging*, pp. 1–3.

Chapter 10

Almekinders, Matthijs. (2005). *High Tech-High Touch*. AARP International Association of Homes & Services for the Aging. Sixth International Conference, pp. 1–26.

Bakker, W. Evolution of living. (2006). *AARP Global Report on Aging*, pp. 1–3.

Belkin, L. (5 March 2006). A virtual retirement home. *The New York Times Magazine*, p. 91.

Bengston, V. et al. (2003). Global aging and the challenge to families. *Global Aging and Challenges to Families*, pp. 1–24.

Brodsky, J. and Morginstin, B. (1999). Balance of familial and state responsibility for the elderly and their caregivers in Israel, pp. 68–81, in Lechner, V. and Margaret, B. (eds) *Work and Caring for the Elderly: International Perspectives*. Ann Arbor, MI: Brunner-Mazel.

Brown, N. (2003). Under one roof: The evolving story of three-generation housing in Japan, in J. Traphagan and J. Knight (eds) *Demographic Change and the Family in Japan's Aging Society*. Albany, NY: State University of New York Press, pp. 53–71.

Brasileira. (8 September 2006). *A House for a Lifetime*, pp. 1–7.

Camargo, E. (2004). Today's private home design and the current metropolitan living habits in Brazil, unpublished paper presented at the ENHR Conference, Cambridge, UK.

Caplan, R. (2005). *By Design*, 2nd edition. New York: Fairchild Publications, Inc.

Daniels, Dwight. (5 January 2004). Respecting and protecting dignity of the elderly. *China Daily*, p.1.

Dychtwald, K. (1990). *Age Wave*. New York: Random House.

Eckholm, E. (20 May 1998). Homes for the elderly replacing family care as China grays. *The New York Times*.

———. (24 May 2006). Mobile Bathing Service. *E-Medica*, p. 1.

Fisk, Arthur D. et al. (2004). *Designing for Older Adult*. New York: CRC Press.

Garcez-Leme et al. (November 2005). Geriatrics in Brazil: A big country with big opportunities. *Journal of the American Geriatrics Society*, vol. 53, no. 11, pp. 2018–2023.

———. (2004). HSBC Survey: *The Future Of Retirement In A World Of Rising Life Expectancies: Attitudes Towards Ageing And Retirement Across 10 Countries And Territories*.

Jackson, Richard and Neil Howe. (April 2004). *The Graying of the Middle Kingdom*. Center for Strategic & International Studies.

Lai-Kwok, Elaine Chung. (12 October 2004). Housing for the elderly: New horizons. *International Conference on Housing for the Elderly Today*, p. 1.

Lee, E. (15 August 2003). HK gets its first retirement home for the middle-class. *South China Morning Post*, p. 1.

———. (23 June 1999). Old folks want to be more independent. *Liaoning Daily*, p. 1.

Liebig, P. (2003). Old age homes and services: Old and new approaches to aged care, in P. Liebig and S.I. Rajan (eds) *An Aging India*. The Haworth Press, pp. 151–178.

Lundberg, S. et al. (2005). Design of an evaluation technology, organization, and care for extended living at home by persons suffering from acquired brain injury or dementia. The Royal Institute of Technology, pp. 1–5.

Marsden, John P. (2005). *Humanistic Design of Assisted Living*. Baltimore: The Johns Hopkins University Press.

Medeiros, M. (30 August 2004). Architecture with a social conscience in Brazil. *Third Sector*, p. 1–3.

Miles, W. (2003). Mid-life crisis, Kibbutz-Style. *Shofar*, vol. 21, no. 2, pp. 82–100.

———. (May 2005). *Ministry of Health & Social Affairs, Sweden*. Fact Sheet #14, p. 1.

———. (21 July 2005). Robots to offer Japan's elderly a new lease on life. *MSNBC*, p.1.

Pacific Research Consulting, Inc. (25 April 2003). *Japan Toy and Game Software Journal*, pp. 1–2.

Peck, R. (14 January 2006). Sobering thoughts from Sweden. *Nursing Homes Magazine*, p.1.

Perito, S. (14 January 2005). Life in Minicities. *City Finance*, p.3.

Quesenbery, W. (28 September 2004). *The Politics of Design at Aging by Design*. Whitney Interactive Design, pp. 1–8.

Rifkin, J. (2000). *The Age of Access: How the Shift from Ownership to Access is Transforming Capitalism*. New York: Penguin Books.

Rosenfeld, J., Chapman, W. and McCullough, E. (February 2007). Going global: learning from India's senior housing. *LiveWire*, pp. 12–13.

Sandstrom, G. (2005). Future houses in Sweden. Royal Institute of Technology, pp. 1–24.

Schwarz, Benyamin and Ruth Brent. (1999). *Aging, Autonomy and Architecture*. Baltimore: Johns Hopkins University Press.

Schwarz, Benyamin. (1999). *Nursing Home Design*. New York: Garland Publishing.

———. (11 June 2004). Home care for the elderly to expand across city. *Shanghai Daily*, p. 1.

Sharma, D. (January 2006). Support systems: Where to go when you need help with new gadgets. *Harmony Magazine*, pp. 70–71.

Sharma, R. (7 August 2005.) Old on the look-out for new-age homes. *The Times of India*, pp. 1–2.

———. (2005). Current developments in care of the elderly in Sweden. *Socialstyrelsen*, p. 11.

Tapscott, D. et al. (2006). *Wikinomics: How Mass Collaboration Changes Everything*.

———. (11 April 2002). The house of the future: Networked appliances make life more convenient. *Japan Information Network*, p. 2.

———. (15 July 2005). Preventive care for the elderly. *The Japan Times*, pp. 1–2.

Toshiba. (2006). Networked home appliances, p. 1.

———. (21 November 2003). Living longer. *Trends in Japan*, p. 1.

———. (4 August 2004). Universal home: Appropriate for a lifetime. *Harmonia*, vol 19, p.36.

———. (2001). *The World Population Prospects: The 2000 Revision*. New York: The United Nations.

Williams, Eugene. (2004). Implementing *Access Through Universal Design In Five Brazilian Cities: Porto Alegre, Curitiba, Sao Paulo, Rio De Janeiro, And Belo Horizonte*. Design for The 21st Century, Plenary Session.

www.building.com.hk/A=T Design Ltd.

www.India.9.com/i9show/RajajiEldersHome.

Web-Japan. (18 August 1997). New ways to help the old: Elderly-care service industry enjoys boom, pp. 1–2.

Wiejers-Hasegawa, Yumi. (2 April 2003). Homes for seniors not all created equal. *The Japan Times*, p. 1.

———. (2005). Accessed 2005, from http://en.wikipedia.org/wiki/Sweden2005

Wu, Y. (21 June 2004). Investors wanted for elderly care in Shenyang. *China Daily*, p. 1.

Yokohama, Y. (2005). *Group Homes in Japan*. AARP Conference on World Aging, pp. 1–16.

———. (25 September 2004). Empty nesters and community centers: How China copes with an aging population. *Xinhua General News Service*, p. 3.

Xu, Qin. (24 October 2005). Facing up to the graying of China. *Beijing Times*, p. 1.

Credits

Intro

I.0   © joSon/Photographer's Choice/Getty Images
I.1   Courtesy Rajaji Elders' Home
I.2   Courtesy Clasic Kudumbam
I.3   Photograph © Michele Panzeri/Courtesy Papa Architects
I.4   Courtesy Gerontech
I.5   Photograph © Mike Stone
I.6   Courtesy Orange County China

Chapter 1

1.0   © Jonathan Nourok/The Image Bank/Getty Images
1.1   Courtesy Kohler
1.2   Courtesy Ashiana Utsav
1.3   Courtesy NAHB Research Center
1.4   Courtesy NAHB Research Center
1.5   Courtesy Kohler
1.6   Photograph © Mike Stone
1.7   Courtesy Heartland House/Richard Bergman
1.8   Courtesy Heartland House
1.9   © AP Photo/Steve Helber
1.10 Courtesy Kohler
1.11 Photograph © Open House Expo: the Vitra Design Museum and Art Center in Pasadena

Chapter 2

2.0   © Mark Scott, Splurge Productions Inc./Riser/Getty Imagse
2.1   Photograph © Jereon Musch
2.2   © Jim Wilson/*The New York Times*
2.3   Courtesy Co-Op City
2.4   Courtesy Pulte Homes & the Communities of Del Webb
2.5   Courtesy Pyatok Architects
2.6   Courtesy ElderSpirit
2.7   © James Estrin/*The New York Times*
2.8   Courtesy Muir Commons
2.9   © AP Photo/Elaine Thompson

Chapter 3

3.0   © Holly Harris/Stone Sub/Getty Images
3.1   Courtesy Avalon Square
3.2   Courtesy Richard Bergman
3.3   Courtesy Mississippi Methodist Senior Services
3.4   Courtesy Fairchild Publications, Inc.
3.5   Courtesy Grand Rapids Dominicans
3.6   Courtesy Alameda Center
3.7   Courtesy Sun Health

3.8   © James West/JWestProductions.com
3.9   Business Visuals/Askew Nixon Ferguson
3.10 Courtesy Collective Architecture
3.11 Courtesy The Intelligent Assistive Technology and Systems Lab at University of Toronto
3.12 Courtesy The Gables at Westminster-Canterbury

Chapter 4
4.0   © Ben Clark/Photonica/Getty Images
4.3   Courtesy SANYO
4.4   Courtesy Yori-soi
4.5   Courtesy New Wing
4.7   Courtesy Green Tokyo
4.8   Courtesy Green Tokyo
4.9   Photograph © Hiroyuki Hirai/Courtesy Kawai Architects
4.10 Courtesy Green Tokyo
4.11 Courtesf Warashiko Nursing home
4.12 Courtesy Green Tokyo

Chapter 5
5.0   © Angelo Cavalli/The Image Bank/Getty Images
5.3   © Alfred Molon - www.molon.de
5.4   Photograph © Ryan Pyle
5.5   Courtesy TianJan Senior Citizen's Welfare Institute
5.6   Photograph © Ryan Pyle
5.7   Courtesy Chang Gung Health and Culture Village
5.9   Photograph © Ryan Pyle

Chapter 6
6.0   © Andreas Kindler/Johner Images/Getty Images
6.1   Photograph © Leo Gullbring
6.2   © VINGBILD/Berndt-Joel Gunnarsson Bildbyrå: Nordic Photos
6.3   Photograph © Mikael Sodersten
6.4   Photograph © Olof Hultin/Arkitektur Magazine
6.5   Courtesy Greger Sandstrom
6.6   Courtesy Greger Sandstrom
6.7   Courtesy Greger Sandstrom
6.8   Courtesy of HSB Omsorg
6.9   © Anders Petersen/Nordic Photos
6.10 Photograph © Carl de Keyzer/Magnum Photos

Chapter 7
7.0   © Christoph Wilhelm
7.1   Courtesy Residencial Santa Catarina
7.2   Courtesy Menotti Parolari
7.3   © Christopher Pillitz/Reportage/Getty Images
7.4   Photograph © iStockPhoto.com
7.5   Courtesy Sandra M. Perito
7.6   Courtesy Sandra M. Perito
7.7   Courtesy Menotti Parolari
7.8   Courtesy Menotti Parolari
7.9   Courtesy Menotti Parolari
7.10 Courtesy Residencial Santa Catarina

Chapter 8
8.0   © Jeremy Horner/Riser/Getty Images
8.2   Courtesy Mishkenot
8.4   Courtesy GeronTech—The Israeli Center for Assistive Technology & Aging and Bezalel Academy of
      Arts and Design, Jerusalem
8.5   Courtesy Sheba Medical Center

8.6   Courtesy Mishan Haifa
8.7   Courtesy Beth Protea
8.8   Courtesy Mishkenot
8.9   Courtesy of Ezrat Avot
8.10 © Emporis Images
8.11 © Israelimages.com / Lev Borodulin

Chapter 9
9.0   © Philip Lee Harvey/Stone/Getty Images
9.1   Marcus Wilson-Smith/Red Cover
9.2   Courtesy Rajaji Elder's Home
9.3   Courtesy Phoebe Liebig
9.4   Courtesy Phoebe Liebig
9.5   Courtesy Phoebe Liebig
9.6   Courtesy Ashiana Village
9.7   Courtesy Ashiana Utsav
9.8   Courtesy Clasic Kudumbam
9.9   Courtesy Clasic Kudumbam
9.10 Courtesy Clasic Kudumbam

Chapter 10
10.0 © Charles Mason/Stone/Getty Images
10.2 Photograph © Mikael Sodersten
10.3 Courtesy CogniFit
10.4 © YOSHIKAZU TSUNO/AFP/Getty Images
10.5 Courtesy Clasic Kudumbam
10.6 Courtesy Phoebe Liebig
10.7 Courtesy Charles Durrett/Senior Cohousing: A Community Approach to Independent Living - The Handbook, by Charles Durrett, Ten Speed Press, 2005.

Appendix
Ap.1, Ap.2, Ap.3, Ap.4a, Ap. 4b Courtesy Wid Chapman
Ap.5, Ap.6a+b, Ap.7a+b Courtesy Studio 16
Ap.8a+b+c+d Courtesy Allan Chapman
Ap.9, Ap.10, Ap.11a+b Courtesy Ellen & Doug Gallow
Ap.12, Ap.13 Courtesy Marianne Cusato (designer)/Wid Chapman
Ap.14, Ap.15a+b, Ap.16, Ap.17, Ap.18, Ap.19, Ap.20 Courtesy Sandra Perito
Ap.21 Courtesy Kyungsung So (Korea)/Wid Chapman
Ap.22 Courtesy Ling-Zhi Hew (Singapore)/Wid Chapman
Ap.23 Courtesy Marlene Mendez (US)/Wid Chapman

Index